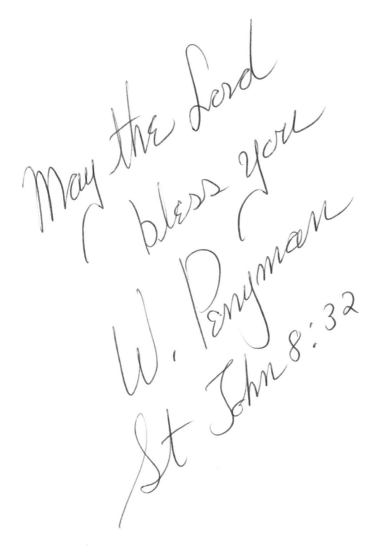

May the Lord
bless you

W. Penyman

St John 8:32

UNVEILING THE WHOLE TRUTH

WHAT THE MEDIA FAILED TO TELL AMERICAN VOTERS

REV. WAYNE PERRYMAN

 BOOK PUBLISHERS NETWORK

Book Publishers Network
P.O. Box 2256
Bothell • WA • 98041
PH • 425-483-3040

10 9 8 7 6 5 4 3 2 1

Printed in Canada

LCCN 2007939190
ISBN10 1-887542-61-2
ISBN13 978-1-887542-61-6

Editor: Julie Scandora
Cover Design: Laura Zugzda
Typographer: Stephanie Martindale

Dedication

I dedicate this book to my four lovely children, Sean, Conner, Latricia and Telisha to my brothers and sisters; Audria, Soncie, Anna, Johnnie and Stanley; to America, the country that I deeply love and to my Lord who gives me the strength and wisdom to serve others.

Table of Contents

.

Special Thanks

Special thanks and my deepest appreciation to Stephen J. Klos of Mercer Island, Washington for believing in me and supporting me in this project.

And my most sincere appreciation to my prayer partners Dr. Cecilia Harris and Dr. Dave and Kathy Brown and to my host of advisors and encouragers including Professor James White, Dr. Frances Rice (Florida), Harold and Cynthia Jenkins (Dallas), Bill Calhoun (Houston), Ms. Devita Dorsey (Seattle) and Pastor John Jenkins of the First Baptist Church of Glenarden in Landover, Maryland.

newspapers, there is a multitude of positive events in the black community that are ignored by major news organizations.

How many African Americans graduate each year with medical degrees or degrees in science, law, or engineering? How many inner-city black students made the honor roll in 2007? How many black churches are providing food for the needy and other social services for the less fortunate? If your main source of information comes from the news media, you may never know the answers to these and other important questions pertaining to African Americans.

Questions like: Why did the media devote so much time to the imprisonment of Paris Hilton and the death of Anna Nicole Smith? Are white girls (such as Natalee Holloway) the only ones missing? In a rare June 16, 2005 article entitled "Spotlight skips cases of missing minorities," Mark Memmott, reporter for USA Today asks a similar question. He writes: *"Those networks that drive such stories* [about missing white girls] *are being asked a tough question: Do they care only about missing white women?"* Mark went on to report that in the FBI files, there are 13,860 cases of missing blacks.

Each day editors from the major news organizations attend in-house editorial meetings to discuss what information should or should not be included in their featured stories. I found this to be true while working on a civil rights case that involved a number of large shipping companies in the Pacific Northwest. During my investigation I discovered that the shipping industry had a specific job classification which they referred to as "Nigger Jobs." My investigation also uncovered a multitude of evidence which proved that racial discrimination was systemic and that the use of the word "nigger" was commonplace in the workplace. When the *Seattle Times* became interested in the story, I provided them with over two thousand pages of internal company documents which verified my findings. When the paper finally released the featured story (with front page coverage) their editors decided to exclude all appropriate references that included the word "nigger." Readers who read the three-page story thought they were getting the "whole truth" (based on the length of the article).

They never knew they were only getting an edited version of what really took place.

When it comes to news, that average American citizen is like a new born baby bird. While the bird waits for his mother to drop food in his mouth, we the general public wait for the news media to drop their thoughts in our minds, and we do so without realizing that the media have the power to reveal or conceal important information that can have a profound impact on our lives and on the future of our country.

The media:

❖ Can promote or demote conservative ideas

❖ Can protect or reject traditional values

❖ And has the power to shape public opinions and affect court decisions.

The media can either show us the way or it can lead us to moral decay.

Because the news media have been our primary source of information, we have all formed opinions about Katrina, the Iraq War, George Bush, and immigration reform through their reporting. But did they give us all of the information? What information did they leave out? Unfortunately, most of the misinformation that we receive today comes from the news media. It was true in 1938 when Orson Wells convinced the public that we were being invaded by People from Mars and it was true sixty-six years later when Dan Rather convinced millions that he, indeed, had the actual military records of George W. Bush.

Unveiling the Whole Truth is a series of editorials based on comprehensive study and research and on common-sense approaches to the problems we face. The editorials cover a wide variety of subjects from the controversies involving weapons of mass destruction to abortions. In this book you will discover just how much information the media decided not to include in some of our major news stories and how the absence of such information affects public opinion.

Weapons of Mass Destruction and the Iraq War

Weapons of Mass Destruction— Who Lied?

Saddam Hussein has been engaged in the development of weapons of mass destruction technology which is a threat to countries in the region and he has made a mockery of the weapons inspection process.

Rep. Nancy Pelosi
December 16, 1998

Contrary to what the media have reported, President Bush and his two key black cabinet members, Colin Powell and Condoleezza Rice, weren't the only ones who claimed that Iraq had weapons of mass destruction. The media conveniently overlooked or forgot to acknowledge that, in March of 1991, a unanimous Security Council of the United Nations was the first to make such claims in Resolutions 687.

The following are a few facts regarding the United Nations Security Council's (UNSC) 687 Resolution and its findings regarding Iraq's efforts to obtain nuclear capabilities in 1991, almost ten years before George W. Bush occupied the White House.

- In April of 1991, UNSC Resolution 687 was adopted enabling the International Atomic Energy Agency (IAEA) to carry out immediate on-site inspections of Iraq's nuclear capabilities and carry out a plan for the destruction, removal or rendering harmless any of the prohibited items.

- August 1991, UNSC Resolution 707 was adopted demanding that Iraq "halt all nuclear activities of any kind, except for use of isotopes for medical, agricultural, or industrial purposes."

- Despite the resolutions, Saddam Hussein retained intellectual capital (scientists) for the possibility of restarting a nuclear program post 1991.

- On November 15, 1991, the first removal of highly enriched uranium from Iraq took place. An IAEA cargo flight carrying forty-two fresh fuel elements from the IRT-5000 5 megawatt light water research reactor at Al Tuwaitha, and 6.6 kilograms of uranium-235 left Baghdad for Moscow.

- Iraq Survey Group's (ISG) inquiry had found Iraq concealed elements of its nuclear program from inspectors after 1991, including the hiding of documents and technology, and attempting to maintain the brain trust of scientists who had earlier worked on the nuclear program; this conclusion echoes the statements made by Hussein Kamel upon his defection in 1995.

After the United Nations Security Council issued its findings, others started making claims that Iraq had acquired weapons of mass destruction. Among those making such claims were President Bill Clinton and several prominent Democrats. You will note that they made their statements a year and a half before Bush announced his candidacy for President. Bush made his official announcement in June 1999. Clinton issued one of his many statements regarding Iraq's weapons of mass destruction program one year earlier, in February 1998. Other Democrats soon followed and issued similar statements, but the media never credited the Democrats as being the progenitors of such statements. Did all of these people lie? The following statements by key members of the Democratic Party are often ignored by the news media.

On February, 17, 1998, President Clinton said:

> *If Saddam rejects peace and we have to use force, our pur-*
> *pose is clear. We want to seriously diminish the threat posed*
> *by Iraq's weapons of mass destruction program.*

On February 18, 1998, Madeline Albright, Clinton's Secretary of State said:

> *Iraq is a long way from [here], but what happens there matters*
> *a great deal here. For the risks that the leaders of a rogue state*
> *will use nuclear, chemical, or biological weapons against us*
> *or our allies is the greatest security threat we face.*

On February 18, 1998, Sandy Berger, Clinton's National Security Adviser said:

> *He* [Saddam Hussein] *will use those weapons of mass destruc-*
> *tion again, as he has ten times since 1983.*

On October 9, 1998 – a letter to President Clinton, signed by Carl Levin (D-MI), Tom Daschle (D-SD), and John Kerry (D – M) included the following statement:

> *We urge you, after consulting with Congress, and consis-*
> *tent with the U.S. Constitution and laws, to take neces-*
> *sary actions (including, if appropriate, air and missile*
> *strikes on suspect Iraqi sites) to respond effectively to the*
> *threat posed by Iraq's refusal to end its weapons of mass*
> *destruction programs.*

On December 16, 1998, Rep. Nancy Pelosi said:

> *Saddam Hussein has been engaged in the development of*
> *weapons of mass destruction technology which is a threat*
> *to countries in the region and he has made a mockery of the*
> *weapons inspection process.*

After the initial attack on Iraq because of its weapons of mass destruction program, the president went on the air and delivered the following message:

> *Earlier today, I ordered America's armed forces to strike military and security targets in Iraq. They are joined by British forces. Their mission is to attack Iraq's nuclear, chemical and biological weapons programs and its military capacity to threaten its neighbors....*
>
> *Their purpose is to protect the national interest of the United States, and indeed the interests of people throughout the Middle East and around the world....*
>
> *On the unanimous recommendation of my national security team- including the vice president, the secretary of defense, the chairman of the joint chiefs of staff, the secretary of state and the national security adviser - I have ordered a strong, sustained series of air strikes against Iraq....*
>
> *The hard fact is that so long as Saddam remains in power, he threatens the well-being of his people, the peace of his region, and the security of world.*
>
> *The best way to end that threat once and for all is with a new Iraqi government -- a government ready to live in peace with its neighbors, a government that respects the rights of its people....*
>
> *This situation presents a clear and present danger to the stability of the Persian Gulf and the safety of people everywhere. The international community gave Saddam one last chance to resume cooperation with the weapons inspectors. Saddam has failed to seize the chance.*
>
> *Our allies, including Prime Minister Tony Blair of Great Britain, concurred that now is the time to strike.*

The decision to use force is never cost-free. Whenever American forces are placed in harm's way, we risk the loss of life. And while our strikes are focused on Iraq's military capabilities, there will be unintended Iraqi casualties.

No, these weren't the words of George W. Bush; they are excerpts of a speech delivered by President Clinton on December 16, 1998. Even after this military effort, leading Democrats still felt that Iraq had weapons of mass destruction. They made their statements regarding Iraq's WMD program, shortly after Mansoor Ijaz, an American Muslim and long time supporter of President Clinton wrote a December 5, 2001 op-ed article that appeared on the *Los Angeles Times.com* internet. The article was entitled: *Clinton Let Bin Laden Slip Away....* As member of the Council on Foreign Relations, Ijaz wrote:

President Clinton and his national security team ignored several opportunities to capture Osama bin Laden and his terrorist associates including one as late as last year [2000]. I know because I negotiated more than one of the opportunities.

From 1996 to 1998, I opened unofficial channels between Sudan and the Clinton administration. I met with officials in both countries, including Clinton, U.S. National Security Advisor Samuel R. "Sandy" Berger and Sudan's president and intelligence chief.

President Omar Hassan Ahmed Bashir, who wanted terrorism sanctions against Sudan lifted, offered the arrest and extradition of Bin Laden and detailed intelligence data about the global networks constructed by Egypt's Islamic Jihad, Iran's Hezbollah and the Palestinian Hamas....

But U.S. authorities repeatedly turned the data away, first in February 1996; then again that August, when at my suggestion Sudan's religious ideologue, Hassan Turabi, wrote directly to Clinton; then in April of 1997, when I persuaded

Bashir to invite the FBI to come to Sudan and view the data; and finally in February 1998, when Sudan's intelligence chief Gutbi al-Mahdi, wrote to the FBI. Gutbi had shown me some of Sudan's data during a three-hour meeting in Khartoum in October 1996...."

On the same day that Ijaz released his op-ed regarding Clinton's failure to capture Bin Laden, leading Democrats re-directed the nation's focus to weapons of mass destruction. On December 5, 2001, Senator Bob Graham (along with the signatures of other Democrats) sent President Bush a letter which included the following statement:

There is no doubt that ... Saddam Hussein has invigorated his weapons programs. Reports indicate that biological, chemical and nuclear programs continue apace and may be back to pre-Gulf War status. In addition, Saddam continues to redefine delivery systems and is doubtless using the cover of a licit missile program to develop longer-range missiles that will threaten the United States and our allies.

On September 19, 2002, Sen. Carl Levin (D- MI), made the following statement:

We begin with the common belief that Saddam Hussein is a tyrant and threat to the peace and stability of the region. He has ignored the mandate of the United Nations and is building weapons of mass destruction and the means of delivering them.

On September 23, 2002, Al Gore said:

We know that he has stored secret supplies of biological and chemical weapons throughout his country. Iraq's search for weapons of mass destruction has proven impossible to deter, and we should assume that it will continue for as long as Saddam is in power.

On September 27, 2002, Ted Kennedy said:

We have known for many years that Saddam Hussein is seeking and developing weapons of mass destruction.

On October 23, 2002, Sen. Robert Byrd said:

The last UN weapons inspectors left Iraq in October of 1998. We are confident that Saddam Hussein retains some stockpiles of chemical and biological weapons, and that he has since embarked on a crash course to build up his chemical and biological warfare capabilities.

On October 9, 2002, Sen. John F. Kerry said:

I will be voting to give the President of the United States the authority to use force- if necessary- to disarm Saddam Hussein because I believe that a deadly arsenal of weapons of mass destruction in his hands is a real and grave threat to our security.

On October 10, 2002, Sen. Jay Rockefeller said:

There is unmistakable evidence that Saddam Hussein is working aggressively to develop nuclear weapons and will likely have nuclear weapons within the next five years . We also should remember __we have always underestimated the progress Saddam__ has made in development of weapons of mass destruction."

On October 10, 2002 Rep. Henry Waxman said:

He has systematically violated, over the course of the past eleven years, every significant UN resolution that has demanded that he disarm and destroy his chemical and biological weapons, and any nuclear capacity. This he has refused to do.

On October 10, 2002 Sen. Hillary Clinton said:

In the four years since the inspectors left, intelligence reports show that Saddam Hussein has worked to rebuild his chemical and biological weapon stock, his missile delivery capability, and his nuclear program. He has also given aid, comfort, and sanctuary to terrorists, including al Qaeda members. It is clear, however, that if left unchecked Saddam Hussein will continue to increase his capacity to wage biological and chemical warfare, and will keep trying to develop nuclear weapons.

On December 8, 2002 Sen. Bob Graham said:

We are in possession of what I think to be compelling evidence that Saddam Hussein has, and has had for a number of years, a developing capacity for the production and storage of weapons of mass destruction.

On January 23, 2003 Sen. John F. Kerry said:

"Without question, we need to disarm Saddam Hussein. He is a brutal murderous dictator, leading an oppressive regime. He presents a particularly grievous threat because he is so consistently prone to miscalculation. And now he is miscalculating America's response to his continued deceit and his consistent grasp for weapons of mass destruction. So the threat of Saddam Hussein with weapons of mass destruction is real."

On one hand the news media consistently reported there were no weapons of mass destruction, and on the other hand the New York Times released a small article on October 24, 2004, claiming "that nearly 380 tons of powerful conventional explosives –used to demolish buildings, produce missile warheads and detonate nuclear weapons are missing from one of Iraq's most sensitive former military installations." CNN reported that the IAEA and the State Department also verified that the weapons had strangely vanished. In 2004, one year after the war was started no one thought to ask: Why would there be explosives to detonate nuclear weapons if Iraq had none or wasn't in the process of developing such weapons?

Although most news sources were reluctant to report the missing weapons story, even fewer news organizations (with the exception of the *Los Angeles Times*) reported that according to a relative of Syrian President Bashar Assad, Iraq's weapons of mass destruction were moved to three locations in Syria. The relative said the "weapons were smuggled in large wooden crates and barrels by Zu Alhema al-Shaleesh" under the direction of Saddam's General Shalish, with the help Assif Shoakat and Bashar Assad's cousin. Shoakat was the CEO of Bhanhja, an import/export company owned by the Assad family. The move took place in February 2003, one month before the coalition's invasion. The specific locations where the weapons are hidden include (1) a mountain tunnel near the village of al-Baidah in northwest Syria (2) a Syrian air force camp near the village of Tal Snan and (3) the tunnels in the small town of Shinshar. You will note that this story did not get the exclusive sustaining coverage that those who opposed the war received.

Democrats and Republicans Voted for the War

In October of 2002, when the vote was taken to go to war, Senators Kerry, Cantwell, Daschle, Feinstein, Clinton, Rockefeller and a host of other Democrats voted for the war. Perhaps they remembered the words from President Clinton during his December 16, 1998, speech when he said:

> *First, we must be prepared to use force again if Saddam takes threatening actions, such as trying to reconstitute his weapons of mass destruction or their delivery systems, threatening*

his neighbors, challenging allied aircraft over Iraq, or mov-
ing against his own Kurdish citizens...."

The records will show that both Republicans and Democrats voted in favor of the war for many reasons, beyond weapons of mass destruction.

Senator John McCain said:

The United States needs to move before Saddam can develop a more advanced arsenal. Giving peace a chance only gives Saddam Hussein more time to prepare for war on his terms, at a time of his choosing, in pursuit of ambitions that will only grow as his power to achieve them grows.

Richard Gephardt, who helped draft the measure to go to war, made the following remarks:

Giving Bush the authority to attack Iraq could avert war by demonstrating the United States is willing to confront Saddam over his obligations to the United States. I believe we have an obligation to protect the United States by preventing him from getting these weapons and either using them himself or passing them or their components to terrorist who share his destructive intent.

Senator Tom Daschel said:

The threat of Iraq's weapons program may not be imminent, but it is real. It is grown. And it cannot be ignored."

The final vote in the United States Senate was 77 for and 23 against. In the House it was 296 for 133 against.

On February 5, 2003, (one month before the Iraqi invasion) Secretary of State Colin Powell, addressed the United Nations. During his speech he emphasized that Iraq, as of that date, had not complied with

Resolution 1441, which meant that Saddam had not provided proof that he had ended his weapons of mass destruction program. Powell told the UN Security Council:

This is an important day for us all as we review the situation with respect to Iraq and its disarmament obligations under UN Security Council Resolution 1441.

Last November 8, this council passed Resolution 1441 by a unanimous vote. The purpose of that resolution was to disarm Iraq of its weapons of mass destruction. Iraq had already been found guilty of material breach of its obligations, stretching back over sixteen previous resolutions and twelve years.

Was It A Lie?

If the claims that Iraq had weapons of mass destruction was a lie, the records clearly show the lie started during the Clinton administration; it was supported by both leading Democrats and the United Nation's Security Council; then it was passed on to the Bush Administration after Bush assumed the presidency. The so-called lie did not start with Bush. Supported by intelligence from the international community as well as intelligence from the Clinton Administration, claims that Iraq had weapons of mass destruction started ten years before Bush took office. So if Bush lied, so did the international community and Clinton Administration. But was it a lie? Not according the scientist that defected from Iraq or the IAEA who reported that a cache of 380 tons of weapons were missing from an Iraqi military base, nor was it a lie according to the reports from the relatives of the Syrian president who claimed that the weapons were moved to Syria.

(Quotes in this editorial were taken from speeches delivered by Democrats and a variety of Internet sources including: World Net Daily, Institute for Public Accuracy, Urban Legends References, Latimes.com, CNN.com, and the New York Times).

Going To War with Iraq over Oil – A Very Wise Security Move

If we turn our backs on his defiance, the credibility of U.S. power as a check against Saddam will be destroyed. We will not only have allowed Saddam to shatter the inspection system that controls his weapons of mass destruction program; we also will have fatally undercut the fear of force that stops Saddam from acting to gain domination in the region....

President Clinton
December 16, 1998

There has been a multitude of news coverage regarding the Bush Administration and how it misled Congress as to the reason why we went to war. Some news reports have suggested that going to war had nothing to do with weapons of mass destruction. It was all about the oil in the Middle East. If this is true, could that be bad? It all depends on who you ask. Many feel that oil would have been a better reason than the weapons.

When we think about our dependency on oil, our thoughts and discussions usually focus on the gas that we use in our vehicles. Seldom do these discussions ever focus on the fact that without petroleum, our Air Force planes cannot not fly, our Army tanks cannot roll and our Navy ships cannot sail. In other words, an inadequate supply of petroleum reserve could be the greatest threat to our national security.

Not only is petroleum essential for the protection and security of our nation (as older citizens can verify from the gas rationing during World War II), major manufacturers will attest that petroleum is one of the central ingredients in hundreds of millions of products that are a part of our everyday life. If we stop the import of oil, or if for some reason a radical dictator took control of the oil reserves in the Middle East and Venezuela, our nation would fall into a utter chaos.

Oil is one of the principal ingredients in making plastics. As we all know, plastic is used to manufacture weapons, vehicles, household products, computers, and a multitude of other products that we use on a daily basis. In addition, oil is a key ingredient in rubber products for our cars; asphalt for our roads; toys for our children; a variety of medical products including bandages, artificial limbs, heart valves, contact lenses; as well as millions of other products - ball point pens, explosives, sunglasses, trash bags, nylon rope, toothbrushes, deodorant, nail polish, lipstick, synthetic fabrics, fertilizers, paint, paint brushes, soap, photographic film, insecticides, tennis shoes, hair shampoo, plywood adhesives, roofing materials, carpeting, water pipes, glue, and the list goes on and on and on.

Americans are as dependent and addicted to oil as a crack addict is dependent and addicted to crack. If a powerful leader from the Middle East were to take over the oil reserves of the Middle East and stop the export of oil to the United States, thousands of businesses would have to close their doors, millions of workers will be out of work, and our economy would be in shambles.

Many of us remember how our lives were radically changed on October 17, 1973, when the Organization of Arab Petroleum Exporting Countries (which included OPEC nations plus Egypt and Syria) announced that as a result of the ongoing Yom Kippur War, they would no longer ship petroleum to nations that had supported Israel in its conflict with Syria and Egypt. Around that same time, OPEC members agreed to use their leverage in the pricing of petroleum and the next thing we (Americans) knew, we were sitting in our cars waiting for a few gallons of rationed gas. It was a time of long lines and short tempers. Fist fights broke out when impatient customers tried to merge ahead of other customers who had been patiently waiting in seemly unending lines, stretching for several blocks. OPEC's decision to increase the price of oil, affected countries worldwide and created a multitude of problems for the U.S. economy. How soon do we forget.

If your recall, angry voters demanded that Congress do something to prevent this from happening in the future. There were discussions regarding alternative fuel, exploratory drilling in places that were preveiously protected by environmental concerns as well as a demand for smaller cars with better gas mileage. (Note: Six years after this crisis Saddam became president of Iraq).

By the time we invaded Iraq in 2003 (thirty years later), we were still dependent on Middle Eastern and Venezuela oil and none of the above was fully accomplished. In fact instead of smaller cars, more drilling and the development of alternative fuel. Car manufacturers started rolling out larger gas-guzzling vehicles (i.e. SUV's and Hummers), while environmenalists continued to block efforts to find new sources of oil and oil companies complained that it was too expensive to develop alternative fuels.

During the past thirty years, Republican and Democratic controlled congresses have failed to live up to their pledge to adequately resolve our dependency on foreign oil. It is apparent that they were influenced more by the powerful lobbyists representing the oil companies, the car manufacturers and the environmentalists than they were about the need to live up to their commitment to find solutions.

We often overlook the fact that the meetings to form the Organization of Petroleum Export Countries (OPEC) took place in Baghdad (Iraq) in September of 1960. Unlike the average American citizen, Saddam Hussein knew the history of OPEC and the power of petroleum. He knew not only this, he knew much more.

❖ He knew that America was addicted to, and dependent on, the import of foreign oil

❖ He knew that America had not lowered its dependency by developing alternative fuels

- ❖ He knew that that our U.S. Congress was influenced by powerful lobbyists from oil companies, environmentalist organizations and car manufacturers.

- ❖ He knew that if he could take control of the oil in the Middle East, he could use the petroleum to purchase technology to develop weapons of mass destruction (including nuclear weapons)

- ❖ He knew that if he could acquire such weapons he could become one of the most powerful leaders in the world, much like Hitler.

- ❖ He knew that with the oil and weapons he could influence and even possibly dictate American policy in the Middle East and elsewhere.

- ❖ And finally, he knew that, in order to accomplish all of the above, he would have to start with a strong military to begin the process.

On September 22, 1980, Saddam tested the first phase of his plan with an invasion of Iran. The purpose of the attack was to take over Iran's oil fields and dominate the Persian Gulf. In addition to attacking Iran, on March 15, 1988, with the use of chemical weapons of mass destruction, he attacked the Kurds in northern Iraq. The Kurds occupied the region that was known for having Iraq's largest deposits of oil.

Two years later, on August 2, 1990 at 0200 Saddam invaded Kuwait, one of the largest oil producing countries in the region. He launched the attack with four elite Iraqi Republican Guard divisions (1st Hammurabi Armoured Division, 2nd al-Medinah al-Munawera Armoured Division, 3rd Tawalkalna al-Allah Mechanized Infantry Division and the 6th Nebuchadnezzar Motorized Infantry Division), along with an Iraqi Army Special Forces units equivalent to a full division. The main attack was conducted by commandos deployed by helicopters and boats with attacks on the main city of Kuwait, while other divisions advanced to seize Kuwait's airports and its two airbases.

Iraq justified its invasion by claiming that Kuwait was illegally slant-drilling into the portion of the Rumaila Oil Field that belonged to Iraq and demanded $10 billion including $2.4 billion in compensation for the oil "stolen" from the Rumaila area since 1980. This resulted in the first Gulf War, a war about oil, a war to take back the oil fields that Saddam had taken with military might.

Like Hitler's ambitions, Saddam's quest for power was relentless. Hitler used his powerful military. Saddam had planned to do the same. George W. Bush wasn't the only president that was concerned with Saddam's plans to dominate the region. Bill Clinton expressed his concerns during his December 16, 1998 speech. In that speech he told America:

If we turn our backs on his defiance, the credibility of U.S. power as a check against Saddam will be destroyed. We will not only have allowed Saddam to shatter the inspection system that controls his weapons of mass destruction program; we also will have fatally undercut the fear of force that stops Saddam from acting to gain domination in the region....

Saddam had to be stopped. If not now, when? Eventually, there would be a showdown. Our only options were:

   a.   Military action

   b.   Developing our own alternative fuel sources

   c.   Drilling more wells in environmentally protected regions

   d.   Passing legislations to force car manufacturers to manufacture fuel efficient cars

   e.   Having Congress to pass legislation to control the profits of oil companies

    f.   And/or to start rationing gas as we had in World War II and the 1970's

Bush knew that if Congress had failed to do any of the above during the past thirty years chances of it doing so in the immediate future was nil and time was running out. The 911 terrorist attacks and the previous attacks on our embassies and ships created an opportunity to do two things: (1) let the terrorist know that we had had enough and (2) stop Saddam from carrying out his plans to dominate the oil reserves of the Middle East.

I am convinced that not only was the initial invasion of Iraq about protecting the oil reserves of the Middle the East which is the second largest reserve in the world. I believe the current internal fighting between the Kurds, Shiites and Sunnis within Iraq is also about oil. According a recent article in U.S. News & World Report (November 13, 2006), the Kurds claim that Iraq's constitution gives them control over the rich oil fields in their region as well as the revenue generated from those oil fields. The Shiite-dominated parliament in Baghdad disagrees. The Sunnis fear that if the Kurds prevail, it may leave them (the Sunnis) in the poorest regions of Iraq with the least amount of oil. According to the article, the Kurds have already invited some of the largest multi-national oil companies in the world to meetings to discuss investing in their new oil fields.

Note: One of the first American companies to invest in Middle East oil was Standard Oil of California in 1933. Together with the government of Saudi Arabia it formed Aramco. It is reported that three years later (1936) the Texas Oil Company purchased fifty percent of the company.

If Americans only knew what life would be like without the oil from the Middle East, they too would want our government to protect our interest, particularly when they discover that it was American companies and their financial investments and technology that helped many of these nations develop their oil industries. Should we protect the oil in the Middle East from dictators and terrorist? Unfortunately yes, because our lives depend on it. Remember, we are not at war with

Iraq. We are at war with the terrorists in Iraq of which many are not citizens of that country. And if these terrorists can create havoc with a fifty-cent box cutter and a ten dollar backpack filled with explosives, think what they can do with the revenue from oil.

It's all about the oil. If you don't believe me, let the OPEC countries stop shipping oil to the U.S. for one year and see the impact that it has on our country. It may even cost you your job.

Bringing Our Soldiers Home: Didn't We Do This Before And It Didn't Work?

The leader was defeated, the government in the region had been overthrown, the terrorist were running rampant, thousands of U.S. troops had died, and even though the president was claiming *to stay the course,* the general public, the news media, along with members of the Democratic Party (with the support of some Republicans) were demanding that the President *"bring our troops home,"* and all of this was happening during an election year. No it wasn't 2006; it was 1876.

In 1876, Democrats had finally gained enough public support to take back the White House. The election was close, so close that some demanded a recount. The Republicans had two choices: give in to the Democrats' demand and bring home the federal troops that were sent to the south to protect the newly freed slaves (during Reconstruction), or ignore their demands and risk loosing the White House.

This is how history recalls the event.

The 1876 election showed a one-vote electoral college majority for the Republicans, but the Democrats protested. Two sets of official results were sent to Congress by Democrats from South Carolina, Florida, and Louisiana. The official Electoral Commission awarded the election to Rutherford Hayes. Southern Democrats retaliated and announced plans to block the Commission's report with a filibuster in the same way that Democratic Senator Al Gore Sr. attempted to block the passage of the 1964 Civil Rights Act. The Democrats had a weak hand-but strong public support. Republicans quickly reached a compromise to keep their opposition quiet. The compromise was reached through a series of secret meetings that were attended by the powerful leaders of both parties. The compromise stated that the South would acknowledge Rutherford Hayes as president if the Republicans acceded to various demands, including the following:

- The removal of all Federal troops that were sent to the South during Reconstruction to establish a new government and protect the newly freed slaves (similar to what U.S. troops are doing in Iraq).

- The appointment of at least one Southern Democrat to Hayes' cabinet. Hayes selected David M. Key of Tennessee and gave him the position of Postmaster General.

The informal agreement satisfied Democrats, and they aborted their plans to filibuster. Hayes was inaugurated on schedule and kept his end of the bargain by removing the troops. The **Compromise of 1877** (as it is now known) was an informal, unwritten agreement that was designed to settled the disputed 1876 U.S. presidential election.

The removal of the federal troops produced choas, the choas produced a reign of terror and the terror devestated an entire race. When the troops were removed Jim Crow, Black Codes and segregation became the unchallenged law of the land. Southern Democrats and their terrorist organizations (much like the terrorist in Iraq) carried out their violent racist agenda without federal interference. During the next one hundred years after the troops were removed the following took place:

❖ Elected black officials were driven from office

❖ Blacks were denied the right to participate in the political process and were denied the right to vote

❖ Millions of acres of land were fraudulently taken from blacks

❖ Patents were denied-inventions were stolen

❖ Entire black communities such as Wilmington, North Carolina, Rosewood, Florida, and the Greenwood District in Tulsa Oklahoma were burned to the ground.

❖ Thousands of blacks were lynched and murdered.

❖ Black churches were bombed.

❖ Blacks became the victims of secret government experiments such as the Tuskegee Experiment.

❖ Hundreds of thousands of blacks from ages seven to seventy-five were forced to work in prison labor camps to help rebuild the south.

❖ Blacks were denied a quality education while their teachers were driven from their classrooms and many were beaten and murdered. Professor James McPherson of Princeton University said: *Southern hostility to Yankee teachers sometimes went beyond ostracism and verbal abuse. ... Many missionaries were threatened, beaten, and murdered. The American Missionary Association (AMA) reported several incidents similar to the one in which a group of masked men took a teacher from his house in North Carolina, tied him up, and after threatening to kill him if he did not leave the state gave him 100 lashes with a bullwhip. The founder and president for nearly 30 years of Shaw University, Henry Tupper of Massachusetts, was often harassed by the Ku Klux Klan and once hid all night in a cornfield with his wife and two children to avoid an assassination attempt. The AMA tried for several years to cooperate with local [southern] school boards* [prior to the removal of the troops]. *So long as Republicans were in power this arrangement worked out reasonably well. But when the Democrats began to regain control of the South* [after the troops were removed] *the dual support foundered and eventually collapsed. In Memphis the Democrats dismissed all AMA teachers, forcing the association to withdraw from the jointly sponsored Lincoln School and found LeMoyne Institute in its place. In 1879, two years after the troops were removed, the Northern Methodists compiled a list of 34 attacks on their missionaries and teachers in the past decade; 19 of the victims were White and 15 Black, three of the whites and four of the Blacks were killed.*

❖ The first black to be elected to Congress from the south after the troops were removed was Barbara Jordan, in 1973 almost one hundred years later.

Many believe similar atrocities will take place in Iraq when American troops are removed.

Iraqi War Casualties Compared to Other Wars

The claims that we are loosing too many soldiers are the same claims that the media and Democrats made 130 years ago in 1877. But compared to all other U.S. wars, the casualties of the Iraq War are very small by comparison. The Iraq War started in March of 2003, and as of this date (June 1, 2007), fewer than 3,600 U.S. soldiers have lost their lives. Of all the wars lasting three years or more, the Iraq War is unique. It has the *fewest* number of U.S. military casualties of any war in American History.

❖ World War I   Over 110,000 casualties   1917-1918

❖ World War II   Over 400,000 casualties   1940-1945

❖ Korean War   Over 40,000 casualties   1950-1953

❖ Viet Nam War Over 100,000 casualties   1964-1975

❖ Iraq War   Fewer than 3600 casualties   2003 to present

U.S. Civil War (1861-1865)

During the U.S. Civil War, which is quite similar to the Iraq War in many respects (in both terrorists killed innocent civilians during their reconstruction phases), over 500,000 died from battles and another 400,000–plus died from accidents, suicides, sickness, murder and executions. During one month of fighting, 65,000 soldiers lost their lives, which is *twenty times* more than those that died during the *entire* the Iraq War.

In 1876, Democrats (along with a few defectors from Republican Party) demanded the removal of our troops from the South. One hundred-thirty years later in 2006 during the congressional races, this same party (along with a few of their Republican counterparts) demanded that the government remove our troops from Iraq. Will history repeat itself? If we remove the troops, will the terrorists take over Iraq as they did in the South? Many predict that they will.

THE BLACK VOTE

AND OUR

TWO PARTY SYSTEM

As President - Barack Obama Can Do Very Little to Help Blacks

Every four years, while the so-called pro-black candidates flock to the black community seeking to get the black vote, major news organizations flock to the black community seeking to get a story. The two leading pro-black candidates that received the most press during the 2008 presidential campaign were Democratic Senators Barack Obama and Hillary Clinton. As with their predecessors who previously campaigned in the black community, the crowds cheered and applauded as each candidate told his or her black audience what they would do if he or she were elected President of the United States. As they cheered and applauded, little did they know that as president, neither one of these individuals would be in a position to help blacks. Why? Because:

1. Presidents cannot sponsor or pass laws; only Congress can.

2. And because Congress can over-ride a presidential veto, presidents do not have the final say-so as to whether a law will be passed.

3. Presidents cannot hire whom they will; Congress confirms or rejects all presidential appointments.

4. Presidents do not have the final say so over the national budget or taxes, that's Congress' job.

5. Presidents cannot declare war or fund wars without Congressional approval.

6. Presidents cannot approve reparation pay for blacks; only Congress can.

7. Presidents cannot fund programs for the African American community nor can they fund relief for disasters such as Katrina without Congressional approval.

Simply put, in domestic matters, presidents are merely individuals with (what they believe to be) good ideas, ideas that they hope will be approved by Congress. George W. Bush had ideas about social security reform, immigration reform and school choice but the bi-partisan Congress rejected them all. Bill Clinton had ideas about health care reform, but again, Congress said no. President Jimmy Carter also had problems with Congress. Of all the presidents, he was least effective in getting Congress to support his ideas. After leaving office, he made the following statement:

I think I have found it is much easier for me in my own administration to evolve a very complex proposal for resolving a difficult issue than it is for Congress to pass legislation and to make that same decision.

The energy legislation is one example. I never dreamed ... when I proposed this matter to Congress that a year later it still would not be resolved. I think I have got a growing understanding of the Congress, its limitations and its capabilities... this was a new experience to me altogether....

Presidents may have good ideas but it is Congress that decides what's best for the people.

To keep the pro-black candidates honest and ensure that they really have the best interest of blacks in mind, both the media and the black community should challenge these candidates by asking the following questions.

Regarding Laws to Help African Americans

❖ As a current member of the legislative (law-making) branch of government, how many programs have you developed and/or specifically funded for blacks, and how many laws have you written, sponsored and/or passed on behalf of blacks?

❖ As a lawmaker (member of Congress), if you did not pass laws or get funding for programs that would specifically address the needs of blacks, how can you do it as president, when the president has no legislative power to do this?

❖ If you have failed to do anything for us as a member of Congress during the past ___ years when you had the opportunity, how can we trust you to do anything for us as president?

Regarding Health Care and Abortions

❖ As a lawmaker in charge of funding, Congress seems to have unlimited funds to give to young black mothers funding to kill their babies(through abortions), but it struggles to find funds to provide funding for pre-natal care if they decide to let their baby live. Tell me, how can you have unlimited funds to kill them (seventeen million black babies since *Roe v. Wade*), but you are hard pressed to find health care funds to heal them?

❖ Let me put it another way. Under the banner that *a woman has the right to choose,* why is it that you lawmakers have unlimited funds to help the black baby die, but limited health care funds to help the baby live?

❖ Isn't it true that the government has spent billions to kill the seveteen million black babies (that have been aborted since *Roe V. Wade)*? Why did the government decide to fund abortions? Was it out of the concern for the poor black mother, or was it to slow down the birth rate of African Americans due to Afro-phobia? Did you realize that had those seventeen million babies lived during the past thirty-four years and each had two children of their own, the black population in America would be close to ninety million, making it the largest ethnic group in America?

Regarding Black Economics and Our Prison Systems

❖ As a senator who approves all budgets that pass through Congress you have provided enough funds to lock up every black man that commits a crime to the tune of $40,000 to $65,000 per year per prisoner. How can you find unlimited funds to give every black man a prison cell with health care at the rate of $40,000 per year, but you cannot find the same kinds of funds to give every black man $40,000 per year to either go to college, or to purchase a home or to start a business?

❖ As a senator, have you ever written a law (as a crime prevention program) to provide blacks with $40,000 per year to start a business or to go to school, as a means to keep them out of jail? If not, why not?

Immigration Reform & Blacks

❖ As a member of Congress, why are you so interested in immigration reform for illegal immigrants from Mexico, but a few years ago you ignored immigration reform when black Haitian refugees attempted to come to America to escape political persecution? How is it that you can effectively keep black Haitians from coming into this country but you cannot stop brown Latinos from coming into this country?

Stopping Drugs from Coming into our Inner-cities

❖ As a senator, you are aware of the countries that produce the illegal drugs that eventually make their way to the inner-cities of America. With modern-day satellite technology, why is it so difficult to stop these drugs from coming into our communities? After-all they can only be transported from those countries by trucks, boats or planes.

Giving Up Legislative Authority to Help Blacks

❖ Why would you as a lawmaker want to give up your legislative powers which can help blacks - for a position of President, which has no legislative authority to help blacks?

Your Track Record of Helping African Americans

❖ Prior to becoming a member of Congress, what *specifically* did do you do for blacks and the black community during the past 25 years?

Since most of the national debates are sponsored by news organizations, the chances of these types of questions being asked are nil, simply because most news organizations are more interested in stories about blacks but not the welfare of blacks.

Blacks Need Both Parties to Succeed

Despite the fact that every piece of legislation and every presidential request must have the approval of a bi-partisan Congress (from the passage of the Civil Rights Act of 1964 to the authorization of the Iraq War), the media has convinced millions of African American voters that who they (blacks) have in the White House is far more important than who they have in Congress. Few are aware that according to congressional records, today all laws are passed with the support of both Democrats and Republicans. These records further reveal that without bi-partisan support newly proposed legislation is seldom ever referred to the appropriate legislative committee for consideration.

What this means is that African Americans can no longer embrace one party while ignoring the members of the other party if they really want to accomplish their objectives. Political experts strongly urge African Americans to work to establish *allies in both parties, and avoid creating enemies in either party*. The media, special interest groups, and our political lobbyist have known this for some time and have successfully courted both parties to get what they want. During a recent Bill O'Reilly Show (aired August 21, 2006), the Reverend Al Sharpton confessed that he receives money from both Republicans and Democrats. Even though blacks need allies on both sides of the aisle, the media coverage of our elections has led many African Americans to focus primarily on the presidential races rather than the congressional races.

Inner-city ministers often quote the scripture which says: *"How shall they hear without a preacher and how can he or she preach, except they are sent..."* (Romans 10:14). One might say (metaphorically speaking), when voters send representatives to Washington, they are really sending political preachers to Congress to deliver policy-changing sermons (messages) on their behalf.

As voters African Americans must establish a practice of never voting for any candidate (Democrat or Republican) without first letting that person know what is expected of him or her (see Appendix A). Therefore candidates for office should never come into the African American community telling blacks what they plan to do. They should come in asking blacks what should be done. After all, elected officials are the employees of the voters and it is the employers' job (the voter's) to tell the newly hired employee (the candidate) what is expected of him or her, not the other way around. Hiring and sending individuals to Washington or to your state legislation to advocate on your behalf is what voting is all about. Therefore, when the voter places a politician on the payroll, it is not only their right to tell the politician what to do, it is his or her responsibility and obligation to do so.

Viewing each candidate as a potential employee is why the interview process is so important. A thorough interview of each candidate will not only determine whether each is qualified to do the job, it will also determine whether or not the candidate has the same core values as you, the voter. African Americans should never vote for any individual (whether Democrat or Republican) without first being assured that the individual has the same core values as themselves and that he or she is willing to reflect and/or include these core values while drafting and voting on future legislation. This is important because our values are the most precious gems that we can ever possess. What we do not value, we will eventually destroy and this can include our families, our faith, our communities and our country. Protecting our values is a process of protecting our people and protecting our people is a process of protecting our future and protecting our future means never compromising our values to be politically popular or politically correct. To accomplish this African Americans will need allies in both political parties who share their values. African Americans must remember this truth: If the president of the United States needs the members of both parties to accomplish his objectives, African Americans will need them as well. Jimmy Carter learned this lesson the hard way.

Republicans Must Include Racism as a Moral Issue to Reach Blacks

Republicans across the country are attempting to woo black conservative Christians to the GOP by placing an emphasis on such moral issues as:

- ❖ Same-sex-marriage

- ❖ Abortion

- ❖ And the Separation of church and state

But their fatal mistake has been their reluctance and unwillingness to include racism as one of the moral issues.

The biggest differences between today's Republican Party and its predecessors, is the fact that their predecessors viewed slavery and racism as monumental moral issues. Their position on slavery and racism not only resulted in the formation of their new political party, but a multitude of civil rights legislation as well.

Contrary to their way of thinking, today the number one moral issue on the minds of African Americans is not abortions, same-sex-marriage or the separation of church and state, even though these are important moral issues. The number one moral issue on the minds of African Americans is still racial discrimination. The media and the Democratic Party have known this for some time and have consistently played the race card to keep their black constituency. Although the Democrats continue to seize the opportunity to talk about racial issues, they have yet to introduce one bill during the past forty years to eradicate racism.

Republicans also overlook the fact that if we solve or resolve the moral issues of same-sex-marriage and abortions, racism would still be a problem for African Americans. It is an issue that they are forced to live with on a daily basis.

From 1854 to 1983, Republicans believed so strongly that the eradication of slavery and the achievement of racial equality were so vitally important that they did the following:

1. Formed a political party to address slavery and racism

2. Opposed the Dred Scott Decision

3. Opposed the Kansas Nebraska Act

4. Opposed Fugitive Slave Laws

5. Issued the Emancipation Proclamation

6. Passed the 13th Amendment, abolishing slavery

7. Passed the 1866 Civil Rights Act

8. Passed Reparation Senate Bill 60 to give blacks forty acres and a mule

9. Passed the 14th Amendment to give blacks citizenship

10. Opposed the Slaughterhouse Case

11. Passed the 1867 Reconstruction Act

12. Passed the 1870 Force Act to force Civil Rights

13. Passed the 1871 Enforcement Act

14. Passed the 1871 Ku Klux Klan Act

15. Passed the 1875 Civil Rights Act

16. Opposed the decision in *Plessy v. Ferguson*

17. Supported the Decision in *Brown v. Board of Education*

18. Passed the 1957 Civil Rights Act

19. Passed the 1960 Civil Rights Act

20. Supported and Passed the 1964 Civil Rights Act

21. Supported and Passed the Voting Rights Act of 1965

22. Supported and Passed the 1968 Civil Rights Act

23. Supported and Passed the 1972 Equal Employment Opportunity Act

24. Started and Introduced affirmative action Programs

25. Supported and Passed a bill to legalize Dr. King's Birthday as a national holiday

Not only did they pass a multitude of legislation and fight against various pieces of racially biased litigation, Republicans distanced themselves from those who supported and promoted racism. During a speech on October 15, 1858, Lincoln told his audience how the moral issue of slavery divided the nation: Lincoln said:

Parties themselves may be divided and quarrel on minor questions, yet it [the moral issue of slavery] *extends beyond parties themselves.*

But does not this question make a disturbance outside the political circles? Does it not enter into the churches and rend them asunder? What divided the great Methodist Church into two parts, North and South? What has raised this constant disturbance in every Presbyterian General Assembly that meets? What disturbed the Unitarian Church in this very city two years ago? Is it not this same mighty, deep seated power that somehow operates on the minds of men, exciting them and stirring them up in every avenue of society – in politics, in religion, in literature, in morals in all the manifold relations of life? Is this the work of politicians. Is it that irresistible power which for fifty years has shaken government and agitated the people to be stilled and subdued by pretending that it is an exceedingly simple thing, and we ought not to talk about it?

Today churches are no longer split over the moral issues of slavery, instead they are faced with other moral issues such as abortions, homosexuality, sex education, the separation of church and state and racism. And it seems as if everyone feels comfortable talking about everything, except the moral issues of racism.

Since the legalization of Dr. King's Birthday as a national holiday, Republicans seem to no longer view racial discrimination as a moral issue, instead they seem to be preoccupied with eliminating the very program that their predecessors started to achieve equality: affirmative action. This is not to say that Republicans should support affirmative action programs (as we know them today), studies have shown that these programs have had limited success. However Republicans (like their predecessors) should classify racism and equality as moral issues and should include them as part of their political platform.

In an effort to reach black pastors, many Republicans point out that since moral issues are biblically based, black pastors should support Republicans, not Democrats. While many black pastors would agree with them, others would point out that the Bible also addresses and condemns racism in both the Old Testament and the New Testament. God Himself confronted Moses' sister who was angry with her brother (Moses) because he had married a black woman. Jesus used a race-relations parable to illustrate *loving our neighbor as ourselves*; and Paul confronted Peter because of his racial prejudice.

In speaking to African American pastors, Republicans must realize that every black congregation in America has (both liberal and conservative) members who have been victims of racial discrimination. They must also realize that while many black pastors will agree that same-sex-marriages and abortions are explosive moral issues, they also believe that racism is an equally explosive moral issue and must be addressed along with the other important concerns that are condemned by the Bible.

Modern-day Republicans must learn from their predecessors who were sensitive enough to start the process of racial equality for African Americans. They must pick up the mantle, embrace the principles of righteousness, and complete the job that their predecessors started.

Blacks Evaluating Black Leadership

My concerns about the failure of America's Black leadership are no different from those of many Blacks, most of whom prefer to keep their feelings private because they are not politically correct among the Black elite.

Tony Brown
Black Lies, White Lies

Of all the truths, none are as difficult to accept as those associated with ineffective black leadership, but seldom will the mainstream media report on this. Each year, more and more African Americans are openly expressing their displeasure with their current leaders and with such organizations as the Congressional Black Caucus (CBC). Writing for *Savoy Magazine*, Deborah Mathis, a Shorenstein Fellow at Harvard University said: *The Congressional Black Caucus, which was founded in 1971 by thirteen Black members of Congress, started out well. But by the 80's, the CBC was weary and worn, with virtually no legislative trophies to show for its scars. By many accounts, the body that was once a force to be reckoned with has not only lost its fervor but its political power as well. Critics say that the Caucus grew complacent under what was generally accepted as a friendly Clinton administration, and many wondered whether the CBC may be past its prime.* In reference to the Caucus' annual conference which draws many famous people including movie stars, Mathis said: *Aside from the daily workshops, the weekend is such a feast of fashion, schmoozing and carousing that it can never be said the CBC is good for nothing.*

Criticism of our black leadership by black citizens and by other black leaders is not a new phenomenon. During the beginning of Dr. King's civil rights movement he told Playboy Magazine that he had talked to a crowd of two-hundred black ministers and challenged them to do more than just preach about the glories of heaven to their people. He told them that *A minister cannot preach the glories of heaven while ignoring the social conditions in his own community that caused men an earthly hell.*

Just three years after the death of Rev. Dr. Martin Luther King Jr., actor Ossie Davies, addressed the 1971 Congressional Black Caucus Conference. On June 18, 1971, he told the audience to stop blaming the white man for their problems. He said, *"It's not the man, it's the plan."* Davis said it is *"very simple,"* Blacks do not need a bunch of *rhetoric* from their leaders. Blacks *"need a map,"* not their leader's *"rap."* He challenged the Caucus to come up with Ten Black Commandments, Commandments, guidlines that would be a simple, moral, intelligent plan that Blacks could carry in their heart.[1] Thirty-six years later, apparently the Caucus is still working on the plan and the Commandments because no one has seen either.[2]

Most African Americans are aware of what the caucus and the Clinton administration did for the gay community, but few to none can specifically state what they did to address the specific needs of Black Americans. Using the black experience as a spring board to launch their own agenda, gay rights groups obtained medical coverage for their live-in lovers, the right to adopt children and the right to marry (in a few states), and a *"don't ask don't tell policy"* in the military. But no one can tell what Jesse Jackson or the Congressional Black Caucus did to address the pressing needs of African Americans.

---

1   (Source: *Black Lies, White Lies* By Tony Brown pp. 245-246
2   *Black Lies, White Lies* pp. 235

Both Jackson and members of the Caucus showed their compassion and concern for the various gay rights groups, but that same compassion and concern has yet to reach the oppressed black community. Some blacks have said, *"If a black leader can travel overseas and successfully negotiate the freedom of American hostages, why can't he devote the same amount of time to free his own people who are hostages and victims of gang violence, drug addiction and teenage pregnancies?"*

Samuel Cotton (the author of *Silent Terror: An African American Journey Into Contemporary Slavery*) wasn't upset with Jesse Jackson because he traveled overseas to negotiate the freedom of American hostages. Cotton was upset because he felt our powerful black leaders have ignored those who are hostage to the black slave trade in Africa. Cotton accused Jackson, the Congressional Black Caucus and other powerful black leaders of consistently ignoring the modern day enslavement of black Africans in Muslim controlled African countries. The Encyclopedia Britannica reports that from 605 AD to 1905 *Black slaves exported from Africa were widely traded throughout the Islamic world. Approximately 18,000,000 Africans were delivered into the Islamic tran-Saharan and Indian Ocean slave trade"* [by Muslims]*).[3]*

During the past decade other blacks have also expressed their concerns about black leadership. In a nationwide poll conducted by Janice Hayes of *Detroit News* and Ellyn Ferguson of *Gannett News Service,* 1,211 blacks reported that: *"Civil rights groups are falling behind the times and not keeping up with the problems facing blacks in the 1990's."* Their findings were highlighted in a front-page article released *by USA Today* on February 24, 1992, entitled: <u>Civil Rights Groups Out of Step</u>. They reported that blacks wanted their leadership to *"fight crime, help the poor and improve education."[4]* NPR talk show host Juan Williams voiced similar sentiments about black leadership in his most recent book (August 2006) entitled: *Enough: The Phony Leaders,*

---

3   Source: *Black Lies, White Lies* By Tony Brown pp. 245-246
4   USA Today February 24, 1992

Dead-End Movements, and Culture of Failure That are Undermining Black America and What We Can Do About It.

Nine years later, after the Janice Hayes National Poll, an international magazine called the *Economist,* expressed similar feelings about today's Civil Rights leaders. The article entitled, <u>The Leadership of Black America: Time to Pass On The Torch</u> said:

> *"Rarely out of the headlines, masters of the stage-managed event and the attention-grabbing sound bite, men like Mr. Jackson and Mr. Sharpton have long used the power of publicity to prod white America into recognizing the claims of black America, and doing something to meet those claims. But, for all their past successes, their grandstanding now looks tired and increasingly irrelevant. To a growing number of blacks, their ideas have gone stale. The problems of America's blacks have changed considerable over the past four decades; but their leadership has not."[5]*

PBS Commentator Tony Brown said in his book *Black Lies White Lies*:

> *"That black leadership in this country has scrupulously avoided having a plan of action or a road map to equality either because they are not smart enough (which I doubt is the case) or because they don't want Blacks to leave the **Democratic plantation**. My concerns about the failure of America's Black leadership are no different from those of many Blacks, most of whom prefer to keep their feelings private because they are not politically correct among the Black elite."[6]*

Today's leaders could learn from black leaders of the past. Booker T. Washington, who was both a Republican and a very powerful black leader of his time, presented the following plan for the black community during his National Negro Conference in 1896. During the conference he told the audience,

---

5 Economist Magazine August 18, 2001 page 21-22
6 Page 235 *Black Lies, White Lies*

1. *"We are more and more convinced, as we gather in these Annual Conferences, that we shall secure our rightful place as citizens in proportion as we possess Christian character, education and property. To this end we urge parents to exercise rigid care in the control of their children, the doing away with the one room cabin and the mortgage habit.*

2. *We urge the purchase of land, improved methods of farming, diversified crops, attention to stock raising, dairying, fruit growing, and more interest in learning the trades, now too much neglected.*

3. *We urge that a larger proportion of our college educated men and women give the race the benefit of their education, along industrial lines, and that more educated ministers and teachers settle in the country districts.*

4. *As in most places, the public schools are in session only three or four months during the year, we urge the people by every means possible, to supplement this time by at least three or four additional months each year, that no sacrifice be considered too great to keep the children in school, and that only the best teachers be employed.*

5. *We note with pleasure, the organization of other Conferences, and we advise that the number be still more largely increased."*[7]

This was the type of plan that Ossie Davis and Tony Brown were referring to. So far, our black leaders have yet to come up with such a plan. Perhaps they are still looking for one of the two political parties to do the planning for them.

One might think that having more black politicians would mean fewer black problems, but such has not proven to be the case. There were seventeen (African American) members of the House of Representa-

---

7 Documentary History of Negro People Vol. 2

tives in 1980. Thirteen years later in 1993, there were forty members, but no major differences in the problems facing African Americans. In some areas, the conditions were slightly worse even with twice as many political representatives. In 1980, with seventeen black members in the House of Representatives, 1,826,000 black families were living in poverty (28%) and 60.1% of blacks had private health insurance. In 1993, when there were forty black members in House of Representatives, the number of black families living in poverty increased to 2,499,000 (31.3%), while the number of blacks having private health insurance decreased to 52%.[8]

According to a University of Michigan study, from 1994 to 1999 black family wealth declined despite a booming economy. According to the study, the net worth of the median black household fluctuated – half were higher and half were lower – decreasing from $8400 to $7500. The study went on to say that for every dollar of wealth, the median white household had in 1999, the median black household held barely 9 cents.

In the 60's, when we had fewer black politicians we had lower unemployment. The chart in Appendix C shows the number of persons receiving unemployment compensation each year. The numbers do not reflect the actual percentage of all who are unemployed, only those receiving unemployment compensation. When people are no longer receiving unemployment benefits they are classified as employed whether they have found a job or not. In 1965, when our unemployment was only 8.5%, we had fewer black politicians, but we also had the Reverend Dr. Martin Luther King Jr. In 1970, when our unemployment went down to 6.7%, Dr. King's residual presence was still a factor. In the mid-70's, after his death, our unemployment reached double digits and has remained there every since. Unemployment increased during the same period when the number of black politicians increased.

This is not to suggest that black elected official aren't needed nor is it to suggest that black elected officials are ineffective. It is to say that

8 Dept. of Commerce Bureau of Labor & Statistics - Statistical Abstract

as taxpayers we must hold all politicians accountable, whether they are black or white, Republican or Democrat. Failure to do so will only prolong our pains and problems.

Many black religious leaders believe the pressing problems facing African Americans are not the results of ineffective black leadership alone, even though effective leadership can make a difference. They believe many of our problems stem from lifestyle choices. That is, choosing to walk away from God and His principles, rather than walking with God and using His principles to unite and change our community. Unfortunately, only a handful of our national leaders today are challenging our people to walk with God and accept responsibility for our own behavior.

Writing for the *Wall Street Journal*, reporter Jason Riley says: "There was a time when black liberals, too, knew the difference between black responsibility and white oppression." "In 1961, Dr. King told a congregation, We know that there are many things wrong in the white world, but there are many things wrong in the black world too. We can't keep on blaming the white man. There are things we must do for ourselves. Do you know that Negroes are 10 percent of the population of St Louis and responsible for 58% of its crime? We got to face that. And we got to do something about our moral standard."[9]

Rev. Joseph E. Lowery of the Southern Christian Leadership Conference said if Dr. King was alive today, he would have as much to say to his people as he would to the politicians and corporate America. Rev. Lowery believes King would "call for a liberation of lifestyles that would make us free at last, in this life. Free from confused priorities, free from dependency on drugs and alcohol. Free from abuse of sexuality, free to support black institutions and businesses. Free to support and love ourselves, and free to turn to each other and not on each other." Benjamin L. Hooks said, "Dr. King, a southern preacher

---

9 Wall Street Journal April 18, 2001 Article: <u>Do Black Americans Still Need Black Leadership</u>

who earned his doctorate in theology, had a consistent message taken from the Scripture."[10]

Rev. Hooks, Rev. Lowery and the Rev. Dr. Martin Luther King Jr., all knew that when we, as a race, walked with God, we made forward progress with each godly step. They and other ministers believe that when we, as a race, walked away from God, our steps took us backwards not forward. They believe that it was our faith in God, not our faith in government that made a major difference in our lives.

Former Congressman Floyd Flake of New York is a prime example of how a person's faith in God (not their political affiliation) can change a community. Many believe that this ordained minister did more for his community as a pastor, than he did as a Congressman. When this former member of the U.S. House of Representative left congress and went back to his community in Queens, New York, he developed expensive commercial and residential developments, private schools and a variety of social commercial and social services enterprises. Pastor Flake and his Allen A.M.E. church of ten thousand members now have the unique distinction of being the largest African American employer in New York City. In his book, *The Way of The Bootstrapper*, Pastor Flake says, "I believe that without God none of it would be possible."[11] Rev. Flake is the true personification of what a modern day black leader should be like.

It is important that we hold everyone accountable who claims that they are working on behalf of African Americans. On an annual basis, every politician and every national leader should be evaluated to determine what efforts, if any, were made on behalf of their African American constitutes. Politicians are the employees of the people. If corporations can conduct annual Performance Appraisals to determine whether or not an employee has fulfilled his or her job requirements, the citizens who employ the politicians should feel obligated to do the same.

---

10 Ebony magazine January 1993 issue pp. 114-116
11 *The Way of A Bootstrapper*, p. 199

While the Japanese, the gay rights movement, environmentalist and energy companies can boast about the many pieces of legislation passed on their behalf during the past thirty years, African Americans would be hard pressed to find one piece of legislation that was specifically written, sponsored and passed on their behalf by their black leadership to address their concerns. This must change. Blacks must develop their own political agenda (See Appendix A). Unfortunately the media will never encourage blacks to do this. They want to be in charge of setting the agenda for blacks.

What Blacks Must Do for Themselves

Black Americans are still captives of the 60's and its political goals. Racism and poverty are not the reasons why we are in the situation we are in today. To try to link our solutions to elective politics is to put government on the hook for things we should do ourselves.

William Raspberry
Newsweek Magazine, April 6, 1992

Problems, heartaches and pains have seemingly been the plight and experience of every African American since we first stepped onto American soil. The realities of our struggles are documented not only in the chronicles of black history, but in American history as well. The injustices that we faced produced pain; the pain produced problems, and the problems produced two types of African Americans: those who put their faith in God and made a difference, and those who simply ignored God and made excuses.

Blacks who made a difference trusted God and turned their stumbling blocks into stepping stones, and built a stairway to success. Others who simply made excuses did not see the blocks as stepping stones, but as obstacles to their future. Thus many became angry, bitter and self-abusive. Instead of viewing the blocks as a means that could take them from the Valley of Despair to the Plateaus of Prosperity - they viewed them as worthless materials, and used them to build a Monument of

Excuses, excuses that eventually destroyed their families, their homes, their communities, their values and, eventually, themselves.

In contrast, those who made a difference were able to do so because they put their trust in God and took the same materials and made a multitude of differences. They made products out of peanuts, schools out of churches and political spokesmen out of preachers. When the stumbling blocks kept blacks out of white restaurants and hotels, they didn't complain; instead, they built their own restaurants and hotels. When the blocks prevented blacks from joining major league baseball teams, Buck O'Neil, director of the Negro Baseball Museum said, "they didn't complain." They used these blocks and formed the Negro Baseball League, a league that "drew more fans than their white counterparts." When major insurance companies would not insure us, we seized the opportunity and started our own insurance companies, institutions such as the North Carolina Mutual Insurance Company. When the blocks of racism prevented blacks from joining various organizations and associations, we took advantage of these obstacles and started our own organizations such as the National Bar Association and the National Negro Business League. And when major news organizations refused to cover events in the Black community, we built our own news organizations like the *Pittsburgh Courier*, *The Chicago Defender*, and *The Negro Digest*.

The stumbling blocks that we face today are the same types of stumbling blocks that our great grandparents faced during their day. The biggest difference between their generation and our generation was their faith in God and their determination to make a difference.

In the late 1800's, Booker T. Washington started a series of Negro Conferences. During one conference in 1896, the following were his opening remarks regarding the need for blacks to do things for themselves.

> *"The aim will be, as in the four previous years, to bring together for a quiet conference, not politicians, but the representatives of the common, hard working farmers*

and mechanics and the back bone and sinew of the Negro race, <u>the ministers and teachers</u>. I want to emphasize the object of these conferences. When they were first instituted, it was to confine ourselves mainly to the conditions within our own power to remedy. We might discuss many wrongs which should be righted; but it seems to me that it is best to lay hold of the things we can put right rather than those we can do nothing but find fault with. To be perfectly frank with each other; state things as they are; do not say anything for mere sound, or because you think it will please one or displease another; let us hear the truth on all matters. We have many things to discourage and disappoint us, and we sometimes feel that we are slipping backwards; but I believe, if we do our duty in getting property, Christian education, and character, in some way or other the sky will clear up, and we shall make our way onward. (pp 770)"[12]

One hundred and six years later, columnist William Raspberry of the *Washington Post* expressed similar feelings during an interview with *Newsweek Magazine*. On April 6, 1992, *Newsweek* reported that Raspberry said, "Black Americans are still captives of the 60's and its political goals. Racism and poverty are not the reasons why we are in the situation we are in today. To try to link our solutions to elective politics is to put government on the hook for things we should do ourselves."[13]

What should African Americans do for themselves? The following is a suggested plan to build character and economic success.

---

12 Documentary History of Negro People Vol. 2
13 Newsweek Magazine April 6, 1992

Perryman's Plan *of* Ten
for
African Americans

As a community African Americans should do the following:

1. Encourage every employed African American to give $10.00 per month - payroll deduction to a National Economic Self-Help Fund for economic development in predominately African American communities and to cover lobbying expenses to lobby state and national legislators on issues pertaining to African Americans.

2. Encourage every African American church to give 10% of its total income to a local economic development fund to help establish local medical clinics and finance various business ventures that will enhance the community.

3. Encourage every African American citizen to commit to donating 10 hours a month to community service projects to better his or her community and 10 hours per week of physical exercise to maintain and improve their health.

4. Encourage every African American doctor, lawyer and accountant to donate a minimum of 10 hours per month for professional services and educational projects in the black community.

5. Encourage every African American to write 10 letters a year in support of new legislation that would benefit African Americans.

6. Encourage every African American parent to attend a minimum of 10 PTSA and/or school board meetings per year.

7. Encourage every African American to attend one of their local churches, a minimum of 10 times per quarter.

8. Encourage every African American child to read a minimum of 10 books each year and commit to 10 hours of homework each week during the school year.

9. Encourage every African American child to save $10.00 per month, preferably in African Americans Credit Unions.

10. Encourage every African American entertainer and athlete to negotiate an additional 10% clause in every movie, media, or sport's contract to be donated to an African American educational fund for our youth.

We all can make a difference - if we stop making excuses

Wayne Perryman 3-01-2005

Let's Look at Numbers

Perryman's Plan of Ten for African Americans

1. If one million African Americans participate in the payroll deduction donation plan, the national fund will take in a minimum of $10,000,000 a month. If 10 million participate, it will generate approximately $100,000,000 a month or over a billion dollars a year.

2. If every African American church gave 10% of their total income to their local economic development fund, they would generate approximately $3.7 billion a year. Members of black church currently give approximately $37,000,000,000 per year to their local churches.

3. If every African American gave an average of 10 hours a month of community service to inner-city projects, their

total combine time of community service would come to 3,600,000,000 hours per year.

4. If every African American doctor, lawyer, and accountant donated 10 hours per month of professional services to the black community the total number of hours donated each year would exceed 120,000,000 hours (based on one million professionals).

5. If every African American wrote an average of 10 letters per year to support black legislation, our legislators would receive over 100,000,000 letters per year.

6. If every African American child was committed to reading 10 books per year, the combined total of books read by our children will exceed 20,000,000 books per year.

7. If every African American child devote 10 hours per week to homework, they will average approximately 360 hours per year of study time and collectively for the entire African American youth population over a billion study hours per year.

8. If every African American child saved $10.00 a month, each month our youth collectively, would be depositing over $20,000,000 per month (in their banks and credit unions) or 240,000,000 per year.

9. If every athlete and entertainer negotiated an additional 10% bonus of their contract to give to a National African American Educational Fund, the fund could receive as much as a billion dollars per contract period.

10. If African Americans can force every movie maker and TV. Producer to take 1% of their gross revenue from films and TV shows that target the black market and donate this money to our African American National scholarship fund we would have an additional billion dollar per year for scholarships.

Business Component

And if every African American buys an average of 10 products and services per month from black owned businesses, their business revenue will more than triple. With this plan we can transform the lives of every African American (physically and spiritually) within ten years, in addition to building economically sound communities.

POLITICAL INFLUENCE
AND THE FUTURE OF THE
CHRISTIAN CHURCH

The Black Church Must Speak Out on Moral Issues for Its Own Survival

We Need a Black Mordecai to Speak to the Black Church

Within the past ten years there has been an unprecedented number of lawsuits attacking Christian symbols, Christian holidays, and the historic relationships between Christians and local and federal governments. These lawsuits (filed by aggressive secularist) have included everything from banning prayer in public schools and at school functions to denouncing the Boys Scouts whose policies excludes gays as scout leaders and an oath that includes "God," as their divine leader. In these lawsuits the secularists have argued that America was not founded on Christian principles and that there is a "separation of church and state," therefore all words, symbols and other references associated with Christianity (as well as other religions) should be removed and banned from government properties and documents.

These aggressive secularists have:

1. Challenged the display of Ten Commandments in the courtrooms.

2. Removed and are attempting to remove crosses from government emblems, as well as from the graves of the cemeteries that are owned by the government.

3. Launched a multitude of efforts to remove the religious elements from Christian holidays (Easter, Thanksgiving and Christmas), by replacing what is perceived as religious references with secular references i.e. exchanging "Merry Christmas" with "Happy Holiday."

4. Condemned the traditional Christian doctrine on gay lifestyles and same-sex- marriages and called such doctrines, homophobic.

5. Placed limitations on the sizes and locations of churches.

6. Expanded the legal parameters of Eminent Domain which can result in the elimination of urban churches in the name of urban renewal and job creation.

7. Restricted the speech of the clergy by classifying and associating certain biblical teachings with "hate crimes" and other teachings on moral issues" as political, while under the freedom of speech granting secular movie producers the right to produce movies such as the *Da Vinci Codes*; the right of secular scientist to produce baseless arguments to challenge "Intelligent Design, and the right of secular researchers to changed the image of Judas from a man who betrayed Jesus to a man who was a friend of Jesus.

Many have asked: "Why isn't the black church speaking out against these attacks? Don't they know that these attacks will affect their future?" Some political experts believe many African Americans pastors have been conditioned to speak out against attacks that affect blacks, but not against attacks that affect their faith. Other political experts believe most African American pastors see these as white-right-wing issues that only affect the (late) J.D. Kennedys and the Jerry Falwells or the Pat Robertsons of the white Christian community, but not issues that will affect the black church, their congregations and their communities. When a black minister does speak out on these issues, seldom does it ever get media coverage.

If it is true that that the black church feels these issues do not and will not affect them, does the Black church need a Mordecai wake up call? In the biblical story of Esther, she was insulated from the attacks against her Jewish people (by the secularist of her day) because of her relationship with the King, that is, until her uncle Mordecai confronted her with the truth. Paraphrasing what Mordecai told her. He may have said something like this: "You a Jew, me a Jew. They kill me and they kill you." It was only then that Esther realized that the attacks on her Jewish brothers and sisters, were essentially attacks on her, even though she apparently did not look like them.

In all of their reporting the media have never even hinted that if today's secular attacks against Christianity affect the white Christian church, they will not only devastate the black Christian church, they will eventually destroy the entire black community. Why? Because the black church is the foundation on which the community rests. In the black community, everything revolves around the black church.

a. The black church is the primary institution that fights against social injustice.

b. It is the institution that produced most of the black schools and colleges.

c. It is the trusted place where most blacks gather on a regular basis.

d. It is the institution that guides us morally, spiritually and politically.

e. Collectively, it is the one black institution that has billions of dollars in real estate assets.

f. It is the institution that is the biggest recipient of black giving, totaling more than thirty-seven billion per year.

g. It is the glue that holds our families and communities together.

h. And it is the only institution that has a successful track record of transforming lives and building godly character.

So if black preachers:

1. Can no longer preach biblically based sermons condemning certain sinful behavior because it would be classified as *hate speech* and therefore a *hate crime.*

2. If they can no longer preach against certain acts of immorality and social injustice because such sermons would be considered political, which means churches would lose their IRS status as a non-profit religious organization.

3. If they cannot build newer and larger churches because of restrictive zoning laws.

4. If they are forced to marry couples of the same sex because refusal to do so, would be in violation of federal laws governing discrimination.

5. If they are forced to hire individuals that do not believe in their Christian doctrine because failure to do so would also violate discrimination laws.

6. If the public schools continue to expand their curriculum to teach subjects that are contrary to the church's Christian doctrine (safe sex, abortion, evolution etc.)

7. And if the inner-city black churches start losing their property because of urban renewal through Eminent Domain: Can the black church survive? The answer is no.

In his dissenting opinion opposing the United States Supreme Court's recent decision on eminent domain, Clarence Thomas said *"urban renewal"* is nothing more than what was previously called, *"Negro removal."* The following is a portion of his dissenting opinion in opposition to eminent domain which he believes would have a devastating affect on the black community.

> *"Of all the families displaced by urban renewal from 1949 through 1963, 63% were of those who were non-white... and had incomes low enough to qualify for public housing.... Public Work projects in the 1950's and 1960's destroyed predominantly minority communities in St. Paul, Minnesota, and Baltimore Maryland. In 1981, urban planners in Detroit, Michigan uprooted the largely lower income and the elderly Poletown neighborhoods for the benefit of General Motors Corporation. Urban renewal projects have long been associated with the displacement of blacks... in cities across the country and came to be known as Negro removal. Over 97% of the individuals forcibly removed from their homes by slum-clearance projects upheld by the United States Supreme Court were black."*

Judge Thomas is convinced that eminent domain will eventually destroy the black church and the entire black community. Very few black preachers are aware of this fact because the media never discusses the impact that it will have on the black community nor will they publish pro-black comments by Justice Thomas.

Each year, over 150 thousand new laws are introduced at the city, state and federal level. Many of these laws are now aimed at limiting the Christian church's influence in our society. Like Esther, many pastors become aware of these efforts only after the Mordecai's of our society bring these issues to their attention. Through Mordecai, Esther finally realized that if she did not impact public policy, public policy would impact her. That's the message for the church today, both black and white.

In Tavis Smiley's new book, *The Covenant*, he mentioned many things that blacks should be aware of, but the possible destruction of the black community through the secularist attacks on Christianity was not one of them. In his book he said very little about the importance of the black church. Most of his concerns and solutions are directed at the government and the community at large, but not the black church. Is it possible that he feels the black church is no longer effective in shaping public policy? Could it be that he feels black apathy will be our destruction? Does he realize that if the black church is destroyed, which is the foundation of the community, there will be nothing left to support the community?

The black church must always remember that according to scripture, the job security and the future of the black preacher (or any preacher) is contingent and dependent on his or her response to the attacks on their Christian faith, and not merely on the attacks on blacks.

The black church must reacquaint itself with the following scriptures and what they mean to us today.

- Romans 10:14-15: How can they [our politicians] hear without a preacher

- Philippians 1:17 & 27-29: Standing together and suffering together [with our white brothers and sisters] in defense of the gospel

- Isaiah 56:10: What Isaiah says about preachers who are uninformed and afraid to speak up

- Hosea 4:6: What will happen to us if we are uninformed

White Church's Fear and Black Church's Mistrust

Two Things That Keep 160 Million Christians From Becoming the Largest Political and Voting Blocks in America

Even though both the Black Christian Churches and the White Christian Churches have many things in common including the same views on many doctrinal issues; and even though the two groups collectively make up the one largest voting blocks in America (over 160 million – see II Kings 6:16), their political effectiveness is hampered by fear, mistrust and ignorance.

As stated in the previous editorial, both churches are faced with pressing social issues that conflict with their Christian faith. These issues include:

1. The Pastor's right to speak out on social and political issues without the fear of losing the church's IRS tax exempt status

2. Eminent domain and its impact on urban and suburban church properties

3. The teaching of evolution in schools

4. The removal of religious symbols in the work place and from public institutions

5. The rising popularity of homosexuality as a legitimate lifestyle

6. Same-sex-marriage and same-sex-unions

7. Abortions

8. The possible removal of the phrase *"One nation under God"* from our Pledge of Allegiance and *"In God We Trust"* from our currency.

9. The Boys Scout's hiring practices involving homosexuals and the use of God in their oath.

10. The Federal Communication Commission's (FCC) lack of enforcement in matters pertaining to shows that affect Christian values and morals.

11. The relentless efforts to secularize Christian holidays such as Thanksgiving, Christmas and Easter.

12. And a multitude of other issues pertaining to the so-called *"separation of church and state"* doctrine.

With so many issues facing the possible elimination or the destruction of the Christian Church in America, why don't the black churches and white churches join together to protect their doctrine and their future? The answer is three-fold, *fear, mistrust, and ignorance*?

Fear among White Churches

Even though we are now in the year 2007, *white fear* still exist. Because many white churches have never had a relationship with a black church and many white pastors have never had a sincere meaningful relationship with inner-city pastors, both are unsure of what would happen if they developed such a relationship. Many whites fear that these relationships may result in more mixed marriages between blacks and whites. Others fear that the black churches may demand too much or that the white churches will be accused of being racist. Many whites wonder if the black will church accept them or reject them. In addition to fear, there is also a power issue: Over the years white churches never needed the support of black churches in order to accomplish their objectives, so why would they need them now?

Mistrust among Black Churches

With black churches *fear* is not a factor, their issue is *mistrust*. Some black pastors ask: Can we really trust the white churches? Do they really want a relationship with us as the Bible requires (St John 17:21) or do they just want to use us to get what they want politically? Others have stated: "Most white churches were never concerned about civil rights issues when it pertained to African Americans they only became concerned when homosexuality became a Civil Rights issue. Even though whites know that our history and culture is rooted in Christianity and that many of our historical figures were Christians, most white churches will not celebrate Dr. King's birthday and/or Black History Month."

Ignorance

a. In the book of Hosea, he tells us (Hosea 4:6) that *"My people* [today's Christians] *are destroyed because of the lack of knowledge."*

b. In the book of Malachi (2:7), it tells us: *"For the priest's lips should keep knowledge, and they should seek the law at his mouth. For he is the messenger of the Lord of Host."*

c. In Romans (10:14-15), it tells us: *"How can the people hear without a preacher and how can he preach, except he is sent."*

d. Then in Matthew 12:25 Jesus says: *"A House* [the Christian Church] *divided against itself cannot stand."*

History tells us that when black and white churches developed meaningful relationships and worked closely together they accomplished the impossible. It was the work of both the black and white Christians that made the Underground Railroad successful. It was the joint efforts of black and white abolitionist (most of whom were Christians) that brought about the Emancipation Proclamation and the end of slavery. It was the work of black and white churches that built black schools and colleges after the Civil War. Working with Booker T. Washington, it was the black and white churches that supplied teachers to teach in those schools. It was the white preacher, Dr. Benjamin Rush along with the assistance of two black pastors (Rev. Richard Allen and Rev. Absalom Jones) that saved thousands of lives during the Yellow Fever epidemic in Philadelphia in 1793. Jews and white Christian pastors joined Dr. Martin Luther King Jr. in many of his marches and assisted in voter registration drives. The Honorable Thurgood Marshall worked with white attorneys in the successful case of *Brown v. Board of Education*. In every war from the Revolutionary War to the Desert Storm, it was black and white soldiers fighting side by side that gave America's its victories. It was a black man that helped Moses organize the children of Israel which enabled them to reach the Promised Land (Jethro, Moses' father-in- law). Another black man helped Jeremiah when he was placed in the dungeon. And it was a black man (Simon of Cyrene) who arrived just in the nick of time to help Jesus accomplish his mission (Luke 23:26).

Even though the chronicles of history clearly documents the successful track record of black and white churches working together on both civil and social issues, these facts are overlooked by our churches, our schools and the news media. History tells us that contrary to what many may have thought, these joint efforts did not result in more mixed marriages, nor did it create mistrust between the races, instead it created beautiful relationships that lasted for a lifetime.

If the 160 million members of the Christian church (both black and white) could just rid themselves of unwarranted fear, mistrust and ignorance and join together as one collective voice (I Cor. 12:21-26), the pressing social issues that we face today, will no longer exist tomorrow. But if we fail to join forces, the destruction of the (black and white) Christian church in America will be just a matter of time.

The collective voices of the black and white Christian churches not only are vital to their future and to maintaining a standard of morality for our society, they are also vital to our national security. Radical Muslims and their clerics (terrorist) often cite our nation's support and endorsement of abortions, homosexuality and same-sex-marriage along with the various manifestations of the *separation of church and state* doctrine as one of the many reasons why they call us hypocrites and infidels. Both moderate and radical Muslims around the world are cognizant of the fact that America (the so called Christian nation) is one of the world's leaders in exporting pornography and R-rated movies. They also know that even though both the Bible and the Torah speak against many of the moral issues that are being legitimized and becoming mainstream in our society, the 160 million plus Jews and Christian (in America), have yet to produce a collective voice to speak against what all three religious books (the Koran, the Bible and the Torah) calls sin (Malachi 2:7). Radical Muslims do not hate us because of President George W. Bush, they hate us because of our new moral standards and support of Israel. On September 7, 2007, Osama Bin Laden told Americans (both Christians and non-Christians) that they should convert to Islam to end terrorism and to secure their future. The Holy Quran says in Sura 5:51: "Take not Jews and Christians for your friends and protectors; they are but friends and protectors to each other. And he amongst you that turns to them is of them. Verily Allah guideth not a people unjust."

With internal attacks by secularist and external threats by terrorist, black and white churches need each other more than they will ever know, but they will never hear this message from the media.

The Bible instructs preachers to do the following: "Let the priest, the ministers of the Lord, weep between the porch and the altar, and let them say, Spare thy people, O Lord, and give not thine heritage to reproach, that the heathen should rule over them: wherefore should they say among the people, Where is their God?

-Joel 2:17 (King James)

The Separation of Church and State and The Boy in the Manger

It is sad to report that some local governments are more willing to accept holiday decorations that may include the Menorah, than they are with decorations that may include the manger. They do so without realizing that the manger and the menorah are both religious symbols and both represent miracles involving lights. The Menorah commemorates the miracle of lights in the Jewish faith and the manger with the Star of Bethlehem commemorates the miracle of the birth of Christ, the child who would later be referred to as the: "*Light of the World.*"

While we have no problem recognizing the birth and the life of other great men such as the Reverend Dr. Martin Luther King Jr., George Washington and Abraham Lincoln; three devout historical figures whose lives were shaped and influenced by the baby in the a manger, our society seemed to have done everything within its power to ignore the influential baby boy. It claims that such recognition would be in violation of the Constitution's *separation of church and state* clause, even though the words *"separation of church and state"* were never part of our Constitution nor were they ever included in the First Amendment.

Secularists have tried to secularize the word *"Christmas"* even though the word means the *Mass of Christ* (a religious service established by the Catholic Church to honor the birth of Christ). And because they were unsuccessful to change its meaning, they now want to replace the greeting *"Merry Christmas"* with *"Happy Holidays*," even though the word "holiday*"* derives from the term *"holy day,"* meaning, *days set aside for religious purposes*. We seem to have the space (and the room) to recognize everything in our society, but no room for the baby boy that ironically found *no room in the Inn*.

Who is this baby that we are attempting to *abort* from our society?

He grew up and became the great philosopher that introduced the Golden Rule and coined the phrase: "Do unto others as you would have them do unto you." He grew up to become the compassionate religious leader whose central theme was to "love your neighbor as yourself." And he grew up to be a powerful civil leader that urged his followers to respect and pay taxes to the very government that would eventually try him. He was an influential leader that never endorsed wars, civil disobedience or encouraged violence and revenge. Because loving, caring and compassion were always a part of his message and mission, many refer to his birth, life and death as the *"greatest love story ever told."*

As an effective communicator, he told stories to establish values and these values became the standards for many societies. From his story of the *Good Samaritan*, we get our modern-day Good Samaritan laws. The story illustrated how a man of one ethnicity went out of his way to help someone of another ethnicity, simply because the person was in desperate need of help (St. Luke 10:25-37). Good Samaritan laws in the United States and Canada were designed to protect indivduals who choose to go out of their way to help others in emergency situations (just like the man in the story told by Jesus). The laws are intended to reduce bystanders' hesitation to assist others for fear of being prosecuted for unintentional injury or wrongful death. The United Good Neighbor Fund (known today as United Way) was also a modern-day expression of the Good Samaritan story and Jesus' teachings to "love our neighbors as ourselves."

From his birth to long after his death, this *manger-born-baby* has been an inspiration to billions of individuals and to those who started a multitude of social services and health organizations around the world. They were all influenced by his life and his teachings on compassion. Thousands of Christian and Catholic hospitals around the world were established to help the sick and afflicted because he demonstrated compassion for the same during his life time. Florence Nightingale, the mother of the nursing industry said she was inspired to do what she did, because of his teachings. Millions of other charities were started to help the poor and the outcast because the baby from the manger taught that when you neglect the poor and the rejects of our society, you have rejected and neglected me (Matthew 25:40). As a result of his teachings, Christians established many of our historical black colleges and a multitude of worldwide social service organizations such as the Red Cross, the Salvation Army, and the YMCA and the YWCA.

Jesus was the inspiration behind many great men and women, including such individuals as Mother Teresa of Calcutta, India; Father Edward J. Flanagan of Boys Town; Jean Henri Dunant of the International Red Cross; and Levi Coffin, the Quaker who started the Underground Railroad to free the American slaves. He was the inspiration behind the work of Henry L. Morehouse and Laura Spellman, two devout Christians who dedicated their lives and spent millions of dollars to establish black schools and colleges in the Jim Crow South (two historical black colleges are named after them). He was also the inspiration behind many of the signers of the United States Constitution and the Declaration of Independence. These were the individuals who wrote and established the First Amendment guaranteeing religious freedom. It was an amendment that stressed that

Congress cannot establish a national religion nor can they (the government) interfere with the exercise of religious expressions, even if such expressions are displayed in the halls of government buildings or the halls of Congress, the same rooms of Congress where many of the framers of the Constitution attended (Christian) worship service each Sunday. Yes, according to noted historians, each Sunday the House of Representatives was converted into one of the largest Christians churches in the Washington D.C. area. There is no evidence that Thomas Jefferson (the person that coined the phrase: separation of church and state) attended these services. But there is evidence that as President of the United States and Chairman of the District of Columbia School District, Jefferson approved the use of Bibles and Isaac Watts' hymns as principle books for teaching District of Columbia students how to read. Jefferson's approval of the use of these Bibles took place nineteen years after Congress passed a bill (September 10, 1782) to have Bibles printed for the public schools. From this, we can conclude that our founding fathers would not have a problem with Christmas celebrations in our public schools or with decorations in our government buildings.

For centuries the birth of Christ has been celebrated in a way that reflects his caring and giving nature. Christmas is one of the most celebrated holidays in the world. It is a time when Christians, Jews and even atheists demonstrate compassion for others by giving to those in need and to those they love. It is a time when families come together. It is a festive time of bright lights, inspirational music and a spirit of peace. Historically it is a time when wars were stopped temporarily as in World War I to honor the day and soldiers who were common enemies the day before, paused and came together to sing familiar Christmas songs in peaceful harmony.

It is also a time when companies around the world depend on Christmas sales to provide jobs for their employees so that they can provide for their families. Because so many companies worldwide depend on Christmas sales for their survival, the celebration of this baby boy's birth (Christmas) is one of the central factors that affect and impact our world's economy. In fact, economists say more trips are taken and more products are purchased during the celebration of this specific holiday than at any another time of the year.

The birth and life of Jesus has impacted the world in more ways than we can ever imagine - spiritually, physically and economically. No other leader in the world, secular or religious, has had such a long-lasting positive impact on our society and no other leader in the world has ever generated the kind of tax revenues that can be traced directly to the celebration of his or her life, death and influence, like the baby born in the manger. And yet these same governments that benefit from the tremendous tax revenues generated by the activities centered around the celebration of his birth (as it was in the days of Mary and Joseph when they came to Bethlehem to pay taxes) – they have no room for him in the *end* (inn).

Separation of Church and State?

According to the 2001 edition of the *Oxford Companion to United States History*, produced by over 900 world renowned scholars: "The origins of the Constitution extend back centuries into Judeo-Christian culture, drawing upon the Bible (the Hebrew scriptures far more than the Christian)...."

BUSH DOESN'T LIKE BLACKS?

Clinton & Bush: Which President Did More for African Americans

It is common knowledge that most African Americans do not like or support President Bush. Like all presidents, Bush has made his share of mistakes which have been highlighted by the media. But do African Americans really have a reason not to like him? During the Katrina crisis one black celebrity took the opportunity to tell the world that "Bush don't like blacks!" Many have asked: What has he done for blacks? The following are a few things that are often overlooked.

1. He has given more money to historically black colleges than any other president in U.S, History, $371 million, a significant increase over President Clinton.

2. He has hired one of the most racially diverse and gender diverse cabinet in US History, far more diverse than most executive teams in corporate America and far more diverse than the media organizations that criticize him. Because the media have never given him credit for his hiring practices,

most African Americans are unaware of his African American appointees beyond Powell and Rice.

3. He is the only President to approve funding for a National Historic Black Museum, even though African Americans have been trying to get such since the early 1900's. The massive design calls for a site as large as two football fields.

4. He pushed for the passage of the Voting Rights Act without amendments, and in May of 2002 his Justice Department assisted with the successful prosecution of Bobby Cherry for the 16th Street Baptist Church bombing that killed four young African American girls. And in May of 2004 his Justice Department re-opened the Emmett Till Case. In contrast, President Clinton filed a reverse discrimination lawsuit against the Illinois State University on behalf of a group of white janitors, but refused to help a group of black longshoremen with their case against 100 major shipping companies in the Pacific Northwest.

5. He approved funding for a memorial for Ms Rosa Parks –

6. Regarding the Jena 6 incident in Jena, Louisiana, President Bush issued the following statement during an interview with Fox commentator, Juan Williams:

"I was saddened by the events. I would hope the hearts of children would grow beyond this notion about insulting somebody through hanging a noose -- which is an inherently bigoted response. And I'm not surprised of people's reaction, of the African American community reacting the way they did because this notion of unequal justice harkens back to a previous time in our history that a lot of folks, including me, are working to get beyond.

7. On September 25, 2007, the media ignored the following statement by President Bush:

"Fifty years ago today, nine students endured bitterness and violence because of the color of their skin and because of their convictions. As an Arkansas high school turned into a battleground for equality, the bravery of the Little Rock Nine inspired a generation of Americans.

Today, we commemorate the 50th anniversary of the integration of Central High School. This anniversary reminds us of our Nation's struggle to fulfill its founding promise for all Americans. We are also reminded of the resilience of the heroes who sacrificed for justice and equality. We honor their courage, and we resolve to continue their work to make America a more perfect Union."

8. Bush voiced his opposition to the United States Supreme Court's decision on eminent domain, a program that could allow private developers to come into the inner-cities of America and take the property of black churches and senior citizens in the name of urban renewal.

9. During his presidency, the Department of Education has reported that the gap between black and white students in the area of math and reading is at the narrowest point in US history. And although the federal government is not responsible for funding public education, he has increased federal spending for education by 38%. The department also report that his programs for the disadvantage increased by 58% and Pell grant funding for colleges and technical schools has increased by 57%.

10. He pushed for School Choice and Vouchers so inner-city children could afford to go to quality private schools, just like the children of Congressmen and Congresswomen.

11. He as worked very hard to encourage black churches to take advantage of the billions of dollars in his faith-based initiative program.

12. He is the first president to allocate federal land for home ownership for the victims of a hurricane. Many of the victims of Katrina had lived in poverty and in termite infested homes years before the Katrina disaster.

13. He is the first president to recognize the inequities in the criminal justice system and has called for better legal representation for African Americans accused of crimes. In contrast, President Clinton's criminal justice program for African Americans was *"three-strikes and you're-out."*

14. He is the first president that called for a re-entry program to help African Americans find suitable employment when they are released from prison.

15. Since he has been president, the number of minority home owners has reached an all time high.

16. During his administration the number of unemployed blacks has decreased to single digits for the first time in fifty years.

17. In 2004 he has increased the funding for small businesses to $19 billion, funding over 88,000 small businesses of which 30% were minority. From 2000 to 2004 more than 283,000 small business received loans through the SBA totaling more than $68 billion. This represent more than what was previously done in the agency's first forty years.

18. He has budgeted and provided more money for AIDS in Africa than has any other previous president.

19. He pushed for Social Security Reform so that citizens would have control over their own money much like the members of Congress. He realized that many African Americans who contribute to Social Security never live long enough to collect it. His reform would give African American citizens control over their own funds.

20. Many claim that Bush does not care for the poor, but according to Democratic Senator Zell Miller, the Bush Administration has allocated more entitlement money for the poor than any other president in U.S. history: $368 billion compared to Clinton's $198 billion

Most of this information has never been included in major news stories.

Affirmative Action:
If George W. Bush Can do it
What's our Excuse?

During Bush's first term he received much criticism for his position on racial preferences in hiring practices, and for calling the University of Michigan's points program for minority students, "constitutionally flawed." For the past thirty years Republicans have argued that our system should be color-blind and that hiring and selection should be based solely on qualifications and not on racial preference and quotas. Democrats have argued that in order to right the wrongs of the past, minorities needed something better than a color-blind system, they needed Affirmative Action. During these ongoing debates neither group could provide one example within its own political organization to prove that its hiring philosophy regarding equality actually worked.

While both groups were busy debating, George W. Bush was busy walking the walk and talking the talk. Without any fanfare, Bush quietly and meticulously practiced what he preached by appointing "qualified" African Americans, Latino's, Asians and women to high paying, policy making positions in his administration, (as department heads and/or assistant deputy secretaries). The following are a few of his key appointees.

State Department (black)

Department on National Security (black Female)

Department of Labor (Asian Female)

Department of Justice (black Assistant Deputy)

Department of HUD (black)

Department of FCC (black)

Department of Education (black)

Department of Transportation (Asian)

Director of Small Business Administration (Latino)

Office of Personnel Management (U.S. Civil Service) (black female)

Department of Commerce (Second Latino)

White House Advisor (White Female)

Chief Chef of the Whitehouse (Filipino)

Second Attorney General (Latino)

As overseers of these vitally important government agencies, Bush's qualified minority men and women took these positions which included handling budgets that exceeded billions and overseeing thousands of employees. From international affairs to domestic affairs, these qualified men and women were entrusted with the responsibility of developing policies, which would provide protection for our country and social services provisions for our citizens.

At the same time, while the DNC, RNC and the NAACP were busy debating about what they thought would work, none was duplicating what Bush had done in the way of color- blind hiring practices. Of these three organizations, not one has a diverse cabinet consisting of qualified African Americans, Latinos, Asians or women in high-paying policy-making positions, with large budgets to match (please note: these are cabinet level paid positions and not support staff). It seems as if the only one who had a system to locate qualified minority and women to head up major departments, was President Bush. While Bush was busy making a difference these other organizations were busy making excuses.

The DNC used the Reverend Al Sharpton, Reverend Jesse Jackson, Ms Donna Brazile, and Carol Moseley-Braun to promote their party, but did not offer them the position to head up the DNC. The Republicans used JC Watts, Michael Steele and Michael Williams to promote their party but did not offer their top RNC position to an African American. And when was the last time you saw a white person or an Asian person head up the NAACP?

The party that promotes affirmative action, and feels that it has the only answer as to how to achieve equality, is the same party that passed over *qualified* African Americans and other minorities and chose a white man to head up the DNC (Dr. Dean). The other party that claims we should be color-blind and that decisions should be based solely on qualifications, apparently felt that there were no *qualified* black Republicans and they too chose a white man to head up their organization (Ken Mehlman) and then replaced him with two other white persons and one Latino. And the organization that is always ready to step to the microphone to condemn all forms of racial discrimination (NAACP), is one that has never had a white person run their organization since its three white founders (two men, one woman). President Bush had the same labor pool to draw from as did the DNC, RNC and the NAACP, so what is their excuse?

Equality has to become a reality and not just a political or social *philosophy*. The only way equality can be achieved is by simply doing what George W. Bush did, and that is to look pass the cover and see the content. If this happens, you will see corporate officers, board of directors and political organizations filled with whites, African Americans, Asians, Latinos and women in high-paying policy-making positions, with adequate budgets and authority to carry out their organization's objectives.

President Bush should be commended for a job well done and the rest of us (from the news media industry and corporate America to the NAACP, DNC and RNC) should be embarrassed for not doing the job - we should have. It reminds me of the following story:

> *"There was an important job to be done and **Everybody** was sure that **Somebody** would do it. **Anybody** could have done it, but **Nobody** did it. **Somebody** got angry about that, because it was **Everybody's** job. **Everybody** thought **Anybody** could do it, but **Nobody** realized that **Everybody** wouldn't do it. It ended up that **Everybody** blamed **Somebody** when **Nobody** did what **Anybody** could have done."*

If President Bush can do it, then what's our excuse?

SOCIAL ISSUES & RACISM

Am I Homophobic?

The dictionary defines homosexuality as: "Having a desire for someone of the same sex [gender] or the act of having sex with someone of the same sex [gender]. In other words it is a sexual behavior carried out with someone of the same gender. It did not define it as two people of the same gender who happens to love one another. It defined it as one who *desires* a person of the same sex. Most would agree that desiring someone and loving someone are not the same. Having said that, Am I homophobic if I do not like, accept or feel comfortable with homosexual behavior? Homophobic meaning: fearing or hating the gay person or the homosexual individual who engage in such behavior? Before answering this question, please let me share with you other behaviors that I do not like.

1. I do not like it when heterosexuals affectionately make out in public when they can do it in the privacy of their homes – Am I hetero-phobic and does this mean that I fear or hate heterosexuals?

2. I do not like it when individuals cheat on their spouse – Because I am opposed to that type of behavior, am I what one would call a spousal cheater-phobic, a person that hates or fears spouses that cheat?

3. I do not like it when my sons sag their pants like gang members – Perhaps this means that I hate or fear my sons, or that I have phobia that is associated with my son's sagging pants. What should we call it, Son's Sagging Pants Phobia?

4. I do not like it when drivers cut other drivers off on the freeway – What would this be called, a driver's-phobia, meaning that I fear or fear hate drivers who do this? Do I have to fear them or hate them because I do not like what they do?

5. I do not like it when my African American brothers and sisters use the "N" word. This must mean I am afro-phobic and fear and hate my African American brothers and sisters?

6. I do not like a lot of <u>my own bad habits</u> – Am I self –phobic and hate and fear myself?

I guess you get my point. Just because I do not like certain behaviors or that I am uncomfortable with certain behaviors, does not mean that I fear or hate the person who engage in such behavior.

We must not allow the media and others to label us or put a guilt trip on those of us who do not like, accept or feel comfortable with the gay lifestyle. I'm sure that even within the gay community there are certain behaviors that they do not like among their own group, but does that mean they *fear or hate* the person demonstrating the undesired behavior? Today several million people have family members who may be on drugs. Because they are uncomfortable wtih that lifestyle, does this mean they hate or fear their family members? Millions of other parents do not approve of their teenager's lifestyle whether it is associated with hip hop or punk rock, but they still love their children.

Do I hate or fear gays? Absolutely not! If I ever came across a situation where an individual was attempting to physically harm a gay person, as a Christian, like the Good Samaritan in the Bible, I would be one of the first to come to his or her rescue. Not because the victim is gay, but because these individuals (whether homosexual or heterosexual), like myself, are loved by God (St John 3:16). Those who accuse others of hating or fearing gays simply because they are uncomfortable with their lifestyle, perhaps are individuals who do not know how to disagree with someone, without fearing or hating the person. These individuals are sick and are in need of professional help.

Final thoughts: Gays often compare their experience with the African American experience, but African Americans have never had the option of removing their black skin and placing it in the closet to escape or avoid persecution. And we were never hated because of our private behavior behind closed doors. We were hated simply because we were publicly, physically and visibly black. There is a difference between homophobia and Afro-Phobia.

Homophobia v Afro-phobia

A Close Look At The Reaction To Tim Hardaway's Comments

During the past two decades, the media have inundated us with the term "homophobia" suggesting that those who oppose the gay rights movement either hate or fear gays. The term surfaced again when NBA star Tim Hardaway made comments about another former NBA player (John Amaechi), who recently came out of the closet (ironically at the same time his (Amaechi) new book was being released).

While I think Tim Hardaway's comments were offensive, very much inappropriate and in some ways misunderstood, I think the rest of society that condemned him were very hypocritical. First of all, I am not convinced that Hardaway hates gays as he indicated. Hate produces the types of behavior that blacks experienced during the past centuries and Hardaway (to my knowledge) has never participated in any lynchings, mutilations, assassinations, or decapitations of gays nor has he worked to pass homophobic legislation to express hatred against gays - as those who hated blacks did.

Like 95 plus percent of all heterosexuals, I believe Hardaway is merely uncomfortable with the gay lifestyles, which is perhaps the reason why 95% of heterosexuals who frequent bars choose not to go to gay bars, including many of the media commentators that covered this story. Just because a person is uncomfortable being around a particular group doesn't mean he or she hate the members of that group. Most blacks do not hang out in country western bars, not because they hate country western people, for many blacks, the country western environment is just not their thing. If the truth be known, you would find that most gays are not comfortable in straight bars. Would this mean that they hate straight people?

The media organizations that gave the story massive coverage (CBS, ABC, NBC, ESPN, FOX, CNN, MSNBC), presented an image to convey or imply that they are very sensitive to discrimination issues, some stating: "How dare anyone make these types of comments in 2007." But none of these so-called 2007 sensitive media organizations are run by blacks, nor have they ever had a black president or CEO (with the exception of Turner Broadcasting). In fact, during this past week (February 16, 2007) NBC, a network that had its fair share of the coverage of the Hardaway story, had a presidential position open for NBC's Universal Integrated Media Division. The job did not go to a black person, instead it went to a white woman (Beth Comstock). In 2007, were there no blacks qualified to fill the NBC position? Do these media organizations hate blacks? Do their actions or their lack of action in the area of hiring and promotions speak louder than Hardaway's words?

ESPN which gave the Hardaway story much coverage, fired one of its top black baseball sportscasters for an alleged sexual harassment, (which never happened) while retaining the employment of white employees who committed some very offensive acts of sexual harassment. The NBA that cancelled Hardaway's involvement in this year's all-star activities (which was a proper move), never had a black commissioner, even though blacks dominate the sport and even though both Bill Russell and K.C. Jones have often talked about the NBA's racist past.

Could afro-phobia, (the fear of losing power to blacks) be the reason why these media organizations in 2007 have yet to place blacks in powerful policy making positions like CEO and President. Afrophobia, unlike homophobia has existed for centuries and the two are very different. With homophobia, there is no real fear of gays taking over the power structure of the country. The only fear is that they may change the moral standards of our society. Persons who are classified as homophobic, are people who simply just do not like the homosexual lifestyle for a variety of reasons regardless of whether the gay person is black or white. But in the case of afrophobia, there has always been a publicly expressed fear that blacks may some day take over the power structure of America and whites will no longer be in charge.

❖ In 1866, after seeing the development of several thriving black communities immediately after the war, southern Democrats feared that blacks would take over the economically prosperous South and urged Andrew Johnson to veto Senate Bill 60 that would have given the four million newly freed slaves forty acres or several million acres of land. The Democratic President granted their wishes and the reparation bill for African Americans was defeated.

❖ During the 1868 Presidential Campaign, the Democrat's theme was: *"This is a white man' country and white men must rule.*

❖ In the Democrat's 1868 Political Platform they wrote, that as a party they wanted: *"The abolition of the Freedman' Bureau and all political instrumentalities designed to secure Negro Supremacy.*

❖ During the debates on the 13th Amendment, Democratic Congressman Fernando Wood of New York said: . *"The proposed Amendment to abolish slavery in the states of the Union... involves the extermination of all white men of the southern states and forfeiture of all the land and other property belonging to them. Negroes and military colonist will take the place of the [white] race that will be blotted out of existence."*

❖ At the turn of the century white employers gave black dock workers cocaine to increase their productivity. When it was determined that the cocaine not only gave black workers superior strength but it increased sexual powers as well (far beyond their white counterparts) they introduced our nation's first anti-drugs laws.

❖ In 1909, Democratic Senator Ben Tillman of South Carolina said: *"We reorganized the Democratic Party with one plank, and the only plank, namely that this is a white man's country and white men must govern it."*

❖ In 1915, the movie *"The Birth of A Nation"* was released by DW Griffith. The movie showed what it would be like if blacks were in charge of our government. The movie featured blacks during Reconstruction, taking over the legislatures while eating chicken and watermelon and taking the opportunity to rape white women. The movie, which is considered by film makers as the greatest movie ever produced, caused afro-phobia rage and mobs of white men around the country left the theaters and attacked and killed blacks at random.

Because most people do not know their own history or the difference between homo-phobia and afro-phobia many were quick to agree with those in the gay rights movement who claimed that their experiences were the same as blacks. Such consensus reduced the entire civil rights struggles of blacks to a mere issue of marriage, implying that blacks wanted civil rights so they could marry white women - much like the gays want civil rights so they can marry people of the same gender. But those who believe that the two experiences are similar or the same, must ask themselves the following questions:

1. When did America ever go to a gay country and bring back over twenty million gays and enslaved them for 400 years?

2. When did our country ever have to past three Constitutional amendments to give gays freedom, citizenship and the right to vote because they were denied the same?

3. When was there ever a United States Supreme Court Case like the *Dred Scott Decision* that reduced our gay brothers and sisters to mere property?

4. When were gay families divided and sold like animals to work on plantations?

5. When were gay inventors denied patents simply because they weren't considered citizens of the United States?

I can go on and on, but my final question is this: When did blacks ever have the option to place their black skin in the closet to avoid persecution? This is not to say that gays, like many others groups, have not suffered. It is just to point out that their experiences in America do not begin to compare with those of the African American race.

Abortions: A Woman's Right To Choose–or an Issue of Racism and Father's Rights?

Children are a gift from God, they are His reward.

Psalms 127:3 *Living*

During each presidential campaign the issue of abortions seems always to surface along with discussions regarding a "woman's right to choose.' Many of the current candidates from both parties including Giuliani and Obama have supported the woman's rights to choose. But how would they and others who hold this position answer the following questions if they were proposed by the media?

1. Isn't it impossible to have an unborn baby in the womb without both the man and the woman's participation? Isn't the unborn the product of the woman's egg and the man's sperm? If this is true, who really owns the unborn fetus? Does it belong to the woman because she is nature's care provider for nine months? Does the fact that the fetus lives within the womb of the woman mean that she has the sole right to determine whether it lives or dies?

2. Since the unborn was produced with a portion of the man's body, if he wanted the abortion and the woman did not,

would he have a say over the portion of the unborn that his body produced?

3. According to society, as long as the baby is in the womb it belongs to the woman. When it leaves the womb only then is the man given ownership (that's why he is obligated to pay child support). Why is this? If the man has ownership outside the womb, why doesn't he have some ownership while it is inside the womb? After all, he is equally responsible for it being in the womb.

The entire abortion program was sold to the general public during the height of the civil rights movement. It was a time when both the general population and Congress were sensitive to the struggles of blacks and women so it was the perfect time for the pro-choice advocates to play the race card. They did so by emphasizing that poor blacks did not have the funds to obtain abortions like many of their white counterparts, consequently many were forced to go to places that were unsafe and unregulated. Congress ignored the fact that as a race, African Americans were never interested in aborting their children. It was not unusual for blacks to have as many as ten or more children. Children worked on farms (often as sharecroppers) and found other odd jobs to help supplement their family's income. Even during the hardship of slavery, blacks as a race never aborted their children. Blacks also believed that abortions were biblically wrong. Nevertheless, by making abortions a woman's right issue and a racial issue, the proponents of abortions gained public and Congressional support. Their support also helped Margaret Sanger (the founder of Planned Parenthood and Director of the "Negro Project") fulfill her dream of reducing the portion of the population that she referred to as "the unfit," meaning African Americans. Because of these factors, I would propose the following questions to the pro-abortion candidates:

4. Senator do you find it strange that Planned Parenthood, the agency that supports abortions and birth control is the same agency that was started by Margaret Sanger, the person that started the Negro Project to control the birth rate of African Americans simply because she felt blacks were inferior?

5. If it is true and seventeen million black babies have been aborted since *Roe V. Wade*, why are the deaths of eight million Jews killed during World War II considered genocide, but the massive death of seventeen million blacks through abortions are not? Don't they know that the seventeen million represent almost 50% of the current black population?

6. Isn't it true that since we started having abortion, such procedures have killed more blacks than the Ku Klux Klan? If we condemned the Klan for killing blacks, why aren't we condemning abortionists for killing black babies?

7. Is it a coincidence that the party that supported segregation, Jim Crow and the Ku Klux Klan is the same party that supports government funding for abortions?

8. Isn't it strange that those who support abortions seems to have unlimited funds to kill black babies (through abortions) but very little funds to provide pre-natal care to keep black babies alive." If the government gave $10.00 or more to fund each abortion, it would mean that they would have spent $170,000,000 to kill 17,000,000 black babies. If the government gave $100 to fund each abortion, the total figure would come to $1,7000,000,000. When you pay someone to kill another, isn't that called, contract killing?

9. Isn't it strange that the party that worked for years to deny blacks the right to vote now support abortions, which during the past thirty-four years eliminated seventeen million black voters through abortions?

10. Did the pro-choice supporters ever report that had those seventeen million babies lived to become adults and had each one gave his or her church an average of $100.00 a month in tithes and offerings, the black churches would have an additional $1.7 billion a month more to help citizens in their communities?

11. In the debates on abortions, why do they fail to mention that both Oprah Winfrey's mother and Jesse Jackson's mother were teens when they became pregnant and because of their unique situation they had every excuse to abort their child but chose not to?

Our society must always remember that all great leaders, from Jesus to Jackie Robinson came through the womb of a woman. The womb of the woman is the *only* pathway to life. We must cherish it, protect it and honor it, recognizing that it is the gateway that God uses to deliver His diversity of gifts to mankind. An abortion however, is just the opposite. An abortion is the process of destroying one of God's most precious gifts, a gift that He personally and meticulously gift wraps with the womb of the woman.

Children are a gift from God, they are His reward (Psalms 127:3 Living)

You [God] made all the delicate, inner parts of my body and knit them together in my mother's womb. Thank you for making me so wonderfully complex. Your workmanship is marvelous (Psalms 139:13-14 Living).

Before I formed thee in the belly I knew thee; and before thou camest forth out of the womb, I sanctified thee.... (Jeremiah 1:5 King James)

Immigration: From Illegal To Legal

Unanswered Questions on Immigration Reform

In Proverbs 30:8-9 it says, "Give me neither poverty or riches.... Lest I be full and deny thee... or poor and steal...." If Americans were perfectly honest, most would probably confess that if they were poor living in Mexico and had the opportunity to come to America illegally to make a living for their family, they too would take advantage of the opportunity. But does the hardship of our Mexican brothers and sisters justify an illegal act to improve their condition? For years, when African Americans turned to illegal activities to take care of their families; when they were caught they were convicted, sentenced and sent to prison. The courts did not offer them amnesty or a guest worker program; they offered them a prison cell. At no time in history has Congress or the president of the United States ever considered passing legislation to legalize the illegal activities of black citizens (or any other citizen) simply because they were trying to provide for their families.

Besides the fact that one study shows that illegal immigrants from Mexico cost American taxpayers over sixty-five billion dollars each year and that over 100,000 are currently incarcerated in our prisons for illegal activity, the need to secure our borders is of the utmost importance.

The issue of illegal immigrants is a problem that existed long before Bush ever thought about running for office. Illegal immigration is not President Bush's problem. It is a problem that Congress has ignored for the past forty years. But what is the solution? If the solution is to grant illegal immigrants a Guest Worker's Permit, one that would allow them to work in the United States simply because they can't find jobs in their own country. Will the Guest Worker Program be limited to our brothers and sisters from Mexico only or will it apply to all of our brothers and sisters around the world who are poor and jobless? What about the poor blacks in the Townships of South Africa, or those in Sudan, Rwanda or Haiti, individuals who are not only poor and jobless, but are suffering and dying from political oppression? What about the Chinese who are brought here in illegally in shipping containers? Will we legalize them as well or is this just a program for the citizens of Mexico? If we exclude illegal immigrants from other countries, would this be considered racist?

Many of us watched, as thousands of Latino citizens and illegal immigrants took to the streets to protest America's immigration policies. Why was the protest in America? Is it America's responsibility to provide jobs for the citizens in Mexico? Why didn't the protest take place in Mexico, the country that has failed to provide jobs for its people? Why is everyone upset with President Bush, but not with President Fox, the president of Mexico? Does Mexico offer a Guest Worker Program to those Americans that come to their country illegally? Will they pass new laws to give Americans citizenship on an accelerated basis?

If China and other countries can use their low wages to develop competitive products for the world market, why can't Mexico? If it is too expensive to manufacture energy efficient hybrid cars in Detroit, why can't they build them in Mexico? Since there is an oil shortage, why can't Mexico (which has an abundance of oil reserves) build more oil refineries and export more oil to the world market? If companies around the world need cheaper ways to manufacture products, why can't they build factories in Mexico? Why can't the beautiful country of Mexico attract investors to build more resorts on its beautiful coast lines to create more jobs? If their immigrants can make beds in American hotels, why can't they make decent wages making beds in the new resorts of their own country?

There used to be a time when we granted immigrants legal residency because of political persecution. Are we now going to have a new immigration policy that grants legal residency to individuals simply because they are poor and jobless? They never offered the thousands of poor black Haitians legal status when they attempted to come to America (in 2004) to escape political persecution. I didn't see our Latino brothers and sisters or other sympathizers protesting on their behalf.

Having said that, I pray that American investors and Congress will partnership with the Mexican government to create millions of jobs within its borders so that these hard working citizens will not have to leave their homeland and risk their lives (to come to America), simply to find suitable employment to provide for their families. As a person who has experienced long term unemployment, I feel their pain.

KATRINA: LOOKING AT ALL THE FACTS

Katrina Disaster:
Enough Blame to Go Around

Most of the media blames President Bush and Michael Brown for the delay in getting the necessary food and water supplies to the victims of the Katrina hurricane disaster. But before we pass judgment on anyone (the president, the mayor or the governor), we must be reminded that the job of the media is not just to inform the public, but to make their news presentations so exciting and so entertaining that advertisers will stand in line to advertise, which means substantial profits for their news organizations. News is a profit making business.

Over the years, the media have not only intentionally kept information from the general public; they have also meticulously decided what information the public should or should not be exposed to. It is a subtle form of mind manipulation and mind control.

But what really happened in the Katrina disaster? And who dropped the ball? To fully understand what transpired, we must look at a variety of news sources as well as sources beyond the media. As a fact-finding investigator, I have uncovered much information regarding the actions at the local (the mayor), the State (the governor) and the federal level (Michael Brown and President Bush) that most of the media has either ignored or failed to report. I will start with the Mayor (the local government) and their responsibility.

The Mayor of New Orleans' Responsibility

The following information is taken directly from the City of New Orleans Comprehensive Emergency Management Plan (cut and pasted with no editing).

❖ The coordination of city and state resources and operations is present throughout all planning, implementation, and resolution of **declared disasters**. This includes the City of New Orleans Office of Emergency Preparedness (NO OEP), New Orleans Health Department (NOHD), the State of Louisiana Office of Emergency Preparedness (La OEP), the LSU Health Science Center (LSU HSC){Medical Center of LA}), the State of Louisiana Department of Social Services (La DSS), and the Louisiana National Guard (LANG). [Note; No mention is made of federal agencies]

❖ Regarding providing shelters for those with special needs, this is what the New Orleans' Emergency Plans mandates.

❖ The Special Needs Shelter (SNS) will only be activated by the Mayor of New Orleans or his designee. Entrance into the SNS does not relieve any individual of the responsibility for their own care. Admission into the Shelter is NOT TO BE INTERPRETED AS A GUARANTEE OF SAFETY, and the City of New Orleans is not assuring anyone protection from harm within the facilities that are being offered or opened for this purpose. It is critical that everyone understands that this shelter will not be able to substitute for the comforts of the individuals' homes, and that all equipment and special furniture, which are normally used, may not be able to accompany them. It is recommended that all persons with special medical needs and/or their responsible family members develop a viable plan for transportation out of the community to a community that will be able to give long term assistance. The potential exists that New Orleans could be without sufficient supplies to meet the needs of persons with special considerations, and there is significant risk being taken by those individuals who decide to remain in these refuges of last resort.

Please note the plan is not assuring anyone "protection," it specifies that the shelters the city provides can not be expected to be a substitute for the comforts of the citizen's own home and that those who take advantage of these shelters do so at their own risks.

Look what their plans says about the evacuation of those with *special needs*.

❖ III. SHELTER POPULATION
   The population for the shelters established in the New Orleans area will consider those individuals without the resources to evacuate. The coordination of transportation and needs for transportation will be coordinated through the SNS Director and NOHD [New Orleans Health Department] EMS Administrator and/or their designee. The organization of the shelter, its staff and direction of all activities in the unit will be the joint responsibility of the Office of Emergency Preparedness (NO OEP), the New Orleans Health Department (NOHD) and the State of Louisiana Department of Social Services (LA DSS)

There seems to be no evidence that the City of New Orleans provided shelters or transportation other than the Superdome at the last minute. The following is what the shelters were supposed to contain.

❖ D.Auxiliary Officer: The Auxiliary Officer will be responsible for all needs of a non-medical or non-direct patient care nature. This individual will report to the SD, or designee. The responsibilities shall include, but will not be limited to: oversight of security personnel, sanitation needs, food and water acquisition and preparation. {Shelters will contain the following] generator power capability, multiple restroom facilities both male and female, a refrigerator that is under the control of generator power, tables that can be used for beds or a minimum of 200 cots for staff and residents of the area. Port-o-lets must be on site in event of rest room failures or disruption. Food will be provided to shelter staff and resident as available by Volume Services of America in the Superdome.

There is no evidence that any of these types of shelters existed and or were used by the city of New Orleans, if such shelters did exist. We have just reviewed the Mayor's Emergency Plan for those residents with *special needs*, but what were his plans for the rest of the population? Again, the following is taken directly from the City of New Orleans Comprehensive Emergency Management Plans.

❖ Authority to issue evacuations of elements of the population is vested in the Mayor. By Executive Order, the chief elected official, the Mayor of the City of New Orleans, has the authority to order the evacuation of residents threatened by an approaching hurricane. [Note: this authority is not given to any Federal agency.]

❖ The safe evacuation of threatened populations when endangered by a major catastrophic event is one of the principle reasons for developing a Comprehensive Emergency Management Plan. The thorough identification of at-risk populations, transportation and sheltering resources, evacuation routes and potential bottlenecks and choke points, and the establishment of the management team that will coordinate not only the evacuation but which will monitor and direct the sheltering and return of affected populations.

❖ The SOP [Standard Operating Procedures] is developed to provide for an orderly and coordinated evacuation intended to minimize the hazardous effects of flooding, wind, and rain on the residents and visitors in New Orleans. The SOP provides for the evacuation of the public from danger areas and the designations of shelters for evacuees.

❖ The Hurricane Emergency Evacuation Standard Operating Procedure is designed to deal with all case scenarios of an evacuation in response to the approach of a major hurricane towards New Orleans. It is designed to deal with the anticipation of a direct hit from a major hurricane. This includes identifying the city's present population, its projected population, identification of at-risk populations (those living outside levee protection or in storm-surge areas, floodplains, mobile homes, etc.),

Again, none of these plans identified any federal agency as a participant. The sole responsibility rested with the Mayor of New Orleans and the State of Louisiana. What about transportation? Whose responsibility is this? Was transportation and food and shelter a federal responsibility? Let us, again, check the city's records.

❖ Conduct of an actual evacuation will be the responsibility of the Mayor of New Orleans in coordination with the Director of the Office of Emergency Preparedness, and the OEP Shelter Coordinator. The evacuation requirements includes identifying the transportation network, especially the carrying-capacity of proposed evacuation routes and existing or potential traffic bottlenecks or blockages, caused either by traffic congestion or natural occurrences such as rising waters. Identification of sheltering resources and the establishment of shelters and the training of shelter staff is important, as is the provision for food and other necessities to the sheltered.

What about feeding the people, is this the federal responsibility?

❖ The City of New Orleans will utilize all available resources to quickly and safely evacuate threatened areas. Those evacuated will be directed to temporary sheltering and feeding facilities as needed.

Did the mayor anticipate that this will be a terrible storm with catastrophic proportions? This is what the Seattle Times quoted the mayor as saying on August 27th days before the storm hit.

"The mayor said that in a worse case scenario, a gigantic storm surge would sweep past the levees and flood the city with 18 feet of water. It would take weeks to pump all the water out. [Mayor] Nagin said he spoke to a forecaster at the hurricane center [who said] that this is the storm New Orleans has feared these many years. Nagin was exploring the idea of ordering a mandatory evacuation. Making matters worse, at least 100,000 people in the city lack transportation to get away. Nagain said the Superdome could be used as a shelter of last resort for people who have no cars, with city bus pick up points around New Orleans. [resident quoted in the article]. I know they're saying, "Get out of town, but I don't have any way to get out, said Hattie Johns 74."

The New York Times reported that Mayor Nagin said:

Hurricane Katrina could bring 15 inches of rain and a storm surge of 20 feet or higher that would most likely topple the network of levees and canals that normally protect the bowl shaped city from flooding.

In another Seattle Times article Mayor Nagin was quoted as saying:

We're facing a storm that most of us have feared... God bless us.

What were the experts telling Mayor Nagin? Before the storm hit Associated Press reported the following:

Joseph Bentley headed to the Superdome yesterday morning, like most of the city's low income residents who had nowhere else to go. New Orleans is one of the nation's poorest cities.

Ivor Van Heerden, deputy director of Louisiana State University Hurricane Center said, "All indications are that this is absolutely the worst case scenario. We're talking about in essence having in the continental United States a refugee camp of a million people. After the storm passes, the water will have no where to go. Emergency management officials are going to be wondering how to handle a giant stagnant pond contaminated with building debris, coffins, sewage and other hazardous materials. We're talking about an incredible environmental disaster.

Regarding the city's ability to handle the floods, this is what Stevan Spencer, the New Orleans' Levee District Chief Engineer said;

Some of the city pumps sit in houses that date back to the 1890's. It really makes you wonder what the French were doing when they built this place.

Regarding whether or not the homes could withstand a storm of this magnitude, city officials including Lou Robinson, captain of New Orleans' Fire Department told the reporters:

"There are a lot of older homes, most of these homes are below sea level, and most of these homes are termite ridden. [Others report that] New Orleans' housing stock is virtually all wood-framed, and often aged and dilapidated. Many structures have been weakened by a relentless exotic termite infestation. [see appendix for more articles from other news organizations]

Knowing all of these factors well in advance and being very familiar with their own Comprehensive Emergency Plans that calls for evacuation and emergency shelters, why didn't the mayor of New Orleans launch a massive evacuation program that included the use of all of the available transportation, including the city's metro and school buses to move people out of the area into shelters days before the storm hit land?

The Responsibility of the Governor and State

In the New Orleans' Comprehensive Emergency Plans it listed the following four those state agencies that would assist the City of New Orleans in the time of a *declared disaster*.

> The State of Louisiana Office of Emergency Preparedness (La OEP),
>
> The LSU Health Science Center (LSU HSC){Medical Center of LA}),
>
> the State of Louisiana Department of Social Services (La DSS), and the Louisiana National Guard (LANG).

There is no evidence that any of these state agencies assisted the mayor in evacuating the city or that these agencies assisted in providing food and shelters for that *at-risk population* that needed to be evacuated. One internet news service reported the following:

> *On Friday night before the storm hit Max Mayfield of the National Hurricane Center took the unprecedented action of calling Mayor Nagin and Governor Blanco personally to plead with them to begin MANDATORY evacuation of New Orleans and they said they'd take it under consideration. This was after the NOAA buoy 240 miles south had recorded 68' waves before it was destroyed.*

The records will show that on August 26, 2005, Governor Kathleen Blanco declared a state of emergency and issued Proclamation No. 48 KBB 2005 activating the Louisiana Homeland Security's emergency response and recovery program which would have included the State's National Guard. However the records will also show that the state's National Guard did not reach the City of New Orleans to assist the local police in securing the city until late Tuesday and early Wednesday, two days after the flood hit. Reports indicate that as of August 28, 2005 the State of Louisiana had a total of 11,500 guardsmen, with 3500 in Iraq and the remaining 8,000 in Louisiana.

Were the National Guard part of the *local law enforcement group* that refused to let trucks loaded with water and food into the city as reported by the president of the American Red Cross? This is what one news organization reported about this incident.

> *Major Garrett told Fox News Wednesday, that the Red Cross had "trucks with water, food, hygiene equipment, all sorts of things ready to go ... to the Superdome and Convention Center. But the Louisiana Department of Homeland Security, told Garret), " they could not go." [Garrett went on to tell Fox News] The Red Cross tells me that Louisiana's Department of Homeland Security said, 'Look, we do not want to create a magnet for more people to come to the Superdome or Convention Center, we want to get them out.' [Garrett continues] So at the same time local officials were screaming where is the food, where is the water, the Red Cross was standing by ready [but] the Louisiana Department of Homeland Security said you can't go."*

Was the slow response from the governor Blanco a pay back because Mayor Nagin had endorsed Republican, Bobby Jindal during the 2003 Louisiana gubernatorial runoff instead of Kathleen Blanco? We hope not, but no one can explain what the Louisiana Homeland Security did with its own resources before the storm hit or what they did right after the storm passed. This brings us to the federal level of involvment.

The Responsibility of the Federal & George Bush

The Seattle Times reported that on Saturday August 27th President Bush did take action. The article said:

> *President Bush, vacationing at his ranch in Texas, declared a state of emergency for the Gulf Coast, a move that cleared the way for immediate federal aid. Mr. Bush also urged people in the storm's potential path to head for safer ground.*

"We cannot stress enough the danger this hurricane poses to the to the Gulf Coast communities," he said.

The President also participated in a videoconference on Sunday with disaster management officials who were preparing for the storm. And he spoke by telephone with the governors of the four states under immediate threat: Louisiana, Mississippi, Alabama, and Florida."

In just the first week after New Orleans' levees had been breached with the assistance of the federal government:

- More than 32,000 people had been rescued by the United States Coast Guard helicopters.

- Shelter, food and medical care had been provided to more than 180 thousand evacuees.

- The Army Corps of Engineers had started the process to pump out water and repair the breaches.

According the National Guard, the federal response to Hurricane Katrina was faster than any other federal response to any other major hurricane in modern-day history, including the federal response to Hurricane Andrew, Hugo, Francine and Jeanne, and all the others major hurricanes that hit the State of Florida, the state where the president's brother (Jeb Bush) was governor. In support of Bush, the White House officials reported the following:

President Bush spent Friday afternoon and evening in meetings with his advisors and administrators drafting all of the paperwork required for a state to request federal assistance (and not be in violation of the Posse Comitatus Act or having to enact the Insurgency Act).

Just before midnight Friday evening the President called Governor Blanco and pleaded with her to sign the request papers so the federal government and the military could legally begin mobilization and call up. He was told that they didn't think it necessary for the federal government to be involved yet.

After the President's final call to the governor she held meetings with her staff to discuss the political ramifications of bringing in federal forces. It was decided that if they allowed federal assistance it would make it look as if they had failed so it was agreed upon that the feds would not be invited in.

Saturday before the storm hit the President again called Gov. Blanco and Mayor Nagin requesting they please sign the papers requesting federal assistance, that they declare the state an emergency area, and begin mandatory evacuation. After a personal plea from the President, Nagin agreed to order an evacuation, but it would not be a full mandatory evacuation, and the governor still refused to sign the papers requesting and authorizing federal action.

In frustration the President declared the area a national disaster area before the State of Louisiana did so he could legally begin some advanced preparations.

The governor's office gives a different story. It reports that the Louisiana governor requested federal assistance on August 28, thereby activating FEMA and her own National Guard. They say a power struggle emerged as federal officials tried to wrestle authority from Gov. Kathleen Blanco. A spokesperson from her office said;

"Shortly after midnight Friday, the Bush administration sent her a proposed legal memorandum asking her to request a federal take over of the evacuation of New Orleans."

If this is true, and the governor was not going to use Louisiana's Homeland Security resources to assist with the evacuation (ie. eight thousand National guardsmen), she should have given up her author-ity rather than to let the people remain in the city and die. On Septem-ber 11th 2005, CNN reported that Governor Blanco finally confessed that she had requested federal troops on Wednesday, two days after the storm and not before the storm. This was her mistake, but the president also made a few mistakes.

President's Bush's Mistakes

Even though the primary responsibility of providing evacuations, shelters and food and water was the City of New Orleans and the State of Louisiana, why did Bush cut funding to secure the levees? The purpose of the levees was to save lives. This is definitely a mis-take on Bush's part. However Bush wasn't the only President that cut funding. The records show:

> *Funding for these projects has generally trended downward since at least the last years of the Clinton administration. Congressional records show that the levee work on Lake Pontchartrain received $23 million in 1998 and $16 million in 1999.*

Would more federal funding to secure the levees guarantee that the levees would hold and prevent flooding? Perhaps, but some experts say that unless the State and federal governments build a comprehen-sive levee system like those in Holland, securing the current system would create a false sense of security and would be a waste of money. Many who witnessed and survived the 1938 hurricane that hit the east coast (New England area) are convinced that there is not a man-made structure in the world that can withstand the force of Mother Nature when she releases all of her power. Hurricane experts report that in ten minutes a hurricane releases more energy than all of the world's nuclear weapons combined.

Michael Brown

Was Michael Brown qualified to head FEMA? Most people would agree—that based on his past work experience, he should have never been given the position, particularly when there are a number of former military officers with disaster experience, as well as fire chiefs and disaster relief professionals from the Red Cross and other agencies who were far more qualified. This was Bush's second mistake even though he did not personally hire Brown. The records show:

❖ Before joining the Bush administration in 2001, Brown spent 11 years as the commissioner of judges and stewards for the International Arabian Horse Association...This was his full-time job...for 11 years.

❖ Brown was forced out of the position after a spate of lawsuits over alleged supervision failures. He was asked to resign, according to Bill Pennington, president of the IAHA.

❖ Soon after, Brown was invited to join the administration by his old Oklahoma college roommate Joseph Allbaugh, the previous head of FEMA.

Brown's appointment is what most African Americans call "*the white man's affirmative action program.*" Employment decisions like theses are the primary reasons why many blacks feel equality programs such as affirmative action are necessary and needed. African Americans are convinced that government sponsored fair employment programs, provides the only assurance that African Americans and other minorities will get a fair shake when these types of employment decisions are made. Brown was eventually fired.

Did the federal government totally blow it in responding to the hurricane? The answer is No. The Wall Street Journal reported the following:

Significant U.S. Military assistance was on alert throughout the week prior to Katrina's landfall. The Pentagon began tracking the storm when it was still just a number in the ocean on August 23ʳᵈ, some five days before landfall in Buras Louisiana. As the storm approached, senior Pentagon officials told staff to conduct an inventory of resources available should it grow into a severe hurricane. Their template for these plans was the assistance the Department of Defense provided Florida last year for its four hurricanes.

And a week earlier than this, Defense Secretary Rumsfeld issued an executive order delegating hurricane decision authority to the head of the Northern Command, Admiral Timothy J. Keating. Four days later, as the tropical storm soon to be named Katrina gathered forced, Adm. Keating acted on that order.

Before the hurricane arrived in New Orleans, Adm Keating approved the use of the bases in Meridien, Miss., and Barksdale, La., to position emergency meals and some medical equipment; eventually the number of emergency-use bases grew to six. And before land fall, Adm. Keating sent military officers to Mississippi and Louisiana to set up traditional coordination with their counterparts from FEMA. As well, Deputy Defense Secretary, Gordon England ordered the movement of ships into the Gulf. The Pentagon carried out these preparations without any formal request from FEMA or other authorities.

In addition to this, the United States Coast Guard was on hand within hours after the hurricane passed and rescued over two thousand residents during the first forty-eight hours.

Nevertheless, the public kept asking: Why was the government so slow? Everyone who has ever applied for social security, veteran benefits, or filed a discrimination complaint knows that the fastest agency in government is still slow. When you have the bureaucracies of the local government, the state government and the federal government all involved in one emergency project, it only makes the response three times slower, not three times faster. Bureaucrats will never change the system, only citizens like you and I can bring about the necessary change (with our vote) when we have had enough.

Claims of Racism

Last but not least, what about claims of racism? While most of the television cameras focused on black looters and conflicts involving blacks at the Superdome, others showed blacks and whites helping one another and white rescue workers rescuing black citizens from roof tops. As a black man, I must say that throughout this whole ordeal I did not witness racism (other than what the news media attempted to portray). What I witnessed was an unprecedented response from people all over the world and a *storm of compassion* that was far more powerful than the *storm of Katrina*.

Katrina's Engineering Disaster

Engineers say the City of New Orleans was a disaster waiting to happen for several years.

According to leading experts in the field of Civil Engineering, Katrina was as much as an engineering disaster as it was a natural and political disaster. Because the news media reported very little about the system failures, many felt that racism is what exacerbated the entire ordeal. But what the media failed to tell Americans is that had New Orleans' antiquated and poorly designed engineering systems functioned as expected, the impact of the storm would have been kept to a minimum.

The Water Pumps

The water pumps which were designed in 1912 were too antiquated to handle the massive flood waters and the fact that these electrical driven pumps were located below sea level made them totally ineffective when the massive flood waters hit and shorted them out. Had they worked properly and had the levees not been breached, it would have only taken from twelve to twenty hours to pump out the flood waters. City officials are currently looking at replacing these antiquated pumps with modern pumping systems and installing them in structures above flood levels.

The Levees

The Levees which were approved by Congress in 1965 also had design flaws. The 1965 design called for driving 25 foot steeling pilings into a spongy soil as a base for the 7 foot concrete levee wall. The Corp of Engineers has replaced the 25 feet steel pilings with pilings that are 79 foot long. Unfortunately they can do very little about the area's spongy soil, which may still be a problem.

The Pontchartrain Bridge

Because the bridge was built so close to the water level, the hurricane force winds were unable to pass underneath the bridge. Consequently the winds collided with the bridge tossing several of the 65 ton sections of the bridge into the lake. The destruction of the bridge, which was the main route in and out of New Orleans, made evacuations virtually impossible. Engineers are currently looking at new design features that will elevate the bridge, allowing hurricane force winds to pass under bridge rather than colliding with the bridge.

The Superdome

The Superdome's engineering flaws allowed the storm to remove portions of the roof, therefore exposing and shorting out the facility's electrical system. The electrical shortage affected several systems including the air conditioning, the refrigeration and cooking facilities and the water pressures in the dome's restrooms. Structural engineers are currently correcting these problems with new design features that will secure the panels on the dome's roof.

Building a City on Sinking Ground

Because most of New Orleans is located ten feet below sea level and is sinking every year, civil engineers have very few options to secure the future of the city.

Rescue Efforts despite Engineering Design Failure

The only federal response that went well was the rescue efforts of the United States Coast Guard. By week's end they had saved over thirty-three thousand persons and shattered the prediction that over sixty thousand persons would die. Although everyone wanted a faster response to Katrina, experts report that this was the fastest response to any hurricane of this magnitude in U.S. history.

The Vulnerable Homes of the Poor

The fact that the poor lived in rat and termite infested shacks was no secret to local government officials and to those black entertainers and tourist that attended Mardi Gras each year. It was also no secret that these individuals (mostly black) had lived in these flood potential areas (the 9th Ward) since the days of Reconstruction (1867) and that their poorly built shacks would not be able to withstand hurricane force winds. But no one spoke on their behalf until Katrina hit. Years prior to the storm, there were no (national) news reports of any efforts or any attempts by Senator John Edwards or by any of our black entertainers and leaders to provide better housing for these individuals.

Historical Relationship Between Blacks and Louisiana

When President Bush delivered his speech on Katrina he briefly referred to the historical role that racism played in the lives of people in that region (State of Louisiana). The following facts support his statement. Some may think the incidents cited below are politically driven because all of these incidents happened under local Democratic control. This is not political; it is factual history.

Except for a short period during Reconstruction, Louisiana had been under Democratic control, or what the historians often referred to as the *Party of White Supremacy*. History Professor, James McPherson of Princeton University reports: *"The focal points of the abolitionist concern* [after the war] *were Louisiana and South Carolina."* McPherson goes on to say that: *"In 1873, Louisiana became almost a synonym for chaos and violence. When Grant sent federal troops to install Kellogg in office* [as governor], *Louisiana Democrats were infuriated. They formed White Leagues which attacked black and white Republicans and took scores of lives."*

The following are just a few of the many racial incidents that took place in the state of Louisiana.

In 1865, over two thousand black men, women and children were murdered in the state of Louisiana alone. That's more deaths than those caused by Hurricane Katrina. Hurricane Katrina was considered to be an *act of God*, these deaths were the acts of a political party that opposed civil rights for African Americans.

In 1866, blacks in Louisiana were forced to return ten thousand acres of farmland to their former slaver owners. The orders came from the Democratic president, Andrew Johnson.

In 1866, Louisiana joined other southern states and passed Black Codes which restricted blacks from performing any job other than those associated with being field hands. Black Codes had many other restrictions as well.

In 1873, the United States Supreme Court issued its ruling on the famous Slaughterhouse Case. The case which originated out of the City of Orleans was a successful attempt to make the 14th Amendment null and void at the state level. The 14th Amendment was drafted to give blacks all the rights of citizenship.

In September 1874 several white Republicans from the Red River Parish who supported the newly freed slaves were victims of the Coushatta Massacre. Among the dead were the brother of Marshall Twitchell, Homer, his three brother-in-laws and seven blacks. Marshall Twitchell was a former Union Army Officer, and the federal agent for the Louisiana Freedman's Bureau. Weeks after the massacre, fearing for their lives, local black leaders and their families sought refuge in the in the nearby woods and swamps, sleeping there at night.

On September 14, 1874, angered that (the Republican) Congress had passed three civil rights constitutional amendments supporting African Americans, the terrorist wing of the Democratic Party invaded the Louisiana State Legislature and removed all black Republican office holders. President Grant responded by sending troops to New Orleans to re-instate the local black officials.

On August 23, 1888, eight black ministers from New Orleans and the surrounding parishes met and wrote a letter to the United States Congress telling Congress how they are treated in the State of Louisiana. The following is a portion of their letter:

To The People of the United States:

We, the citizens of New Orleans, as well as of our neighboring parishes, from which we been driven away without warrant or law, assembled in a mass meeting at New Orleans, Louisiana on Wednesday August 22, 1988, at Geddes Hall declare and assert: That a reign of terror exist in many parts of the state; that the laws are suspended and the officers of the government, from the governor on down, afford not protection to the lives and property of the people against armed bodies of whites, who shed innocent blood and commit deeds of savagery unsurpassed in the dark ages of mankind.

For the past twelve years we have been most effectively disfranchised and robbed of our political rights. While denied the privilege in many places of voting for the party and candidates of our choice, acts of violence have been committed to compel us to vote against the dictates of our conscience for the Democratic Party, and the Republican ballots cast by us, have been counted for the Democratic candidates. The press, the pulpit, and the commercial organizations, and executive authority of the State have given both open and silent approval of these crimes. In addition to these methods, there seem to be a deep scheme to reduce the Negroes of the State to a condition of abject serfdom and peonage.

These acts are done in deliberate defiance of the Constitution and the laws of the United States, which are so thoroughly nullified that the Negroes who bore arms in defense of the

Union have no protection or shelter from them within the bor-
ders of Louisiana. During the past twelve months our people
have suffered from the lawless regulators as never before and
since the carnival of bloodshed conducted by the Democratic
Party in 1868.

A single volume would scarcely afford sufficient space to enu-
merate the outrage our people have suffered and are daily
suffering at the hands of their oppressors...."

The letter was signed by Rev. Lyon, Rev. Albert, Rev. Coker, Rev. Stamps, Rev. Mason, Rev. Green, Rev. Kennedy and Rev. Wilson.

Two years later, in 1890 the Louisiana General Assembly passed an act requiring separate railway carriages for the white and colored passengers. Six years later, this law was challenged by a Mr. Homer Plessy in the landmark case of *Plessy v. Ferguson* of 1896. This case, which originated out of the State of Louisiana is what (legally) established segregation throughout the United States.

NEWS THE MEDIA
REFUSED TO USE

News the Media Refused Used

Dear Readers:

   After extensive research, I discovered that it was the Democratic Party that supported slavery, the Dred Scott Decision, Jim Crow, the Ku Klux Klan and the institution of racism. As a result of my findings, I sent a letter to the Democratic National Committee (DNC) requesting that it issue an apology to African Americans for the role it played in establishing and supporting racism. When it refused to respond, I filed suit in U.S. District Court to force an apology.

In response to the lawsuits, the Democrats stipulated that in the past they may have had members who engaged in such behavior, but argued that since I could not prove how I have been personally harmed by such practices, I did not have *standing* or the authority to bring such a lawsuit on *behalf of all African Americans*. The court agreed with the high powered attorney representing the Democratic Party and dismissed the case, stating that my injuries;

- *"Stem from the injury inflicted on all African Americans over two-hundred years ago and affect the entire African American community."*

Even though the court's reason for dismissing the case was precisely the reason why I filed the case, the court maintained that I must establish how I have been personally harmed by the Democrat's racist practices before the case could proceed. The Democrats cited and used the same arguments and case law that other defendants used to dismiss other African American reparation cases.

Since this case was never covered by the news media, I have included the letters written to the Democratic Party along with the briefs filed in all three federal courts (District Court, U.S. Court of Appeals and the U.S. Supreme Court) for your review. The mainstream media ignored all press releases pertaining to these cases.

Note: To prepare the briefs for this publication, minor editing was required. During this process we maintained the integrity of the briefs by not changing, altering or embellishing any of the facts, allegations, or the primary arguments.

Final Thoughts: On January 28, 1999, members of the Congressional Black Caucus sent former Congressman, JC Watts a letter demanding that he and his Republican counterparts apologize and "Clearly and publicly distance themselves from the CCC [Council of Conservative Citizens] and any other white supremacist or hate groups...."

On October 30, 2007, the Associated Press reported that the Reverend Al Sharpton demanded that Vice President Dick Cheney "apologize" and "denounce" the Clove Valley Rod & Gun Club (that Cheney had visited on October 29th), claiming that the club had displayed a Confederate flag inside one of its garages and that the club "represents lynching, hate and murder to black people." Although the Congressional Black Caucus and the Reverend Al Sharpton have consistently condemned groups and organizations with historical roots in racism, they have yet to condemn the Democratic Party for their historical racist past, nor have they asked the Party to apologize to blacks. While the Associated Press publicized Sharpton's demand for an apology (from a member of the Republican Party), they have consistently ignored the press release(s) regarding the lawsuit that demanded an apology from the Democratic Party.

Letter to Black Leaders and the Democratic Leadership

from the office

of

Rev. Wayne Perryman

P.O. Box 256 Mercer Island, WA 98040 (206) 232-5575

Doublebro@aol.com

January 9, 2006

Congressional Black Caucus	National Bar Association
NAACP	National Urban League
Dr. Cornell West	Professor Charles Ogletree
Senator Hillary Clinton	Senator Joseph Biden
Senator Barack Obama	Senator Edward Kennedy
Senator Joseph Lieberman	Senator Barbara Boxer
Senator Pat Roberts	Senator Carl Levin
Senator Diane Feinstein	Cong. John Conyers
Cong. Jesse Jackson Jr.	Cong. Harold Ford
Senator Mary Landrieu	Senator Sam Brownback
Senator Bill Frist	Cong. Elijah Cummings

Attention Congressional & Community Leaders:

I thought it would only be fitting and proper to provide an explanation as to what brought about the Reparations lawsuit against the Democratic Party. Before I share with you the chain of events that led to the lawsuit, I thought that perhaps I should give you a brief background on myself and my past political affiliation.

I am the author of several books, a former radio talk show host, a corporate consultant, a community activist and an inner-city minister located in Seattle Washington. In addition to working with gang members and professional athletes, I spend my leisure time doing research. In 1993, based on personal research, I challenged major

Christian publishers and scholars that continued to produce publications promoting the *Curse of Ham* theory (a theory that justified slavery from a Christian perspective). My efforts resulted in a public apology and the removal of the 400-year-old *curse theory* from all of their publications, including removing it from the Encyclopedia Britannica (see attached letters and articles). My book: *The 1993 Trial on the Curse of Ham* was based on that research.

Most of my adult life I have voted for and worked with a number of Democratic candidates at the local level. In 1996, I served as a member of the Washington State Black Clergy to Re-elect President Bill Clinton and worked closely with the co-chair. After President Clinton was re-elected, I was challenged by a group of young people from our church regarding the history of the Democratic Party and its relationship with blacks. Their challenge prompted me to devote a considerable amount of time researching the subject.

My research included reviewing Congressional Records from 1860 to present, reading the works of several renowned history professors (both black and white) and looking at the Democratic Platform from the early 1800's to 1954. In addition to these documents I reviewed the research of those who produced the books: *Without Sanctuary* and *100 Years of Lynchings* and added to my library PBS and the History Channel's series on <u>The Rise and Fall of Jim Crow</u> and <u>Reconstruction: The Second Civil War</u>. Excerpts from those books and film documentaries were included as exhibits in my Reparations lawsuit against the Democratic Party.

The graphic depictions of whites fighting over the private parts of black men (penises, fingers, ears) after hanging them and igniting them with kerosene, is forever embedded in my mind. I can still hear the cries of the victims' wives and children pleading and begging for the lives of their loved ones while **Democratic** national and local elected officials joined the crowd and cheered. The lynching of Mary Turner, the nine-month pregnant mother was even more horrific and graphic. All of these events took place under the banner of **"States Rights"** in regions controlled by Democratic governors, mayors, judges, sheriffs, Congressmen and U.S. Senators. Like Dr King, my parents lived through those times in Atlanta and I never fully appreciated what they and other blacks went through until I had completed my research.

In addition to lynchings and terrorist attacks by the Democrat's terrorist organizations (as revealed in the 1871 Senate hearings), Democrats legislated Black Codes, Jim Crow laws and a multitude of other repressive legislation at the federal and state levels (and repealed other key pieces of Civil Rights legislation) all in an effort to deny blacks their rights as citizens. The entire system of racism in America was meticulously thought-out and carried-out by a powerful political machine. And that political machine according to historians, was the Democratic Party - the party of *"White Supremacy."*

Based on these findings, I wrote my latest book: ***Unfounded Loyalty***, and sent the attached (November 7, 2004) letter to the DNC requesting that it issue an apology to African Americans. In 2005, I sent a second letter to the DNC, again requesting an apology. When the DNC ignored the first request, I filed my first lawsuit on December 10, 2004. Prior to my letters, members of the Congressional Black Caucus sent former Congressman, JC Watts the attached letter (on January 28, 1999). In that letter the Caucus told Mr. Watts and his Republican counterparts to: *"Clearly and publicly distance themselves from the CCC and any other white supremacist, anti-semitic or hate groups...."* In my letter to the DNC, I expressed similar sentiments. I told the DNC *"An apology is one of the only ways modern-day Democrats can distance themselves from the party's racist past while bringing some closure to the African American Community."* Instead of apologizing, Howard Dean hired one of the most powerful law-firms in the country, to defend the party's racist past.

Without an apology and repentance, there is no way the Democratic Party can ***ever*** **sincerely** honor Dr. Martin Luther King Jr. and Ms. Rosa Parks; two individuals who literally gave their lives to destroy the racist programs, policies and practices that were established by the Democratic Party. And without an apology and repentance there is no way the Democratic Party can ever respect African Americans. Its past programs and practices from slavery through Jim Crow which literally destroyed the lives of ***millions*** of blacks, amounts to an **act of mass murder**. And to hire an attorney to defend that racist past is not only an official endorsement of murder - it is an insult to the entire black race and to those whites who gave their lives to eliminate racial injustice.

I look forward to your response.

Sincerely

Rev. Wayne Perryman

cc. Senator Maria Cantwell

Letter to the Democratic Party

from the office
of
Rev. Wayne Perryman
P.O. Box 256 Mercer Island, WA 98040 (206) 232-5575
Doublebro@aol.com

November 7, 2004

Democratic National Committee
Mr. Terry McAuliffe, Chairman
430 S. Capital St. SE
Washington, D.C. 20003

Dear Chairman McAuliffe:

My name is Rev. Wayne Perryman. I am an African American inner-city minister in the Seattle area and the author of the enclosed book, *Unfounded Loyalty.* All of my life I have voted Democrat. In the past, I worked with several Democratic candidates and served on the committee of the Washington State Black Clergy to Re-elect President Clinton in 1996. As you know, during the past 70 years African Americans have consistently supported the Democratic Party and put five Democratic presidents in the White House.

The purpose of this letter is to <u>humbly</u> and <u>respectfully</u> request that the DNC offer a formal apology to African Americans for the party's past racist policies and practices toward African Americans, and further request that this apology be issued during the upcoming 2004 convention.

According to the renowned African American history professor, John Hope Franklin, the atrocities committed against African Americans in regions controlled by Democrats and their Klan supporters, *"were so varied and so numerous as to defy classification or enumeration."*

One news reporter documented one of these acts against a Mr. Sam Hose, a black man who was falsely accused of killing his white employer and raping his employer's wife. The reporter wrote:

> "After stripping Hose of his clothes and chaining him to a tree, the self-appointed executioners stacked kerosene-soaked wood high around him. Before saturating Hose with oil and applying the torch, they cut off his ears, fingers, and genitals, and skinned his face. While some in the crowd plunged knives into the victims flesh, others watched with un-feigning satisfaction, the contortions of Sam Hose's body as flames rose, distorting his features, causing his eyes to bulge out of their sockets and rupturing his veins. The only sounds that came from the victim's lips, even as his blood sizzled in the fire. were, Oh my God! Oh, Jesus." Before Hose's body had even cooled, his heart and liver were removed and cut into several pieces, and his bones were crushed into small particles. The crowd fought over these souvenirs. Shortly after the lynching, one of the participants reportedly left for the state capitol, hoping to deliver a slice of Sam Hose's heart to the Democratic governor of Georgia, who would call Sam Hose's deeds, "the most diabolical in the annals of crime."

Another historian reported what the Democratic terrorists did to Mary Turner, a pregnant black woman. Mary was nine months pregnant at the time. She had reported that she was going to file charges against those who had lynched her husband. This is what historians from the PBS special: The Rise & Fall of Jim Crow, and author Leon f. Litwack, had to say about her sadistic murder:

> "After tying her ankles together, they hung her from a tree, head downward, dousing her clothes with gasoline, and burned them [the clothes] from her body. While she was still alive, someone used a knife ordinarily reserved for splitting hogs to cut open the woman's abdomen. The baby fell from her womb to the ground and cried briefly, whereupon a member of the [terrorist] mob crushed the baby's head beneath his

heel. Hundreds of bullets were then fired into Mary Turner's body...."

Other noted history professors also wrote about these atrocities as well, including:

    a.   Professor James McPherson of Princeton University

    b.   Professor David Herbert Donald of Harvard University

    c.   Professor Allen W. Trelease of North Carolina University

    d.   Professor Howard O. Lindsey of DePaul University.

Both the chronicles of history and Congressional Records show that from 1792 up to the 1960's the Democratic Party and its members engaged in the following racist practices:

    a.   On the issue of slavery, Democrats fought for and gave their lives to **expand it** while Republicans fought and gave their lives to **ban it**. Some called it the Civil War, others called it the War between the States. But to African Americans and President Lincoln it was the war between the Democrats and Republicans concerning the State's Rights to maintain the institution of slavery. On March 4, 1865 during his second Inaugural Address, Lincoln said, *"Both parties deprecated war, but one of them would make war rather than let the nation survive, the other would accept war rather than let it perish...."*

    b.   Democrats opposed the Freedman's Bureau and other social programs to help the newly freed slaves.

    c.   Democrats passed Fugitive Slave Laws, Jim Crow Laws, Black Codes and other repressive pieces of legislation to deny blacks their rights as citizens. Democratic Senator Ben Tillman of South Carolina said, *"We reorganized the Democratic*

Party with one plank, and only one plank, namely that this is a white man's country and white men must govern it."

d. Democrats used every means possible to destroy Reconstruction including lynching, whippings, murder, intimidation, assassinations and mutilations. Professor Allen W. Trelease of the University of North Carolina said, *"Democrats by a kind of tortured reasoning, sometimes accused Negroes and Republicans of attacking each other so that the crimes would be blamed on the Democrats; investigations revealed that Democrats had committed the acts themselves."*

e. Democrats filed and financed the lawsuit in the Dred Scott Case and praise the decision that classified blacks as property, but not as people.

f. Democrats murdered blacks who attempted to vote Republican and banned many from participating in primaries.

g. Democrats established rigid testing requirements in southern communities to discourage, disqualify and disfranchise black voters.

h. In 1866, Democrats murdered 40 blacks in the process of driving out every black elected official in Louisiana's State Legislature.

i. Democrats fought for the *Dred Scott Decision* and celebrated after the court issued its ruling that blacks would be classified as ***property***.

j. Democrats formed several terrorist organizations including the Ku Klux Klan to terrorize blacks. During the Congressional debates on the Ku Klux Klan Act of 1871, it was revealed that the Klan was the terrorist arm of the Democratic Party.

k. Democrats praised the court's decision in *Plessy v. Ferguson* which legally established segregation.

l. Democrats opposed and fought against anti-lynching laws.

m. Democrats sued and fought to have the 1875 Civil Rights Act declared unconstitutional by the United States Supreme Court.

n. When Democrats regained control of Congress in 1892, they passed the Repeal Act of 1894 to repeal portions of laws that were designed to help African Americans.

o. Democrats debated and voted against the following:

1. Thirteenth Amendment

2. Fourteenth Amendment

3. Fifteenth Amendment

4. The Civil Rights Act of 1866

5. Reconstruction Act of 1867

6. Enforcement Act of 1870

7. The Ku Klux Klan Act of 1871

8. The 1875 Civil Rights Act (which later became the 1964 Civil Rights Act)

9. The Civil Rights Act of 1957

10. The Civil Rights Act of 1960

p. Southern Democrats debated against and voted against the passage of the 1964 Civil Rights Act and the Voting Rights Act of 1965. Political experts agree that had the Democrats attempted to pass these same types of laws in 1864 (that *certain* members of their party decided to support in 1964), the laws of 1964 would not have been necessary. Instead (prior to 1964), they chose to pass Jim Crow Laws and other repressive legislation to deny blacks their rights as citizens.

q. Entire black communities were destroyed in democratically controlled states including Wilmington, North Carolina,

Rosewood, Florida, and the Greenwood District in Tulsa, Oklahoma, to name a few.

r. Under Democratic rule, an estimated 200 black farmers were massacred in Elaine, Arkansas (1919).

s. In regions controlled by Democrats, hundred of thousands of African Americans were used as free labor by placing them in inhumane prison labor camps. Some called this the new form of slavery.

t. Under the New Deal, Democratic President Franklin D. Roosevelt refused to assist Black sharecroppers who had difficulty in obtaining relief benefits through the Department of Agriculture and refused to assist Blacks that had problems getting loans to purchase land and build homes. Black newspapers were banned from the military, and lynchings and other forms of racial violence continued during his administration.

u. Democrats fought against quality education for African Americans in the 1954 case of *Brown v The Board of Education,* and prior to this case they had a history of murdering our teachers and burning down black schools and churches

v. Under Democratic rule (according to the Associated Press in 2001) African American land ownership in the south decreased from 15 million acres in 1910 to less than two million today. AP reported that the land was lost through fraud, murder and the deliberate destruction of court records.

w. In 1995, while the Clinton Administration proudly supported a group of **White janitors** in their *"reverse discrimination"* lawsuit against Illinois State University, his administration refused to support a group of black, Hispanic and female longshore workers in their discrimination lawsuit against 100 shipping companies and their unions. The workers won their lawsuits without the support of the Clinton Administration and collectively walked away with several million dollars.

    x. From 1792 to 2004, the Democratic Party (the oldest political Party in America) has <u>never</u> elected <u>a black man</u> to the United States Senate.

Many African Americans agree with those psychologists who believe that the horrors of institutional racism established in part by the racist legislation of the Democrats, still haunt African Americans today. Despite these factual truths, the Democratic Party has never issued or offered an apology to African Americans in its 212-year history.

Some have argued that the Republicans also owe African Americans an apology for abandoning them when they reached a compromise (with the Democrats) to remove federal troops from the South, in exchange for giving Rutherford B. Hayes the presidency. History notes that the compromise did indeed take place and troops were removed from the South. However experts say that like the problems facing today's American troops in the <u>Reconstruction of Iraq</u>, it was impossible to have enough federal troops to cover the entire region (13 states) during the<u> Reconstruction of the South</u>. History reveals that from 1866 to 1877 Democrats and their Klan supporters launched a multitude of terrorist attacks against African Americans while federal troops were stationed in the region. Professor David Donald of Harvard writes*: "Congress could require federal troops to supervise the registration of voters, but Negroes were waylaid and butchered on the roads to the registration office...."* The troop's presence had little affect on the reign of terror initiated by Democrats and their Klan supporters.

When it comes to offering apologies, the one factor that may excuse Republicans is the fact that unlike the Democrats, Republicans have always had abolitionists and ***"Radical"*** members like Senator Charles Sumner and Thaddeus Stevens to consistently and effectively challenge racist individuals ***within*** their party (racist Republicans like President Abraham Lincoln). Professor James McPherson of Princeton said, *"The abolitionists became the respected spokesmen of the **radical wing** of the Republican Party."* From 1792 to 1960, the ***"radicals"*** in the Democratic Party weren't spokespersons <u>for</u> African

Americans they were the assassins that brought terror and death to African Americans.

After giving the Democratic Party support for the past 40 years, many African Americans believe that an apology for the role that the Democratic Party played in establishing the institution of racism during the past 168 years is the least that the party can do. The apology should be issued for:

- Fraud

- Murder

- The Formation of Terrorist Organizations

- Economic Deprivation

- Racist Legislation

- Negative Communications

- Promoting Substandard Education

- Terrorist Intimidation

- Landmark Litigation

- Brutal Assassinations

- Racially Flawed Adjudication

I pray that you will earnestly and sincerely consider my request. An apology is one of the only ways that modern-day Democrats can distance themselves from the party's racist past while bringing some closure to the African American community. On May 16, 1997, President Clinton issued a formal apology to African Americans and to those who were victimized by the Tuskegee Experiment; a government sponsored program that allowed Blacks to die from syphilis. Clinton's apology came after the 25,000 black members of the National Medical Association requested such. I pray that the DNC will do the same. If not for the living, the party should do it for the

millions of blacks that lost their lives during this horrible period of history. I'm looking forward to your reply.

Sincerely,

Rev. Wayne Perryman

PS

The enclosed book and attached materials supports the factual claims made in this letter. The book *Unfounded Loyalty*, is a fact-finding investigation covering a period from 1832 to 2002, highlighting the relationship of Blacks with each political party. The book has received rave reviews and a consistent five star rating on Amazon.com.

cc. Associated Press
       National Association of Black Journalists
       National Association of Black Student Unions
       National Bar Association
       National Newspaper Publishers Association
       National Medical Association

Special Note
Perryman's Past Research Resulted In Apologies From Christian Publishers & Scholars

In 1994, my research book, *The 1993 Trial On The Curse of Ham* resulted in an apology and reprinting of several books by our nation's largest Christian publishers, including Thomas Nelson, Zondervan Publishing House and the Encyclopedia Britannica. In this book, I provided proof from a theological perspective that the descendants of Noah's son, Ham (people of Africa) were not cursed as many scholars had previously stated for the past 400 years. The so-called curse was used as a biblical justification for slavery.

Brief to
United States District Court
Western District – Seattle,
Washington

1

2

3

4

5

6

7

8   UNITED STATES DISTRICT COURT

9   WESTERN DISTRICT OF WASHINGTON

10   AT SEATTLE

11   WAYNE PERRYMAN on behalf of himself and | No. **CV04-2442**

12   AFRICAN AMERICAN CITIZENS of the | COMPLAINT—CLASS ACTION

13   UNITED STATES | LEAD PLAINTIFF CLASS ACTION

14   Plaintiff, | COMPLAINT FOR REPARATION

15   v. | PAY FOR CONSTITUTIONAL &

16   DEMOCRATIC NATIONAL COMMITTEE and | CIVIL RIGHTS VIOLATIONS

17   the NATIONAL DEMOCRATIC PARTY | WITHOUT ORAL ARGUMENTS

18   Defendants.

19

20

21   Lead Plaintiff Wayne Perryman ("Lead Plaintiff" or "Plaintiff") individually and on behalf

22   of all other persons similarly situated, by the undersigned Pro-Se litigant, for its first

23   official complaint, alleges to have experienced some of the acts, and upon information

24   and belief to all other matters, based upon the investigation made by the Pro Se Litigant,

25   which investigative research includes, *inter alia,* Congressional Records, chronicles of

26   history, news articles, PBS documentaries, and the works of our nation's top history

27   professors regarding the Democrat's ("Defendant" or "Democratic Party") violation of the

28   Constitutional Rights of African Americans as documented in the Lead Plaintiff's book:

1 Unfounded Loyalty and the enclosed video exhibits. Lead Plaintiff believes that further

2 substantial evidentiary support exists for the allegations set forth below after a reasonable

3 opportunity for discovery.

4

Nature of Action

6 1. Plaintiff brings this action as a class action pursuant to the Civil Liberties Act of 1988,

7 Section 1983 of Title 42 of the United States Codes, and *Jablonowski v. Modern Cap Mfg.*

8 312 Mo. 173, 279, S.W. 89. 95, all of which afford Plaintiff's *redress of an injury and*

9 *amends for the wrong inflicted.*

10

11 2. The Civil Liberties Act of 1988 is one of three pieces of legislation passed by Congress

12 that authorizes *redress for injury.* Senate Bill 60 was the first Reparation Bill submitted on

13 behalf of African Americans in February of 1866. The Senate bill was designed after General

14 William Sherman's Special Field Order #15, which provided African Americans with a

15 tract of land of *40 acres plus a mule*. Although the bill passed both houses (dominated by

16 Republicans), **Democratic** President Andrew Johnson vetoed the bill. Throughout his tenure

17 as president, Johnson carried out the Democrat's agenda by attempting to veto other key

18 pieces of Civil Rights legislation that were designed to give and protect the constitutional

19 rights of African Americans. Title 42 is the third piece of legislation that was passed by

20 Congress which allows redress. Under Section 1983 of Title 42 of the U.S. Code it states

21 that *"deprivation of any rights, privileges, or immunities secured by the Constitution and*

22 *laws, shall be liable to the injured party in an action of law, suit in equity or other proper*

23 *proceeding for redress...."* Section 1983 originated from the **1866 Civil Rights Act** and the

24 **1871 Ku Klux Klan Act**.

25

26 3. The Plaintiffs in this case allege that in an effort to impede and or deny African Americans

27 the same constitutional rights afforded to all American citizens, the Defendants established

28 a *pattern of practice* of promoting, supporting, sponsoring, and financing racially biased

1 entertainment, education, legislation, litigations, and terrorist organizations from 1792 to

2 1962 and continued certain practices up to 2002. The Plaintiffs allege that the Defendants'

3 racist actions were in violation of the **United States Constitution** (as later proven in the case

4 of *Brown v Board of Education* and in subsequent Civil Rights Legislation); and further

5 allege that these racist actions have had an on-going residual effect on today's generation

6 of African Americans.

7

8 4. The Plaintiffs allege that the Defendants' 210 years of racist practices and cover-ups

9 not only negatively *affected* the *entire black race*; but these practices *infected* our *entire*

10 *nation* with the most contagious and debilitating social disease known to mankind, *racism*.

11 In 1866, Republican Congressman John Broomall of Pennsylvania made reference to this

12 *social disease* during his argument for the passage of the 14th Amendment. Broomall said:

13 *"It was also expected that the six Johnsonian new converts to the **Democracy** would also*

14 *oppose and vote against this measure; commencing with the gentleman from New York* [a

15 Democrat], *who, I believe, **has the disease** in the most virulent form, thence down to the*

16 *gentleman from Kentucky* [also a Democrat], *who preceded me on this question, and who*

17 *has the mildest and most amiable type of the **infection**."*

18

19 5. With landmark litigation, racist legislation, and profane defamation, the Defendants

20 spent substantial amounts of money to produce racist campaign literature and to support

21 racist entertainment (i.e., Jim Crow minstrel shows, stage plays, *"The Klansman,"* and

22 movies, *"The Birth of a Nation"*), all in an effort to prove to the world that African

23 Americans were a racially inferior group that should be treated and classified as *"property"*

24 and not as *"citizens."*

25

26 6. The Plaintiffs allege that during the past twenty-one decades the Defendants successfully

27 disguised and concealed their horrific acts against the Plaintiffs by operating and committing

28 these acts under the following aliases: "the Confederacy," "Jim Crow," "Black Codes," the

"Dixiecrats," and the "Ku Klux Klan." Congressional records, historical documents, and the letters and testimonies from several brave black citizens revealed that these groups weren't separate independent organizations, but were various auxiliaries and divisions of the Democratic Party. The debates on the Ku Klux Klan Act of 1871 further revealed that these auxiliaries were committed to use every means possible including: lynchings, murder, intimidation, mutilations, decapitations, and racially flawed adjudication to carry out the Defendants' racist agenda of "*White Supremacy.*"

7. The Plaintiffs allege that to further conceal the truth of their racist history and in an effort to deceive the public, the Defendants made a conscious decision not to mention or disclose their true and complete history. (See exhibit 1.) On their official website they failed to disclose that:

- Democrats opposed the abolitionists' efforts
- Democrats supported slavery and fought and gave their lives to expand it
- Democrats supported and passed the Fugitive Slave Laws of 1793 & 1854
- Democrats supported and passed the Missouri Compromise to protect slavery
- Democrats supported and passed the Kansas Nebraska Act to expand slavery
- Democrats supported and backed the Dred Scott Decision
- Democrats supported and passed Jim Crow Laws
- Democrats supported and passed Black Codes
- Democrats opposed educating blacks and murdered our teachers
- Democrats opposed the Reconstruction Act of 1867
- Democrats opposed the Freedman's Bureau as it pertained to blacks
- Democrats opposed the Emancipation Proclamation
- Democrats opposed the 13th, 14th, and 15th Amendments to end slavery, make blacks citizens, and give blacks the right to vote
- Democrats opposed the Civil Rights Act of 1866

1   •   Democrats opposed the Civil Right Act of 1875 and had it overturned by U.S.

2   Supreme Court

3   •   Various Democrats opposed the 1957 Civil Rights Acts

4   •   Various Democrats argued against the passage of the 1964 Civil Rights Acts

5   •   Various Democrats argued against the passage of the 1965 Voting Rights Acts

6   •   Various Democrats voted against the 1972 Equal Employment Opportunity Act

7   •   Democrats supported and backed Judge John Ferguson in the case of *Plessy v.*

8   *Ferguson*

9   •   Democrats supported the School Board of Topeka, Kansas, in the case of *Brown*

10   *v. Board of Education of Topeka, Kansas.*

11   •   Various Democrats opposed desegregation and integration

12   •   Democrats started and supported several terrorist organizations, including the Ku

13   Klux Klan, an organization dedicated to use any means possible to terrorize Afri-

14   can Americans and those who supported African Americans.

15

16 8. The Plaintiffs further allege that according to the renowned African American history

17 professor John Hope Franklin, the atrocities committed against African Americans in regions

18 controlled by Democrats and their Klan supporters, *"were so varied and so numerous as to*

19 *defy classification or enumeration."*

20

21 **Example 1**: One news reporter documented one of these acts against a Mr. Sam Hose, a

22 black man who was falsely accused of killing his white employer and raping his employer's

23 wife. The reporter wrote: *"After stripping Hose of his clothes and chaining him to a tree,*

24 *the self-appointed executioners stacked kerosene-soaked wood high around him. Before*

25 *saturating Hose with oil and applying the torch, they cut off his ears, fingers, and genitals,*

26 *and skinned his face. While some in the crowd plunged knives into the victim's flesh, others*

27 *watched with unfeigning satisfaction, the contortions of Sam Hose's body as flames rose,*

28 *distorting his features, causing his eyes to bulge out of their sockets and rupturing his*

veins. The only sounds that came from the victim's lips, even as his blood sizzled in the fire, were, 'Oh my God! Oh, Jesus.' Before Hose's body had even cooled, his heart and liver were removed and cut into several pieces and his bones were crushed into small particles. The crowd fought over these souvenirs. Shortly after the lynching, one of the participants reportedly left for the state capitol, hoping to deliver a slice of Sam Hose's heart to the Democratic governor of Georgia, who would call Sam Hose's deeds, "the most diabolical in the annals of crime.' "

Example 2: Another historian reported what the Democratic terrorists did to Mary Turner, a pregnant black woman. Mary was nine months pregnant at the time. She had reported that she was going to file charges against those who lynched her husband. This is what historians from the PBS special: "The Rise & Fall of Jim Crow," and author Leon F. Litwack, had to say about her sadistic murder: *"After tying her ankles together, they hung her from a tree, head downward. Dousing her clothes with gasoline, and burned them* [the clothes] *from her body. While she was still alive, someone used a knife ordinarily reserved for splitting hogs to cut open the woman's abdomen. The baby fell from her womb to the ground and cried briefly, whereupon a member of the* [terrorists] *mob crushed the baby's head beneath his heel. Hundreds of bullets were then fired into Mary Turner's body...."* (See Exhibit 3, "Under Democrat Rule.")

These horrific acts were just the tip of the iceberg. Other noted history professors also wrote about atrocities committed by Democrats and their terrorist organizations, among them include: Professor James McPherson of Princeton University, Professor David Herbert Donald of Harvard University, Professor Allen W. Trelease of North Carolina University, and Professor Howard O. Lindsey of DePaul University.

9. The Plaintiff allege that when the federal government launched various investigations to prosecute those who committed these racist acts, elected officials from the Democratic Party

1 including Democratic governors, judges, mayors, sheriffs, state legislators, and U.S. Senators

2 exhausted every means to block their investigations. Loyal members of the Democratic

3 Party were too loyal to cooperate with the investigations and with rare exception, most

4 African Americans who witnessed the horrific atrocities were too frightened to participate

5 in the investigations. The terrorist attacks by the Defendants and their Klan supporters

6 were so numerous that the Plaintiffs believe that from 1792 to the 1960s this political

7 party is responsible for killing and terrorizing more African Americans than the terrorist

8 activities attributed to Osama Bin Laden, the Al Qaeda, the Baath Party, and the Taliban of

9 Afghanistan. From 1792 to 2002, there are no official records where the Democratic Party

10 officially and publicly apologized and denounced their past racist practices.

11

12 10. The Plaintiffs allege that throughout their history, prominent Democrats openly expressed

13 how they felt about African Americans and where they thought their place should be in

14 our society. On April 29, 1861 Democratic President Jefferson Davis told his Democratic

15 Confederate Congress that: *"Under the supervision of **the superior race**, their* [**blacks'**]

16 *labor had been so directed not only to allow a gradual and marked amelioration of their own*

17 *condition, but to convert hundreds of thousands of square miles of wilderness into cultivated*

18 *lands covered with a prosperous people; towns and cities had sprung into existence, and*

19 *had rapidly increased in wealth and population under the social system of the South...; and*

20 *the productions in the South of cotton, rice, sugar, and tobacco, for the full development and*

21 *continuance of which the labor **of African slaves was and is indispensable,** had swollen to*

22 *an amount which formed nearly three-fourth of the exports of the whole United States and*

23 *had become absolutely necessary to wants of civilized man...."*

24

25 During the 1868 Presidential Campaign Democrats publicly referred to Republicans

26 as *"Nigger Lovers"* and proudly displayed their campaign posters which said: *"This*

27 *is a White Man's Country - Let The White Men Rule*." (See Exhibit 3 video "Under

28 Democrat Rule.")

1 During Reconstruction Georgia Democrats stated that they could never *elevate an inferior*
2 *race over a superior race.* After making the statement, Democrats drove all of their Negro
3 legislators out of office.

4

5 In 1898 during a major election in Wilmington North Carolina, the Democrat's campaign
6 slogan was one word, *"Nigger."* (See Exhibit 3 video "Under Democrat Rule.")

7

8 Senator Ben Tillman of South Carolina told America: *"We reorganized the **Democratic***
9 ***Party** with one plank, and the only plank, namely, **that this is a white man's country, and***
10 ***white men must govern it.*** On March 23, 1909 Tillman told the United States Senate that he
11 defended violence against black men, claiming that "*southern white women will not submit*
12 *to the black man gratifying his lust on our wives and daughters without lynching him.*"

13

14 Senator James K. Vardman (1913-1919), another powerful Democratic Senator from
15 Mississippi said: ***"I am just as opposed to the Negro educator, Booker T. Washington as a***
16 ***voter, with all his Anglo-Saxon re-enforcements as I am to the coconut-headed, chocolate-***
17 ***colored, typical little coon, Andy Dotson, who blacks my shoes every morning."***[14]

18 # Jurisdiction & Venue
19
20 The Democratic Party, also known as the Democratic National Committee, is an official
21 political party operating within the United States since 1792 and currently operates in all
22 fifty states. According the Democratic Party's official website, the DNC and the Democratic
23 Party are one and the same. Their official website makes the following connection:

24

25 "*In 1848, the National Convention established the Democratic National Committee....*
26 *The Convention charged the DNC with the responsibility of promoting the Democratic*
27 *cause between conventions and preparing for the next convention.* Since 1848 their *cause*

28

---

14 *Black Americans*, 59.

1 has included themes like those printed on campaign posters during the 1868 presidential

2 campaign which stated: ***"This is a White Man's Country - Let The White Men Rule."***

3

4 Note: The Democratic Party did not condemn these statements at the time nor have they

5 condemned them since that time.

6

7 The alleged acts contained in this brief took place within the United States from 1792 to

8 2002. The venue is proper in this District Court under 28 U.S.C. §§ 1331 and 1337-67; and

9 pursuant to 28 U.S.C. § 1367.

10 # Class Action Allegations

11

12 1. Plaintiff brings this action as a class action pursuant to Federal Rules of Civil

13 Procedure 23(a) and (b)(3) on behalf of a class consisting of all African American

14 citizens of the United States that are currently alive at the time of this suit.

15 2. The members of the Class are so numerous that joinder of all members is imprac-

16 ticable. While the exact number of Class members is unknown to the Plaintiff

17 at this time and can only be ascertained through appropriate discovery, Plaintiff

18 believes that there are, at a minimum, thirty million African American citizens.

19 3. Common questions of law and fact exist as to all members of the Class and

20 predominate over any questions affecting solely individual members of the

21 Class. Among the questions of law and fact common to the Class are whether,

22 *inter alia*:

23 a. the Civil Rights of African Americans was violated by Defendants' acts as

24 alleged in the Plaintiff's Substantive Allegations from 1792 to 2002.

25 b. the members of the Class have sustained damages and, if so, what is the

26 proper measure of damages?

27 4. Plaintiff's claims are typical of the claims of the members of the Class as Plaintiff

28 and members of the Class sustained damages arising out of Defendants' wrongful

conduct like those who received benefits under the Civil Liberties Act of 1988.

5. Plaintiff will fairly and adequately protect the interests of the members of the Class and will retain counsel competent and experienced in class actions. Plaintiff has no interests antagonistic to or in conflict with those of the Class.

6. A class action is superior to other available methods for the fair and efficient adjudication of the controversy since joinder of all members of the Class is impracticable. Furthermore, because the damages suffered by the individual Class members are so similar, the expense and burden of individual litigation makes it impracticable for the Class members individually to redress the wrongs done to them. There will be no difficulty in the management of this action as a class action.

Substantive Allegations from 1792 to 2002

1792 The Democratic Party was officially formed in 1792 and was dominated with pro-slavery members. Five years earlier the leaders of this party had won a major victory during the Constitutional Convention when the convention relented and gave slave states the legal authorization to classify or count each slave as *three-fifths of a person* for sole purpose of increasing the number of pro-slavery members in Congress. **Democrats** not only used blacks as slaves they also used their numbers to increase their seats in Congress.

1793 Democrats successfully passed the first Fugitive Slave Law of 1793. The law mandated that runaway slaves must be returned to the states from which they came. A new and more powerful Fugitive Slave Law was passed sixty-one years later in 1854.

1820 Democrats used their political muscle to push through legislation that would protect the future of slavery, with the passage of the Missouri Compromise. The Compromise would assure that there would always be an equal number of slave-states and free-states as more states were added to the union.

1831 More individuals joined the many voices opposing the Democrat's pro-slavery platform. One of those individuals was William Garrison, founder of "The Liberator," an

1 anti-slavery publication.

2

3 **1833** Abolitionists formed formal organizations to combat the pro-slavery Democrats.
4 Philadelphia was one of the first cities to organize an anti-slavery society in 1833.

5

6 **1847** Dred Scott filed a lawsuit claiming that he should be given his freedom because his
7 master had taken him to Minnesota, a free-state. Democrats fought hard to defeat Dred
8 Scott and argued that under the current Fugitive Slave Laws he should be returned to his
9 slave master.

10

11 **1852** Harriet Beecher Stowe's book, *Uncle Tom's Cabin*, took center stage as it revealed
12 the horrors of the institution of slavery, an institution that was strongly supported by the
13 pro-slavery wing of the Democratic Party.

14

15 **1854** Democrats passed the Fugitive Slave Law of 1854 and successfully pushed through the
16 Kansas Nebraska Act. The Kansas Nebraska Act gave each state the right to decide whether
17 they would be a free state or a slave state, thus overturning the Missouri Compromise. The
18 anti-slavery members of the Democratic Party were very angry with these turn of events
19 and decided to start their own political party.

20

21 **1854** In July of 1854, anti-slavery members of the Democratic Party formed a new political
22 party in Jackson, Michigan. They called themselves the Republican Party. The party's
23 founders were firmly linked in common opposition to the Democratic Party and their
24 position on slavery. (See Exhibit 4 video.)

25

26 **1856** Republicans had their first national convention. They adopted a platform that stated,
27 ***"Congress did not have the right to recognize slavery, but should have an obligation and***
28 ***a right to abolish it."***

1 **1856** Democrats won their first landmark court decision in the ***Dred Scott*** case. Nine years
2 after Dred Scott filed his lawsuit to re-gain his freedom, the United States Supreme Court
3 (dominated by pro-slavery judges), ruled that the Constitution protected the rights of citizens
4 to own *private property* and that since the Constitution classified slaves as **property** and
5 not as ***citizens*** of the United States, the private property [the slaves] must be returned to its
6 rightful owner. In giving his decision, Chief Justice Taney said *"The Constitution protects*
7 *private property and makes no distinction between the various types of property owned by*
8 *its citizens."* Democrats not only praised the decision they included the Dred Scott decision
9 as part of their political campaign in 1856 and proudly passed out copies of the decision to
10 their constituents. (See Exhibit 4 video.)
11
12 **1856** The Democrats' pro-slavery forces invaded Lawrence, Kansas. Lawrence was a small
13 integrated abolitionist community that supported efforts to make Kansas a free state. Several
14 people were killed and several buildings were destroyed. The invasion proved that whether
15 on the battlefield or on the Senate floor, the Democratic Party felt so strongly about their
16 right to own African Americans that they were willing to engage in war, fist fights or any
17 other violence to defend their position on slavery. Shortly after the invasion in Lawrence,
18 Kansas, Republican Senator, Charles Sumner delivered a fiery speech to Congress (May 21,
19 1856) condemning slavery and the Kansas invasion. While he was yet speaking, Preston
20 Brooks, (a Democratic Congressman from South Carolina) crept up behind Sumner and
21 attacked him with a walking cane. When Preston knocked Sumner to the floor, several
22 Republicans came to Sumner's rescue. The Democrats retaliated on behalf of Brooks and the
23 Senate brawl was on, Democrats and Republicans in a fist fight on the Senate floor, ignited
24 by a speech about slavery. Brooks' behavior and hostile attitude was typical of how most
25 Democrats felt about maintaining the institution of slavery as you will see from Professor
26 David Donald's (of Harvard University) account of what happened after the dust settled:
27
28 *While Brooks was being led off, Sumner partially supported by Morgan, lay at the side of*

1 *the center aisle, his feet in the aisle, and he leaning partially against a chair. He remained*

2 *senseless as a corpse for several minutes, his head bleeding copiously from the frightful*

3 *wounds, and the blood saturating his clothes. Dr. Cornelius Boyle, who had been hastily*

4 *summoned, dressed the wounds, which were still bleeding profusely, and put two stitches*

5 *in each. Sumner's shirt around the neck and collar was soaked with blood. The waistcoat*

6 *had many marks of blood upon it; also the trousers. The broadcloth coat was covered with*

7 *blood on the shoulders so thickly that the blood had soaked through the cloth even through*

8 *the padding and appeared on the inside; there was also a great deal of blood on the back of*

9 *the coat and its sides.* [At the hospital] *Before falling into a dazed sleep, Summer remarked:*

10 *I could not believe that a thing like this was possible.*

11

12 *Arrested on a charge of assault, Brooks was immediately freed under a $500 bail and*

13 *became the hero of the extreme pro-slavery clique. Armed and menacing,* **Southern**

14 **fire-eaters talked of imitating Brook's example, and made violent threats against**

15 **other Northern leaders.** [Saying] *"It would not take much to have the throats of every*

16 *Abolitionist cut. If the northern men had stood up, the city would now float with blood.*

17 *And if Congress dared to discuss Brooks' actions, the House of Representatives would*

18 *ring vollies* [sic] *from revolvers."* [15]

19

20 **1858** Using the *Dred Scott* decision as the basis for his decision, the U.S. Attorney ruled

21 that slaves could not patent inventions. This right was given to citizens only. The slave

22 master not only made money from his slaves' labor; he also made money from their

23 inventions as well.

24

25 **1859** Abolitionist John Brown and his band of thirteen whites and five blacks took matters

26 into their own hands and battled the Democrat's pro-slavery forces at Harpers Ferry,

27 Virginia. Two blacks were killed, two escaped, and one was captured along with John

28

15 Donald, *Charles Sumner* 297-298.

Brown who was later put on trial and executed .

1860 The divide between the Democrats and Republicans widened as they both took firm positions on the issue of slavery during the Presidential elections. On December 17, 1860, South Carolina was the first Democratic state to secede from the Union over of the issue of slavery (State's Rights).

1861 One year after South Carolina's secession, pro-Democratic forces launched a terrorist attack on Fort Sumter. This marked the official beginning of a war between the Democrats and the Republicans, more commonly called: The Civil War.

1862 As commander and Chief of the U.S. Armed Forces, President Lincoln issued the Emancipation Proclamation freeing all slaves in the rebellious states, effective January 1, 1863. His anti-slavery efforts infuriated loyal Democrats like John Wilkes Booth.

1864 Lincoln was re-elected for a second term and chose Andrew Johnson, a devout Democrat to be his Vice President. Lincoln felt that choosing Johnson would improve his relationship with Democrats and accelerate the healing process between the north and the south. But he was wrong. The war continued and the battle ground switched from the fields of Gettysburg to the halls of Congress.

1864 The Thirteenth Amendment

The first battle in Congress was over the 13th Amendment. The 13th Amendment was sponsored by Republican Senator Lyman Trumbull of Illinois to *"free all slaves and abolish slavery in the United States and its territories."* **Democrats' Opposition**: During the debates on March 19, 1864, **one of the spokespersons for the Democrats was a northern Democratic Congressman Fernando Wood of New York**. He argued: *"The proposed Amendment to abolish slavery in the states of the Union is unjust, a breach of good faith and utterly*

1   *irreconcilable... It involves **the extermination of all white men of the southern States**, and*

2   *the forfeiture of all the land and other property belonging to them. Negroes and military*

3   *colonists will take the place of the race* [that will be] *blotted out of existence."*

4

5   **Republican James Wilson's** opening remarks included the following statement: ***"It was***

6   ***perfectly natural for the comparatively few men who held four million human beings***

7   ***in bondage*** *which put to shame all other kindred systems which ever cursed man for their*

8   *mildness, not only to resort to cruel and despotic laws for aid in their diabolical act, but*

9   *also to seek refuge in the anti-republican dogma that "the right to govern resides in a very*

10   *small minority.... Mr. Chairman we can cast our eyes upon no page of this nation's history*

11   *whereon it is not written, 'Slavery is incompatible with a free government.' We have tried*

12   *to close our eyes against this constantly repeated and self-evident truth. We have tried to*

13   *reason it away, to practice arts which should carry us around it, over it, or under it. We*

14   *have failed to accomplish the desired results. As immutable as the laws of God stands*

15   *the declaration, 'Slavery is incompatible with a free government....' No religion which*

16   *recognizes God's eternal attribute of justice and breathes that spirit of love which applies*

17   *to all men the sublime commandments, 'Whatsoever ye would that men should do unto you,*

18   *do ye even so them' can ever be allowed free exercise where slavery curses men and defies*

19   *God. No religious denomination can flourish or even be tolerated where slavery rules with*

20   *surrendering the choice jewel of its faith into keeping of that infidel power which withhold*

21   *the Bible from the poor...."*

22   Note: The 13th Amendment, which was proposed to free all slaves, was opposed by

23   Democrats who overwhelmingly voted against the Amendment. (See Exhibit 4 video.)

24

25   **1865** The war ended. Some called it the Civil War, others called it the War between the States.

26   But to African Americans and President Lincoln it was the war between the Democrats and

27   Republicans concerning the State's Rights to maintain the institution of slavery. On March

28   4, 1865, during his second Inaugural Address, Lincoln said, ***"Both parties deprecated war,***

but one of them would make war rather than let the nation survive, the other would

accept war rather than let it perish…." A month later the President was assassinated by John Wilkes Booth, a loyal Democrat.

1865 On January 16, 1865, General William Sherman initiated the first Reparation program for African Americans with Special Field Order #15. Under the order, each family would receive **40 acres and a mule to work the land**. In February of 1866 this program was introduced to Congress as Senate Bill 60. Although the bill passed both houses (dominated by Republicans), when it finally reached President Andrew Johnson's desk, he showed his true Democratic colors and vetoed the bill. Because of Johnson's pro-Democrat positions and his track record of vetoing key pieces of Civil Right legislation (such as Senate Bill 60 and the Reconstruction Act of 1867), Republicans sought to impeach him but failed. The Democratic president escaped impeachment by one vote.

1865 Black Codes In 1865, shortly after the war, **Democrats** of the south continued their efforts to enslave African Americans by legislating Black Codes. The Black Codes suppressed, restricted and denied African Americans the same constitutional rights and privileges afforded to whites. The Codes established whom African Americans could or could not work for, the type of employment they could pursue, and called for restrictive travel and evening curfews. Many blacks were forced to work for their former slave masters as apprentices. The Black Codes virtually re-enslaved the African Americans.

1866 1866 Civil Rights Acts

Purpose: Introduced by Senator Lyman Trumbull of Illinois, the law was designed to challenge Black Codes by prohibiting discrimination on the basis of race and assuring that every citizen had the same rights to contract, sue, purchase and dispose of property; and *to "bring action and give evidence to and equal benefit of all laws of the security of person and property."*

1   **Democrats' Opposition: One of the spokespersons for the Democrats was Reverdy**

2   **Johnson, a Democrat from Maryland,** who argued against the law. Johnson argued that

3   under this law, the black man would have "*the same right to enter into a contract of*

4   *marriage with a white woman as a white man has.*"

5

6   Republican Senator William Fessenden of Maine responded: "*He* [the black man] *has the*

7   *same right to make a contract of marriage with a white woman that a white man has with*

8   *a black woman.*"

9

10   The **Democrat from Maryland** went on to argue that the 1866 Civil Rights Act could not

11   apply to blacks because, "*The Supreme Court had already ruled in the Dred Scott case that*

12   *a person of African descent, whether born free or not whether free by birth or free by after*

13   *events, is not within the meaning of the Constitution of the United States, a citizen.*"

14

15   **Willard Saulsbury, a northern Democrat from Delaware** said "*I regard this bill*

16   *as one of the **most dangerous that was ever introduced into the Senate of the United***

17   ***States....*** *During the last four or five years I have sat in this Chamber and witnessed the*

18   *introduction of bills into this body which I thought obnoxious to many very grave and*

19   *serious constitutional objection: but I never since I have been a member of the body seen a*

20   *bill so fraught with danger, so full of mischief, as the bill now under consideration.*" Please

21   **note: those opposing this bill were northern Democrats**. The debates started on January

22   29, 1866, the same year that the Ku Klux Klan was organized.

23

24   **Martin Thayer the Republican from Pennsylvania** responded: "*Sir, this bill is the just*

25   *sequel to, and the proper completion of, the great measure of national redress which opened*

26   *the dungeon doors of four million human beings. Without this, in my judgment, that great*

27   *act of justice will be paralyzed and made useless. With this, it will have practical effect, life,*

28   *vigor, and enforcement....*

1   *"Sir, if it is competent for the new-formed* [Democratic] *Legislatures of the rebel States*

2   **to enact laws which oppress this large class of people who are dependent for protection**

3   **upon the United States Government, to retain them still in a state of real servitude;** *if it*

4   *is practicable for these Legislatures to pass laws and enforce laws* [Black Codes] *which*

5   **reduce this class of people to the condition of bondmen;** *laws which prevent the enjoyment*

6   **of the fundamental rights of citizenship;** *laws which declare, for example, that they shall*

7   *not have the privilege of purchasing a home for themselves and their families; laws which*

8   *impair their ability to make contracts for labor in such a manner as virtually to deprive*

9   *them of the power of making such contracts, and which then declare them vagrants because*

10   *they have no homes and because they have not employment; I say, if it is competent for these*

11   [Democratic] *Legislatures to pass and enforce such laws, then I demand to know, of what*

12   *practical value is the amendment abolishing slavery in the United States? ...For one, sir,*

13   *I thought when I voted for the amendment to abolish slavery that I was aiding to give real*

14   *freedom to the men who had so long been groaning in bondage. I did not suppose that I was*

15   *offering them a mere paper guarantee."*

16

17   In Response to Martin Thayer's comments, **Michael Kerr the Democrat from Indiana**

18   said, *"...The Constitution of Indiana, adopted in 1851,* **forbids any Negro or mulatto to**

19   *come into or settle in that State after the adoption of that Constitution and declares all*

20   *contracts made with any Negro or mulatto coming into the State contrary to the provision*

21   *of that Constitution* **shall be void.** *This bill* [1866 Civil Rights Act] *proposes to annul those*

22   *constitutional provisions and* **all State laws passed to secure their execution** *.... I might go*

23   *on and in this manner to illustrate the practical working of this extraordinary measure. But*

24   *I have said enough to indicate the inherent viciousness of the bill. It takes a long and fearful*

25   *step toward the complete obliteration of State authority and the reserved and original rights*

26   *of the States...."*

27

28   Note: The Civil Rights Act of 1866 was designed to improve the conditions of our African

1 Americans, but the Democrats strongly opposed this law and voted against it.

2

3 **1866 The Birth of the Ku Klux Klan**

4 After the Civil War, when Republicans passed various laws and developed a number of

5 social programs (such as the Freedmen's Bureau) to assist blacks, the Democrats became

6 very angry and resentful. From their deep-seated anger several terrorist organizations were

7 born - and in their efforts to gain the upper hand, the Democrats became the "_daddy_" of

8 the Ku Klux Klan (in 1866). The Encyclopaedia Britannica reported that the **"_Democrats'_**

9 _resentment led to the formation of the secret terroristic organizations such as the Ku Klux_

10 _Klan and the Knight of the White Camelia. The use of fraud, violence and intimidation_

11 _helped Southern conservatives regain control of their state governments...."_[16]

12

13 Professor Allen Trelease said: "_Klansmen in disguise rode through Negro neighborhoods_

14 _at night warning Negroes either to cast **Democratic** ballots or stay away from the poll. The_

15 _Klan also sent notices to Republican office holders, warning them of death and telling them_

16 _to either resign or leave the vicinity. Similar notices went to active **Republicans of both**_

17 _**races** and often to the teachers of **Negro schools as well**. Klan activities created a reign of_

18 _terror in many localities and sometimes had the desired effect of demoralizing Negroes and_

19 _Republicans.... **Republicans** of both races were threatened, beaten, shot, and murdered_

20 _with impunity. In some areas Negroes stopped voting or voted **the Democrat** ticket as the_

21 _Klan demanded._" Trelease went on to say, "**_Democrats_**_, by a kind of tortured reasoning,_

22 _sometimes accused Negroes and Republicans of attacking and even killing each other so_

23 _that the crimes would be blamed on the **Democrats**...._"[17]

24

25 Professors John Hope Franklin and Alfred Moss, authors of _From Slavery to Freedom_,

26 report that, "_The Camelias and the Klan were the most powerful of the secret orders. Armed_

27

28 16 1992 _Encyclopaedia Britannica_, 979.
17 _Reconstruction: The Great Experience_

1   with guns, swords, or other weapons, their members patrolled some parts of the South day

2   and night. They used intimidation, force, ostracism in business and society, bribery at the

3   polls, arson, and even murder to accomplish their deed. Depriving the Negro of political

4   equality became, to them, a holy crusade in which a noble end justified any means. Negroes

5   were run out of communities if they disobeyed orders to desist from voting; and the more

6   resolute and therefore insubordinate blacks were whipped, maimed, and hanged. In 1871

7   several Negro officials in South Carolina were given fifteen days to resign and they were

8   warned that if they failed to do so, then retributive justice will as surely be used as night

9   follows day. For many white Southerners violence was still the surest means of keeping the

10   Negroes politically impotent, and in countless communities they were not allowed, under

11   penalties of reprisals, to show their faces in town on Election Day. It had looked as though

12   the Civil War would break out anew as the **Democrats resorted to every possible device to**

13   **over throw the radicals**.[18]

14

15   Professor Franklin went on to say, "*It was reported that in North Carolina the Klan was*

16   *responsible for 260 outrages, including 7 murders and the whipping of 72 whites and*

17   *141 Negroes. In one county in South Carolina 6 men were murdered and more than 300*

18   *were whipped during the first six months of 1870. The personal indignities inflicted upon*

19   *individual whites **and Negroes were so varied and so numerous as to defy classification***

20   ***or enumeration.***"[19]

21

22   In his book, *The Abolitionist Legacy*, Professor James McPherson reported, "*In 1873,*

23   *Louisiana became almost a synonym for chaos and violence. When Grant sent federal*

24   *troops to install Kellogg in office* [as governor], ***Louisiana Democrats*** *were infuriated.*

25   *They formed White Leagues which attacked black and white Republicans and took scores*

26   *of lives.*"[20]

27

28
18 *Reconstruction–The Great Experience*, 226-233.
19 *Reconstruction after the Civil War*,157.
20 McPherson, *The Abolitionist Legacy*, 40.

1 From his book entitled *Charles Sumner*, Harvard Professor, David Hebert Donald reached

2 the following conclusion: *"Congress could give the Negro the vote, but all over the South*

3 *the **Ku Klux Klan** and **other terrorist organizations systematically intimidated the***

4 ***freedmen**, flogged or slaughtered their leaders and drove whites who worked with them*

5 *into exile. Congress could require federal troops to supervise the registration of voters, but*

6 *Negroes were waylaid and butchered on the roads to the registration offices. Congress could*

7 *suppress outright violence by military force, but it could do nothing to protect Negroes from*

8 *landlords who told them bluntly: If you vote with that Yankee* [Republican] *party you shall*

9 *not live on our land."[21]*

10

11 Professor Howard O. Linsay, the author of *A History of Black Americans,* says, *"Blacks and*

12 *sympathetic Whites were attacked and threatened. African Americans were discouraged*

13 *from seeking elected office and even from trying to vote. Any and all means were used from*

14 *threats to violence to outright murder."[22]*

15

16 **1866 Freedman Bureau Extension Act of 1866**

17 Purpose: Sponsored by Republicans, the Freedman Bureau was first established in 1865 to

18 provide basic health and educational services for the newly freed slaves and displaced whites.

19 **Democrats' Opposition**: The Democrats opposed the Freedman Bureau, particularly the

20 portion that assisted blacks and argued that the Bill of Rights gave each state the right to

21 establish their own laws to govern their own states. Through the Black Codes (which were

22 established under state law) Democrats prohibited blacks from going to school and forced

23 blacks to work for their former slave masters thus making the Freedman's Bureau null and

24 void in many states when it came to services for blacks.

25

26

27

28
21 Donald, *Charles Sumner*, 420.

22 Linsay, *A History of Black Americans*, 88-89.

1866 <u>The Fourteenth Amendment</u>

The Purpose: Introduced by Republican Congressmen John Bingham of Ohio and Thaddeus Stevens of Pennsylvania, the bill was drafted in conjunction with the Reconstruction Act to make all slaves citizens and give them the same rights as citizens.

Republican Congressman John Broomall of Pennsylvania said: *"It was to be expected that the measure now before the house would meet the opposition and denunciation of the unrepentant thirty-three* [Democrats] *of this body. The gentlemen* **[northern Democrats]** *who have voted **on all occasions upon the rebel side of all questions** that have been before the country for six years could hardly be expected to change their position at this time. It was also expected that the six Johnsonian new converts to the Democracy would also oppose and vote against this measure; commencing with the gentleman from New York,* [Mr. Raymond] *who, I believe, **has the disease** in the most virulent form, thence down to the gentleman from Kentucky,* [Mr. Smith] *who preceded me on this question, and who has the mildest and most amiable type of the **infection**. Upon them, too, arguments are useless.... I know that the unrepentant **Democracy** of this body who voted against the Civil Rights Bill* [of 1866] *upon the allegation that it was unconstitutional. And I rather expect to see them exhibit their usual consistency by voting against making it constitutional upon the ground that it is so already."*

Democrats' Opposition: During the two year debate (from June 16, 1866 to July 28, 1868), the Democrats argued that the Dred Scott decision by the U.S. Supreme Court had already determined that blacks were merely *property*, not *citizens*, and that Congress had no right or power to overturn the court's decision with this bill. **One of the spokespersons for the Democrats was Democratic Congressman Andrew Rogers from New Jersey.** He said the proposed Amendment was *"...An attempt to in-graft upon the Constitution of the United States one of the **most dangerous, most wicked, most intolerant, and most outrageous propositions ever introduced into this house**. I have no fault to find with the*

1 colored race. I wish them well, and if I were in a State where they exist in large numbers

2 I would vote to give them every right enjoyed by the white people – except the right of a

3 Negro man to marry a white woman and the right to vote. God save the people of the South

4 from degradation by **which they would be obliged to go to the polls and vote side by side**

5 **with the Negro!"**

6

7 **Democratic Congressman George Shanklin argued**: *"There are two prominent and*

8 *distinct ideas contained in this proposition. The first idea is to strike down the reserved*

9 *rights of the States those rights which were declared by the framers of the Constitution to*

10 *belong to the States exclusively and necessary for the protection of the property* [reference

11 to slave property as in the Dred Scott Decision] *and the liberty of the people.... It then*

12 *proposed to disfranchise the people of the southern States* [states originally controlled

13 by Democrats] *who have gone into this rebellion, until the party in power* [Republicans]

14 *could fasten and rivet the chains of oppression for all the time to come, and hedge*

15 *themselves in power, that they may rule and control those people at will. Those are the*

16 *two ideas contained in this proposition.... But how are you going to humble and degrade*

17 *these people? By disfranchising them, by oppressing them with taxes, by denying them*

18 *representation, by dragging them **down** to the loyal political and social equality with the*

19 ***servile African race***."

20

21 Republican Congressman, John Bingham of Ohio said, *"Allow me to say that this*

22 *amendment takes from no State any right that ever pertained to it. No State ever had the*

23 *right under the forms of law or otherwise to deny to any freeman the equal protection of*

24 *the laws or to the Republic, although many of them have assumed and exercised the power*

25 *and that without remedy."*

26

27 In the Senate debates, Republican Senator Jacob Howard of Michigan argued, *"This*

28 *abolishes all class legislation in the States and does away with the injustice of subjecting*

one caste of persons to a code not applicable to another. It prohibits the hanging of a black man for a crime for which the white man is not to be hanged. It protects the black man in his fundamental rights as a citizen with the same shield which it throws over the white man. Is it not time, Mr. President, that we extend to the black man...equal protection of the law?" Note: The 14th Amendment was designed to give citizenship to our nation's **entire black population**, along with the rights that came with citizenship, but the Democrats strongly opposed this law and voted against it. (See Exhibit 4 video.)

1867 <u>The First Reconstruction Act of 1867</u>

Purpose: This (Republican) bill was designed to rebuild the south with a bias-free government system that would be more favorable to the newly freed slaves. The Act included the following: *"Whereas no legal State governments or adequate protection for life or property now exists in the Rebel States of Virginia, North Carolina, South Carolina, Georgia, Mississippi, Alabama, Louisiana, Florida, Texas, and Arkansas; and whereas it is necessary that peace and good order should be forced in the said States until loyal and Republican State governments can be established: Therefore: Be it enacted that said rebel States shall be divided into military districts and made subject to military authority of the United States.... (2) That it shall be the duty of the President to assign to the command of each of said districts an officer of the army, not below the rank of brigadier-general, and to detail a sufficient military force to enable such officer to perform his duties and enforce his authority within the district to which he is assigned...."*

Democrats' Opposition: Democrat's terrorist organizations such as the Ku Klux Klan worked relentlessly to defeat and undermine the Republican's reconstruction efforts. African American Professor John Hope Franklin said**,** *"When Southern whites had almost complete charge of Reconstruction, a kind of guerrilla warfare was carried out against both blacks and whites who represented the Washington government in the South. It had looked as though the Civil War would break out anew as **Democrats** resorted to every*

1 *possible device to overthrow the radicals* [Republicans]. *"*

2

3 Like many of the terrorists groups in Iraq today (2003), the **Democrat's terrorists** of
4 1867 were determined to stay in power and defeat the efforts to reconstruct the South. The
5 obstacles that the Republicans faced in 1867 are quite similar to the obstacles that the Bush
6 Administration faces in Iraq. In both situations, the Bush Administration in 2003 and the
7 Republican Administration in 1867 did not properly plan for Reconstruction. At no time
8 did they anticipate terrorist attacks by the loyal members of the Baath Party during Iraq's
9 Reconstruction or the terrorist attacks by the loyal members of the Democratic Party during
10 the South's Reconstruction. In reference to the 1867 Reconstruction, Professor David
11 Herbert Donald of Harvard said: *"Congress could give the Negro the vote, but all over the*
12 *South the Ku Klux Klan and other terrorist organizations systematically intimidated the*
13 *freedman, flogged or slaughtered their leaders, and drove whites who worked with them*
14 *into exile. Congress could require federal troops to supervise the registration of voters, but*
15 *Negroes were waylaid and butchered on the road to the registration office. "*

16

17 **1868** In 1868, Georgia Democrats publicly stated that *the Negro is unfit to rule the state*
18 and claimed that they would protect Negroes but they *would not let them be governors,*
19 *congressmen or judges.* After stating that they could never *elevate an inferior race over*
20 *a superior race,* Democrats expelled from the legislature all of the Negro legislators. (See
21 Exhibit 3 video "Under Democrat Control.")

22

23 **1868** The nation was engaged in its first presidential election after Reconstruction.
24 Throughout the campaign, Democrats referred to Republicans as *"Nigger Lovers"* and
25 proudly displayed their motto on large campaign posters: ***"This is a White Man's Country***
26 ***- Let The White Men Rule.*** *"* Democrats received tremendous support from Democrats in
27 New York and New Jersey.

28

1869 <u>The Fifteenth Amendments</u>

The Purpose: Introduced by a Republican Senate, the purpose of this amendment was to give blacks the constitutional right to vote. **Democrat Opposition: One of the spokespersons for the Democrats was DeGarrett Davis, the Democratic Congressman from Kentucky.** Davis said, *"Sir, these amendments of the Constitution, your Freedmen's Bureau bill, your civil rights bill, and all of your monstrous and unconstitutional laws will be decided in the course of a few years by sovereign people of the United States of America in their paramount power and sovereignty, to be null and void, mere debris that you have thrown over the Constitution. They will be swept away from it."*

Thomas Hendricks a Democrat from Indiana added, ***"I do not believe that the Negro race and the white race can mingle in the exercise of political power and bring good results to society.*** *We are of different races. Men may argue about it as much as they please; we know that in many respects there is a great difference between the races. There is a difference not only in their physical appearance and conformation, **but there is a difference morally and intellectually, and I do not believe that the two races can mingle successfully in the management of government.** I do not believe that they will add to the common intelligence of the country when we make them voters."*

Republican Senator William Stewart said, *"This amendment is a declaration to make all men, without regard to race or color, equal before the law. The arguments in favor of it are so numerous and so convincing that they carry conviction to every mind. It is the only measure that will really abolish slavery...."*

Republican Senator James Patterson of New Hampshire added: *"I hope that this proposition will be adopted, for all the amendments which have been offered I think it is the best. Our object is to meet **a wrong done to a class of black native citizens**; to give them the same privileges that other citizens of the United States possess...."* Debates took place on

1 January 11, 1869.

2

3 Note: The 14th Amendment was designed to give our nation's **entire black population** the

4 right to vote but the Democrats opposed this law and voted against it. As stated before, a

5 Democratic Senator from Mississippi said: *"I am just as opposed to the Negro educator,*

6 **Booker T. Washington as a voter**, *with all his Anglo-Saxon re-enforcements, as I am to the*

7 *coconut-headed, chocolate-colored, typical little coon, Andy Dotson, who blacks my shoes*

8 *every morning."*[23]

9

10 **1870 The Enforcement Act of 1870**

11 The Purpose: The new bill was introduced by Republican Congressman John Bingham of

12 Ohio. He said the purpose of the bill *was "to enforce the legal right of the citizens of the*

13 *United States to vote in the several States of this Union – a right which had been defiantly*

14 *denied in violation of the Constitution."* **Democrats' Opposition**: The Democrats opposed

15 the legislation, because it was designed to force compliance with the Fifteenth Amendment.

16 **One of the spokespersons for the Democrats was James Bayard, the Democrat of**

17 **Delaware**. Bayard said, **"...*This bill is intended not to prevent discrimination between*

18 *various races of men, but to discriminate directly against the white race in favor of the*

19 *black race*....** *I consider this bill not an act of appropriate legislation fairly to enforce*

20 *that amendment, but it is only another attempt to bolster up by violence, intimidation, in*

21 *the shape of penal enactments,* **the inferior capacities of the Negro race in the struggle**

22 **for racial and political equality**.... *Now, sir, for whom has all this been done? For whose*

23 *protection? It has been only for* **the ignorant, semi-barbarous race unfit for voting,**

24 *manufactured into* **votes and allies of the Republican Party** *to sustain themselves a little*

25 *longer in power...."*

26

27 **Republican Senator William Stewart** of Nevada responded: *"Mr. President, I congratulate*

28

---

23 *Black Americans*, 59

1 *the Senate and the country that we are about to assert some of the powers of Congress for*

2 *the protection of voters; for the protection of down-trodden; for the protection of persons*

3 *in their political and civil rights; that we are about to get a bill which asserts something*

4 *of dignity and power of this action. It has been stated by some, in the course of the debate,*

5 *that no legislation is necessary, and by others that this Fifteenth Amendment is a fraud and*

6 *shall be of short duration. I tell the Opposition that it is no fraud, and that its duration will*

7 *be perpetual. **Rights guaranteed and granted to the people cannot be taken from them.***

8 ***No party can stand on the basis of taking away such rights.** When the high sounding phase*

9 *came from certain pretended or real leaders of the **<u>Democratic Party</u>** that they intended*

10 *to acquiesce in the Fifteenth Amendment, I did not then believe in the good faith of the*

11 *declaration so made. The states which have come from the other side since this debate has*

12 *begun, convinced me that I was right; that they did not intend to do it in good faith.... We have*

13 *commenced legislation in the right direction by attempting to guard the ballot-box in New*

14 *York against the trampling of it down by the **<u>Democratic Party</u>**. Why should the gentlemen*

15 *talk about our want of faith in the people? Sir, our faith in the people is unlimited; but we*

16 *have no faith in a **<u>Democratic</u>** oligarchy in New York City or New Orleans or Georgia,*

17 *which by its power shall drive loyal men from the polls.... **Ever since the war closed you***

18 ***have been trying to point out how we could not reconstruct. You have been quibbling***

19 ***and complaining at every attempt we have made.** You have been occupying whole nights*

20 *here in uttering condemnations of the just and the liberal measures of a patriotic Congress.*

21 *You have failed and you will fail again. Let me advise you now to turn your attention to*

22 *enforcing the laws, to turn your attention to the only means by which peace can be had,*

23 *and we will meet you in brotherly love. We have no enmity against the **<u>Democratic Party</u>** as*

24 *such, but while it goes wrong, while its motto is anarchy, injustice, inequality, fraud, we will*

25 *conquer it every time.... Your now fighting the Fifteenth Amendment is only another of your*

26 *usual blunders.... Come out on the side of humanity, justice, peace, law, the Constitution;*

27 *take the Constitution as it is, uphold it, and defend it, and you will have peace...."* Debates

28 took place on May 16, 1870.

1871 <u>The Force Act of 1871</u>

The Purpose: The propose of the Force Act of 1871 was to supplement the 1870 Enforcement Act by supplying an independent enforcement machinery which would affirmatively insure vindication of the right to vote in all congressional elections. The machinery contemplated was to be provided by the appointment of federal officials to supervise the election process in each election district (in cities and towns with over 20,000 inhabitants) Democrats' Opposition: **One of the spokespersons for the Democrats was Charles Eldredge, a Democrat from Wisconsin.** Eldredge opened up the debate with these words: *"Of all the legislation proposed by this or any other Congress, there is none, in my judgment, more unwarrantable and unjustifiable than that proposed by this bill. It is absolutely atrocious. It is hideous and revolting.... It provides a system to drive citizens from the polls, and to disgust all honest men with our elections....* ***By conferring suffrage upon the colored race have we lost the rights our fathers secured to us by the Constitution? In giving freedom to the slaves have we become slaves ourselves?"***

The Democrats dominated the debates; only a few Republicans were able to speak. **John Churchill, a Republican** from New York, was one of the few who spoke. Churchill said, *"For some years past grave doubts have prevailed in different portions of this country as to whether the declared results of the elections truly expressed the will of the people.... The object of this bill is simply to perfect the bill of last summer and to make it more likely to accomplish the real objective of which was desired and intended to be accomplished by it. And that is, that while it shall exclude no honest man from the polls and hinder no honest man in his effort to vote, it shall prevent the repetition of such acts and many other acts of offense against the elective franchise as have been detailed...."* (Debates took place on February 15, 1871.)

1871 Several southern blacks were interviewed regarding their voting preferences and the intimidation that they experienced at the polls by **<u>Democrats</u>**. The interviews were documented by the Joint Select Committee to Inquire Into Conditions of Affairs In The Late Insurrectionary States. The interviews became a part of *Senate Report No. 579* in the 48th Congress. On November 1, 1871 John Childers of Livingston, Alabama was interviewed by the Select Committee. The following is a portion of his interview as documented by Herbert Aptheker (in his book, *Documentary History of The Negro People In the United States Vol. 2)*:

Question: *Did you ever hear any threats made by* **Democrats** *against Negroes of what would be done* [to him] *if he voted the radical* [meaning Republican] *ticket?*

Answer: *I have had threats on myself. I can tell them.*

Question: *What kind of threats were made to you?*

Answer: *I have had threats that if we all would vote the* **Democratic ticket** *we would be well thought of, and the white men of the county – the old citizens of the county – would protect us; and every struggle or trouble we got into we could apply to them for protection, and they would assist us.*

Question: *Where did you hear that said?*

Answer: *I have heard it often. At the last election it was given to me. There was a man standing here in the court-house door; when he started to the ballot-box he told me he had a coffin already made for me, because he thought I was going to vote the radical* [meaning Republican] *ticket.*

Question: *Who was that man?*

Answer: *Well, I am afraid to tell his name, sir.*

Question: *Were the colored folks generally alarmed by these threats, and afraid to vote their true sentiments?*

Answer: *Yes sir, they were.*

Question: *I have heard that a great many colored people voted the* **Democratic ticket** *at the last governor's election.* [Is that true?]

Answer: *Yes sir.*

1 **Question**: *What made them do it?*

2 **Answer**: *For fear. I voted myself, I voted the **Democratic Ticket**.*

3 **Question**: *Were you afraid if you voted the radical ticket you would be harmed?*

4 **Answer**: *I was sir; because as I just stated to you, there was a man that told me he had a*

5 *coffin already made for me. Yes, sir, I voted it, and don't pretend to deny it before nobody.*

6 *When I was going to the polls there was a man standing in the door and says, Here comes*

7 *you, God damn your soul, I have a coffin already made for you. I had two tickets in my*

8 *pocket then; a **Democratic ticket** and a radial ticket; I pulled out the **Democratic ticket** and*

9 *showed it to him, and he says. You are all right, go on.*

10

11 **1871** What triggered the Senate investigations were letters to Congress from blacks in

12 several southern states. In those letters black citizens reported a multitude of acts of terror

13 by the Democrats and their Klan auxiliaries. On March 25, 1871, a group of blacks from

14 Kentucky sent a petition to Congress and stated the following:

15

16 Blacks From Kentucky

17 *We believe you are not familiar with the description of the **Ku Klux Klan** riding nightly*

18 *over the country going from county to county and in the county towns spreading terror*

19 *wherever they go, by robbing, whipping, ravishing, and killing our people without*

20 *provocation, compelling Colored people to break ice and bathe in the chilly waters of*

21 *the Kentucky River.*

22

23 *The Legislature has adjourned - they refused to enact any laws to suppress Ku Klux disorder.*

24 *We regard them as now being licensed to continue their dark and bloody deeds under the*

25 *cover of the dark night. They refuse to allow us to testify in the state courts where a white*

26 *man is concerned. We find their deeds are perpetrated only upon Colored men and white*

27 *Republicans. The **Democratic Party** has here a political organization composed only of*

28 ***Democrats**—not a single Republican can join them.... We pray that you will take some*

1 *steps to remedy these evils listed below* [in their home state of Kentucky which was under
2 Democrat control].

3

December 24, 1867	A Colored schoolhouse was burned by incendiaries in Breckinridge.
January 28, 1868	Jim Macklin was taken from jail in Frankfort and hung.
May 28, 1868	Sam Davie was hung by a mob in Harrodsburg.
July 11, 1868	George Rogers was hung by a mob in Bradsfordsville Martin County.
July 12, 1868	William Pierce was hung by a mob in Christian.
July 31, 1868	A Colored school exhibition was attacked by a mob in Midway.
August 3, 1868	Cabe Fields was shot and killed by disguised men near Keen Jessamine County.
August 7, 1868	Seven persons were ordered to leave their homes in Standford.
August 1868	Silas Woodford age sixty badly beaten by disguised mob. Also beaten were Mary Smith Curtis and Margret Mosby near Keene Jessemine County.
August 1868	James Gaines was expelled from Anderson by Ku Klux Klan.
August 1868	James Parker was killed by the Klan in Pulaski County.
August 1868	Noah Blankenship was whipped by a mob in Pulaski County.
August 1868	William Gibson and John Gibson hung by mob in Washington County.
August 21, 1868	Negroes attacked, robbed and driven from Summerville.
August 28, 1868	F.H. Montford was hung by a mob near Cogers Landing in

1		Jessamine County.
2	September 1868	Negro hung by a mob.
3	September 1868	A U.S. Marshall named Meriwether was attacked, captured
4		and beaten to death by a mob in Larue County.
5	September 5, 1868	William Glassgow was killed by a mob in Warren County.
6	September 11, 1868	Two negroes were beaten by Klan in Anderson County.
7	September 11, 1868	Oliver Stone's house was attacked by mob in Fayette
8		County.
9	September 18, 1868	Mob attacked Cumins' house and killed his daughter and a
10		man named Adam in Pulaski County.
11	September 28, 1868	A mob killed Crasban Richardson at his home in Conishville.
12	October 26, 1868	Mob hung Terry Laws and James Ryan at Nicholasville.
13	December 1868	Two Negroes were shot by the Klan at Sulphur Springs in
14		Union County.
15	December 1868	Negro was shot at Morganfield Union County
16	January 20, 1869	The Klan whipped William Parker in Lincoln County.
17	January 20, 1869	Albert Bradford was killed by men in disguise in Scott
18		County.
19	March 12, 1869	The Klan whipped a boy at Stanford.
20	March 1869	Mr. Roberts was killed at the home of Frank Bournes in
21		Jessamine County.
22	March 30, 1869	A mob hung George Bratcher on Sugar Creek in Garrard
23		County.
24	May 29, 1869	A mob hung John Penny at Nevada Mercer County.
25	June 1869	The Klan whipped Lucien Green.
26	July 1869	A mob attacked Mr. Ronsey's home and killed three men and
27		one woman.
28	July 2, 1869	The Klan whipped Mr. Miller.

1	July 1869	A mob killed Mr. & Mrs. Chas. Henderson on Silver Creek in
2		Madison County.
3	July 17, 1869	A mob hung George Molling.
4	August 9, 1869	A mob hung James Crowders near Lebanon County.
5	August 1869	A mob tarred and feathered a citizen in Harrison County.
6	September 1869	The Klan burned down a Colored meeting house in Carol
7		County.
8	September 1869	The Klan whipped a Negro at John Carmin's farm in Fayette
9		County.
10	September 1869	A mob raided a Negro cabin and killed John Mosteran, Mr.
11		Cash and Mr. Coffey.
12	October 1869	The Klan killed George Rose in Madison County
13	October 1869	Mob shoots Mr. Shepherd near Parksville.
14	November 1869	Klan shoots man at Frank Searcy's house in Madison
15		County.
16	November 1869	Mob hangs Mr. Searcy in Richmond.
17	November 1869	Klan shoots Robert Mershon's daughter.
18	November 1869	Mob whipped Pope Hall in Willett Washington County.
19	December 1869	Mob takes two Negroes from jail and hangs one.
20	December 1869	Mob kills two Negroes while in custody near Mayfield.
21	December 24, 1869	Klan kills Allen Cooper in Adair County.
22	December 1869	Negro whipped while on Scott's farm in Franklin County.
23	January 20, 1870	Mob hangs Charles Field in Fayette County.
24	January 31, 1870	Mob takes two men to Springfield jail and hangs them.
25	February 1870	Klan whipped two Negroes in Madison County.
26	February 1870	Mob hangs Mr. Simms near Kingston Madison County.
27	February 1870	Mob hung up Douglass Rodes and whipped him.
28	February 18, 1870	Mob hung R.L. Byrom at Richmond.

1	April 5, 1870	Mob hung Mr. Perry near Lancaster Garrad County.
2	April 6, 1870	Mob hung Negro at Crab-Orchard in Lincoln County.
3	April 1870	Mob attacked Mr. Owen's home and shot and killed Mr.
4		Saunders.
5	April 11, 1870	Mob shot and hung Mr. Sam Lambert in Mercer County.
6	April 11, 1870	Mob released five White prisoners from Federal officers.
7	April 1870	Mob kills William Hart at Mr. Palmer's house.
8	May 1870	Mob hangs three men near Gloscow Warren County.
9	May 1870	Klan kills John Reman in Adair County
10	May 14, 1870	Mob hangs Mr. Pleasanton, and Daniel and Willis Parker.
11	May 14, 1870	Klan robbed Negroes and harassed them.
12	May 1870	Negro Schoolhouse burned by incendiaries in Christian
13		County.
14	May 1870	Mob hangs Negro at Greenville Muhlenburgh.
15	June 4, 1870	Mob burns Colored schoolhouse in Woodford County.
16	June 1870	Mob attacks jail and kills two men in Whitley County.
17	August 4, 1870	Riot during elections in Harrodsburg and four persons killed.
18	August 10, 1870	Mob kills Turpin and Parker at Versilled.
19	August 1870	Band of men kill Simpson Grubbs in Montgomery County.
20	September 1870	Mob hangs Frank Timberlake at Flemingburg.
21	September 1870	Klan shots and kills John Simes and his wife in Hay County.
22	September 1870	Klan hangs Oliver Williams in Madison County.
23	October 9, 1870	Klan shoots Howard Gilbert in Madison County.
24	October 1870	Klan drives Colored people out of Bald-Knob Franklin
25		County.
26	December 6, 1870	Two Negroes shot on Harrison Blaton's farm near Frankfort.
27	December 18, 1870	Two Negroes killed while in civil custody.
28	December 1870	Klan murdered Howard Million in Fayette County.

December 12, 1870	John Dickerson driven from home while his daughter was raped.
January 7, 1871	Mob hung Negro named George at Cynthiana Harrison County.
January 7, 1871	Klan killed Negro near Ashland in Fayette County.
January 17, 1871	Mr. Hall was whipped and shot near in Shelby County.[24]

1871 Ku Klux Klan Act of 1871

The Purpose: To stop the Klan's terrorist activities against blacks and their white supporters (Republicans), primarily in the south. The law was designed to (1) provide civil and criminal sanctions to deter infringements upon civil rights; and (2) to provide authority to the government to meet with force unlawful combinations and violence which interfered with civil rights or the execution of justice or federal law. **Democrats' Opposition: One of the spokespersons for the Democrats was George Morgan, a Democratic Congressman from Ohio.** Morgan said, *"I maintain that if such offenses are committed they have been caused in good part by the mistaken legislation of Congress.... Now sir, if you want to preserve peace to the South, if you want to preserve peace and tranquility to the whole country, if you are not determined to strike a blow which may end the total subversion of our free institutions, change your policy to the South."*

Senator William Stoughton, the Republican from Michigan, countered with the following words:

The evidence taken before the Senate committee in relations to the outrages, lawlessness and violence in North Carolina establishes the following propositions:

---

24 The National Archives, Washington D.C., Records of the U.S. Senate, 42nd Congress first session as reported by *Documentary History of The Negro People in the United States Volume 2*, 594-599.

1 *1. The Ku Klux Klan organization* [which] *exists throughout the State, has a political*

2 *purpose, and is composed of the members of the **Democratic** or Conservative Party.*

3

4 *2. This organization has sought to carry out its purposes by murders, whippings, intimidation,*

5 *and violence against its opponents.*

6

7 *3. It not only binds its members to execute decrees of crime, but protects them against*

8 *conviction and punishment, first by disguises and secrecy, and second, by perjury, if*

9 *necessary, upon the witness-stand and in the jury box.*

10

11 *4. All of the offenders in this order, which has established reign of terrorism and bloodshed*

12 *throughout the State not one has yet been convicted.*

13

14 *We may concede, Mr. Speaker, that if this system of violence is to continue in the South,*

15 *the **Democratic Party** will secure the ascendancy. If political opponents can be marked for*

16 *slaughter by secret bands of cowardly assassins who ride forth with impunity to execute the*

17 *decrees upon the unarmed and defenseless, it will be fatal alike to the Republican Party and*

18 *civil liberty. But sir, we may well ask where will this end? **How long will it be before the***

19 ***Tammany Hall Democracy**, who are now furnishing arms to the Ku Klux Klan of the South*

20 *to murder southern Republicans, **will introduce this new element of Democratic success***

21 ***into the northern politics?*** [The Senator was concerned that the Democrats' social disease

22 of *racism* and *terror* would eventually spread and ***infect*** the entire nation.]

23

24 During an interview with a Klan member by the name of James E. Boyd, Boyd told the

25 Senate Investigation Committee that he was *"initiated into the Ku Klux Klan as an **auxiliary***

26 ***of the Democratic Party."***

27

28 The Senator went on to say: *"I have quoted largely from the testimony of this witness for*

1 *the purpose of showing the dangerous character of this organization. I also make an extract*

2 *from the testimony of Honorable Thomas Settle, one of the judges of the Supreme Court,*

3 *showing the same state of things and strongly corroborating the materials statements of*

4 *Mr. Boyd:*

5

6 [by the Chairman]

7 **Question**: *Give us your belief as to the true position of the political organizations with*

8 *reference to this organization* [Ku Klux Klan].

9

10 **Answer**: *We, sir, I must think that the present* **Democratic Party** *there, judging from the*

11 *circumstances, are encouraging it. I do not think it is accidental. In the course of our*

12 *investigation last summer it leaked out in the testimony that Hamilton C. Jones, present*

13 *member of the Legislature, gave the signs of the Invisible Empire to James E. Boyd, who then*

14 *a* **Democratic** *candidate for the house of common for Alamance County. Dr. Moore, also*

15 *who had been a member of the previous house, gave the signs of the Invisible Empire....*

16

17 The Senator continued.

18

19 *The testimony of Thomas W. Willeford, formerly a member of the Ku Klux Klan, throws*

20 *additional light upon the secret working of this order and discloses the means by which these*

21 *results are brought about in the State and local courts. This witness testifies as follows:*

22

23 **Question**: *Did they tell you what the object was?*

24

25 **Answer**: *Yes, sir; in the first meeting. I was initiated in Kennedy's barn.*

26

27 **Question**: *Did you take the oath?*

28

Answer: *Yes, sir, and then the next Saturday went to the meeting.*

1   **Question**: *What did they tell you then was the object of the organization?*

2

3   **Answer**: *They told me it was to damage the Republican Party as much as they could,*

4   *burning, stealing, whipping **niggers** and such things as that.*

5

6   **Question**: *Murder?*

7

8   **Answer**: *The leading men- it was to murder.*

9

10   **Question**: *Have you ever heard of a Ku Klux being convicted of any offense there?*

11

12   **Answer**: *No, sir.*

13

14   **Question**: *Was there anything in the obligation you took or the rules of the order as to your*

15   *being obliged to defend me by your oath, or otherwise.*

16

17   **Answer**: *Yes, sir: if he could get you in as a witness you had to swear him out, let you be*

18   *swearing a lie or not. If you swore against him, why you might just as well be a-traveling*

19   *at onct* [sic].

20

21   **Question**: *You mean by that you would be in danger of your life from the order?*

22

23   **Answer**: *Yes, sir.*

24

25   **Question**: *Anything about getting on the jury?*

26

27   **Answer**: *Yes, sir, if we could get on the jury we could save him, do what you please* [sic].

28

Question: No matter what the proof?

Answer: *Yes, sir, you could not bring proof enough to convict.*

During an interview with a Negro who was a victim of the Klan, the victim told the Senate Investigation Committee, how he was shot and left for dead. The following are portions of that interview. The victim reported:

...The one [Klan member] said, "Open the door." I said, "I shouldn't do it." Then one said, "Blow his brains out." Just as he said that they all fired through the door.... They shot a half a dozen times or more. I clapped my hand on here [placing his hand on his breast] and said, "They've shot me. My boy knew where there were some loose planks in the floor. He jerked up two of them and they all run through under the house—all the biggest of them, but the three little girls I had.

Question: *What occurred afterwards?*

Answer: *The next morning I sent for the doctor to come and take out the balls* [gun shots]. *Dr. Montgomery came and took out the balls and told them they had better move me to Graham... or else they won't move me at all. That evening they carried me to Graham and got me there at night.*

Question: *How many balls did they fire into you?*

Answer: *There were five balls."* [The witness indicated where he had been shot – in both arms and in his chest.]

Question: *What has been the effect of such proceedings upon the colored people of that*

1 *county? Do they feel safe?*

2

3 **Answer:** *They don't feel safe there at all. I can tell you that a great many of them have taken*

4 *the notion to leave.... They wanted to run them all off because the principal part of them*

5 *voted the Radical* [Republican] *ticket.*

6

7 **Question**: *Wanted to run all of them off who voted the Radical Ticket?*

8

9 **Answer:** *Yes, sir.*

10

11 **Question**: *Did you hear that said?*

12

13 **Answer:** *Yes, sir, I heard it talked and I saw them try it. They tried to turn me from voting*

14 *the Republican ticket, but I didn't turn and that is why they shot me.... That is the case*

15 *every election that has been there. They have been trying to get us to vote the Conservative*

16 **[Democratic]** *ticket....*

17

18 **Question**: *Were those that would not vote the Conservative ticket the ones that had these*

19 *outrages committed against them?*

20

21 **Answer**: *Yes, sir. You never saw one bothered at all that voted the Conservative Ticket.*

22

23 After sharing these interviews with the Senate, Senator Stoughton went on to say; *"The*

24 *report, Mr. Speaker, to which I have referred shows over one hundred and fifty authenticated*

25 *cases where persons have either been murdered, brutally beaten, or driven away at the peril*

26 *of their lives. The **Democratic Party** first denied their association* [with the Ku Klux Klan],

27 *then excused the outrages. In Tennessee and other southern states, the laws passed by*

28 *Republican Legislatures to suppress and punish the **Ku Klux Klan** were repealed as soon*

1 *as the **Democratic Party** came back into power. The relation of the **Democratic Party** to the*

2 ***Klan** is precisely that of the receiver of stolen property to the thief. The murder of leading*

3 *Republicans, terrifying the colored population and putting whole neighborhoods in fear so*

4 *that the **Klan** can control an election is heralded as a **Democratic** victory.*

5

6 *"The whole South, Mr. Speaker, is rapidly drifting into a state of anarchy and bloodshed,*

7 *which renders **the worse Government on the face of the earth**.... There is no security of*

8 *life, person or property. A few days ago, over 100 Alabama Klansmen made a raid on upon*

9 *Meridian Mississippi, and carried off their victims for execution."*

10

11 The **Republican Congressman from Mississippi (George McKee)** responded, *"Mr.*

12 *Speaker, I did not intend to take part in this debate but statements have been made upon*

13 *this floor that demand refutation. The Meridian massacre was in my own district. It has*

14 *often been alluded to in this debate, and I cannot pass it in silence. The Alabama Klan*

15 *has made frequent incursions into our State. They participated in this bloody massacre at*

16 *Meridian, invited there by our home Ku Klux. They had been in that County before that*

17 *time. Prior to the late butchery, two colored officials had been murdered. Other outrages*

18 *had been committed, but still it was deemed that enough had not been done, and the bloody*

19 *work of death culminated in that infamous scene of riot and blood at Meridian which can*

20 *neither be denied or excused. I do not care to go into details. One single statement tells*

21 *the whole story. One, and perhaps two white men killed, eight or ten colored men killed,*

22 *according to the **Democratic** authority, while Republicans claim that twenty-five or thirty*

23 *have been killed in the streets and shot or hung in the swamps; and yet amongst all this red*

24 *list of slaughter you do not find the name of a single **Democrat**. The dead and wounded,*

25 *the maimed and the scourged, are all, all Republicans."* Debates took place on March 28,

26 1871. (See Exhibit 3 video.)

27

28 **1874** Blacks from Alabama sent a letter to Congress reporting racist acts by Democrats.

1 (Portions of) Petition to President of the United States and to U.S. Congress From Blacks

2 of Alabama in 1874

3

4 *...As a race, and as citizens, we never have enjoyed, except partially, imperfectly, and*

5 *locally, our political and civil rights in this State. Our right to vote in elections has been,*

6 *in a large portion of this state, denied, abridged, and rendered difficult and dangerous*

7 *ever since we became voters. The means used by our political opponents* [Democrats]

8 *to destroy or impair our right have been various; but chiefly consisted of violence*

9 *in the form of secret assassinations, lynching, intimidation, malicious and frivolous*

10 *prosecutions and arrest. And by depriving or threatening to deprive us of employment*

11 *and renting of lands, which many of us, in our poverty and distress, were unable to*

12 *disregard. These acts of lawlessness have been repeated and continued since our first*

13 *vote in 1868, and their effect has been such that from 10 to 15,000 of the votes of our*

14 *race have in each election been either repressed or been given under compulsion to our*

15 *political opponents.*

16

17 *A secret, powerful, vindictive, and dangerous organization composed exclusively of*

18 *white men belonging to the* Democratic Party *in this state, and whose objects were to*

19 *control the labor and repress or control the votes of the Colored citizens of this state. That*

20 *organization, or a substitute and successor to it, under a changed name and a somewhat*

21 *changed wardrobe and personal manifestation, still exists in all its hideous and fearful*

22 *proportions. This organization we solemnly believe pervades all of the late rebellious States,*

23 *and contains more than 100,000 arm-bearing men, most of whom are experienced and*

24 *skilled in war. The definite political object of this organization is, by terror and violence, to*

25 *make the citizenship and franchise of the Colored race, as established by the Constitution*

26 *of the United States practically and substantially a nullity....*[25]

27 _____

28 25 Executive Document No. 64 House of Representatives, 43rd Congress, 2nd session, transmitted to Congress by the President on December 22, 1874 as reported by *Documentary History of the Negro People in the United States Vol. 2*, 600-604.

1   Professor John Hope Franklin said, ***"With the new franchise laws, with careful***

2   ***administration by white registrars who knew what they were doing and with effective***

3   ***exclusion of Blacks from <u>Democratic</u> primaries, white supremacy in the realm of politics***

4   ***seemed to be permanently established."***

5

6   **1875 <u>Jim Crow Laws</u>** Southern Democrats of Tennessee legislated our nation's first Jim

7   Crow Laws. The law mandated that blacks be confined to separate sections of trains, depots

8   and wharves. Southern states under Democratic control expanded the use of such laws

9   to include many other facilities as well, including separate restrooms, drinking fountains,

10   public parks and cemeteries. Eventually blacks were banned from white barbershops, hotels,

11   restaurants, theaters, and in some states they were required to swear on separate Bibles

12   in courtroom proceedings. The Jim Crow Laws along with the new Black Codes (both

13   initiated by Southern Democrats) had a devastating impact on the newly freed slaves. Some

14   historians believed that these laws and codes created conditions far worse than slavery. The

15   Jim Crow Laws were merely laws specifically designed by southern Democrats to keep

16   African Americans in their place, and the Democratic Party did not condemn these laws.

17

18   **1875 <u>1875 Civil Rights Act</u>**

19   The Purpose: To obtain equality in Public Accommodations. The law stated the following:

20   *"Be it enacted by the Senate and House of Representatives of the United States of America*

21   *in Congress assembled. That all persons within the jurisdiction of the United States*

22   *shall be entitled to the full and equal enjoyment of the accommodation, advantages,*

23   *facilities and privileges of inns, public conveyances on land or water, theaters, and other*

24   *places amusement; subject only to the conditions and limitation established by law, and*

25   *applicable alike to citizens of every race and color, regardless of any previous condition of*

26   *servitude...."*

27

28   **Democrats' Opposition**: The bill was introduced by Republican Senator Charles Sumner.

1 He died in March 1874 one year before the bill was passed. **Republican Senator Frederick**

2 **Frelinghuysen of New Jersey** opened up the debate. The Senator said, *"There is but one*

3 *idea in the bill, and that is: The equality of races before the law. The language of this bill*

4 *secures full and equal privileges in schools subject to laws which do not discriminate as*

5 *to color. The bill provides that full and equal privileges shall be enjoyed by all persons*

6 *in public schools supported by taxation, subject only to the limitation established by law,*

7 *applicable alike to citizens of every race and color and regardless of previous servitude.*

8 ***The object of the bill is to destroy, not recognize the distinctions of race."***

9

10 One of the spokespersons for the Democrats was **Willard Saulsbury, a Democrat from**

11 **Delaware. Saulsbury** gave this response to Frelinghuysen's statement. *" ...There is coming*

12 *a day when the American people will hold you and your party [Republican] to a strict*

13 *responsibility for present indifference to their wishes and for the great wrong you propose*

14 *by this bill to inflict upon them. What is this measure? Disguise it as you may, it is nothing*

15 *more nor less than an attempt on the part of the American Congress to enforce association*

16 *and companionship between the races in this country. The object of this bill is not to confer*

17 *upon the color race any political rights. It proposes to enforce familiarity, association, and*

18 *companionship between the white and colored people of this country. Is not that true? That*

19 *is the object of this bill. It proposes so far as hotels are concerned that the white and the*

20 *colored people shall have the save advantages, equal advantages; that they shall enter with*

21 *equal right into every part of the inn; that the keeper of the inn shall make no discrimination*

22 *on account of their race or color; **that colored men shall sit at the same table beside the***

23 ***white guest, that he shall enter the same parlor and take his seat beside the wife and***

24 ***daughter of the white man,*** *whether the white man is willing or not, because you prohibit*

25 *discrimination against him. If the object was not to enforce companionship, why do you not*

26 *permit in this bill the landlord to set apart a portion of the parlor for white people, so that*

27 *he might have one table for the colored man and another table for the white man, giving*

28 *to one as good accommodations as the other? Why is it that there is not a provision which*

*allows that? Simply because, I say, the object and **purpose of this bill is forced association and companionship between the races.*** The debates took place April 29 – May 22, 1874.

Note: In 1964, the Democrats, in their arguments *against* the 1964 Civil Rights Act, claimed that the 1964 Civil Rights Act was merely the Republican's 1875 Civil Rights Act that they (the Democrats) had the Supreme Court overturn. See 1964 Civil Rights Act.

1877 Republicans reached an ill-advised compromise with the Democrats. The compromised gave the Republicans the White House but required that the government remove federal troops from the south. Although the Democrats had their way with blacks while the troops were present, **Democrats** felt the removal of the troops would give them more flexibility to rule the South without the possible interference of the troops.

1884 On February 18, 1884, the U.S. Senate interviewed Mrs. Violet Keeling regarding blacks voting Democrat. The following is just a portion of that interview:

Question: *Are any of the colored people in your county, **Democrats**?*

Answer: *I don't know. I don't have nothing to do with that sort.*

Question: *I ask you if any of them are **Democrats**.*

Answer: *I am telling you just what I know; I don't have nothing to do with that sort.*

Question: *Why do you have such a dislike to a colored man that votes the **Democratic** ticket?*

Answer: *I will tell you as near as I know. I think that if the race of colored people that has got no friends no how, and if they don't hang together they won't have none while one party* *is going one way and another the other. I don't wish to see a colored man sell himself when he can do without. Of course we all have to live, and I always like to have a man live even if he works for 25 cents a day, but I don't want to see him sell himself away.*

Question*: Cannot a colored man vote the* **Democratic** *ticket without selling himself?*

Answer*: I think if a colored man votes the* **Democratic** *ticket he has already sold himself, because the white man is no friend to him anyway.*

Question*: Suppose your husband should go and vote a* **Democratic** *ticket?*

Answer*: I would just pick up my clothes and go to my father's, if I had a father, or would go to work for 25 cents a day.*[26]

1888 Several black ministers from New Orleans came together and wrote a letter to Congress. The following is a portion of that letter:

To the People of the United States:

We, citizens of New Orleans, as well as of neighboring parishes, from which we have been driven away without warrant or law, assembled in mass meeting at New Orleans, La. on Wednesday, August 22, 1888 at Geddes Hall, declare and assert: That a reign of terror exists in many parts of the state; that the laws are suspended and the officers of the government, from the governor down, afford no protection to the lives and property of the people against armed bodies of whites, who shed innocent blood and commit deeds of savagery unsurpassed in the dark ages of mankind.

---

26 *Documentary History of the Negro People in the United States Vol. 2, 739-740.*

1 *For the past twelve years we have been most effectively disfranchised and robbed of our*

2 *political rights. While denied the privilege in many places of voting for the party and*

3 *candidates of our choice, acts of violence have been committed to compel us to vote against*

4 *the dictates of our conscience for the Democratic Party, and the Republican ballots cast by*

5 *us have been counted for the <u>Democratic candidates</u>. The press, the pulpit, the commercial*

6 *organizations, and executive authority of the State have given both open and silent approval*

7 *of all these crimes. In addition to these methods, there seems to be a deep scheme to reduce*

8 *the Negroes of the State to a condition of abject serfdom and peonage.*

9

10 *These acts are done in deliberate <u>defiance of the Constitution and the laws of the United*

11 *States</u>, which are so thoroughly nullified that the Negroes who bore arms in defense of the*

12 *Union have no protection or shelter from them within the borders of Louisiana. During the*

13 *past twelve months our people have suffered from the lawless regulators as never before*

14 *and since the carnival of bloodshed conducted by the <u>Democratic Party</u> in 1868.*

15

16 *A single volume would scarcely afford sufficient space to enumerate the outrage our people*

17 *have suffered, and are daily suffering at the hand of their oppressors. They are flagrantly*

18 *deprived of every right guaranteed them by the Constitution; in many parts of the State they*

19 *are free only in name; they cannot assemble in places to indicate and discuss an equitable*

20 *rate of wages for their labor; they do not feel safe as property holders and tax-payers, and*

21 *are permitted to enjoy but very few public conveniences.*

22

23 *To our people we advise calmness and a strict regard for law and order. If your homes are*

24 *invaded expect no mercy, for none will be shown, and if doomed to die, then die defending*

25 *your life and home to the best of your ability. If convinced that you will not be permitted to*

26 *live where you are in peace and perfect security, quietly go away.*

27

28 *Invoking the guiding favor of Almighty God and the sympathy of mankind, we are your*

brethren in affliction and the common bond of humanity.[27]

The letter was signed by, Rev. Ernest Lyon, Rev. A.E.P. Albert, Rev. J.H. Coker, M.D., Rev. T.B. Stamps, Rev. M.C.B. Mason, Rev. W. Paul Green, Rev. J. D. Kennedy and the Rev. C.B. Wilson. The problems were so severe that President Grant had to send troops to the South to protect Black voters from the Democrats and their Klan supporters.

1894 The Repeal Act of 1894

The Purpose: After the Democrats won the Presidency and both houses in 1892, they attempted to repeal various portions of certain civil rights legislation. They introduced this bill to repeal all statues relating to supervisors of elections and deputy marshals, as well as federal protection of the right to vote. **Republican Opposition**: Leading the debate against the bill included: **Republican Congressman Marriott Brosius of Pennsylvania and Republican Senator George Hoar of Massachusetts.** On October 10, 1893 it passed in the House with 201 voting for it and 102 against it. On February 7, 1894 it passed in the Senate. Thirty-nine voted for it and 28 voted against it.

Just before the final vote, Republican Senator Hoar of Massachusetts presented the following argument:

*Wherever there is a crevice in our protection of the freedom of the ballot there you will find the **Democratic Party** trying to break through. Where ever we have left open an opportunity to get possession of an office contrary to the true and constitutional will of the majority there you will find that party pressing; there you will find that party exercising an ingenuity before which even the great inventive genius of American People exerted in other directions fails and is insignificant in the comparison.*

[27] *Documentary History of the Negro People in the United States, Vol.2,* 741-743.

1   *In one state, Mississippi, in order to **disfranchise Republicans who can not read and write***

2   *and let **Democrats** who can not read and write vote, there is a constitutional provision by*

3   *which **Democratic** election officers determine whether the understanding of the voters who*

4   *can not read or write is a fit and sufficient understanding of the Constitution; and, although*

5   *that was denounced by able **Democrats** holding high public positions both in Washington*

6   *and Mississippi, the proposition finds defenders on this floor, Senators gravely comparing*

7   *it to the provision of the constitution of Massachusetts....*

8

9   *In Delaware, it is necessary that a tax should be paid a certain time beforehand, and,*

10   *accordingly, unless they are much belied, the **Democratic** tax collector runs away when the*

11   *Republican come to pay their taxes....*

12

13   *Mr. President, this is a question of fraud or no fraud. They tell us that there have been some*

14   *Republican invasions of the elective franchise, and it is quite possible, but where can you*

15   *find one well-authenticated case of a man who has been deprived or inconvenienced in the*

16   *exercise of his franchise by these United States marshals or other officers, I will pledge*

17   *myself to find ten thousand well established by evidence on record here where without*

18   *those securities Republicans have been deprived of their votes by **Democratic** practices.*

19   *I incur no danger in making that challenge. If you will produce me a citizen of the United*

20   *States, a **Democrat,** who lost his honest vote in consequence of intimidation or impediment,*

21   *created by these United States marshals, I will find on record here the proof of ten thousand*

22   *Republicans who have lost their votes by **Democratic** practices....*

23

24   *Mr. President, the nation must protect its own. Every citizen whose right is imperiled if he*

25   *be but one, when it is a right of national citizenship and a right conferred and enjoyed under*

26   *the Constitution of the United States, has the right to demand for its protection the entire*

27   *force of the United States until the Army has spent its last man and the Navy fired its last*

28   *gun. Most of us have nothing else than the right to vote.... The urn in which the American*

1 *cast his ballot ought to be, aye, and it shall be, as sacred as a sacramental vessel.*

2

3 **1896** Democrats won another major landmark court decision in the case of ***Plessy v.***

4 ***Ferguson.*** The case legalized and endorsed the Democrats' Jim Crow segregation policies.

5 This ruling had a profound affect on the **entire black race** in both the north and the south.

6

7 **1898** The **Democrats** carried out their racist political objectives in Wilmington, North

8 Carolina, when they successfully drove Black Republicans out of office by rigging

9 the 1898 election, and killing several blacks in the process. The Democrats' campaign

10 theme was: ***"saving our white women"*** [from the middle class Blacks who controlled

11 Wilmington at the time] and their official campaign slogan was one word, ***"Nigger."***

12 Shortly after the Wilmington massacre, riots broke out in other parts of the south, and

13 101 blacks were lynched.

14

15 **1899** In 1899, the *New York Tribune* published the concerns of the National Afro-American

16 Council of the United States (on May 4, 1899). Herbert Aptheker records the following in

17 his *Documentary History of the Negro People in the United States.*[28]

18

19 *The National Afro-American Council of the United States has issued a proclamation*

20 *calling upon the colored people of this country to set apart Friday, June 2nd, as a day of*

21 *fasting and prayer, and has called upon all colored ministers to devote the sunrise hour*

22 *of the following Sunday, June 4th, to special exercises in order that God, the Father of*

23 *Mercies, may take our deplorable case in His own hands, and that if vengeance is to be*

24 *meted out, let God Himself repay.*

25

26 *We are dragged before the courts by the thousands and sentenced to every form of*

27 *punishment, and even executed, without the privilege of having a jury composed in whole*

28

28 *Documentary History of the Negro People in the United Sates, Vol. 2,* 799-803

or part of members of our own race, while simple justice should guarantee us judges and juries who could adjudicate our case free from the bias, caste and prejudice incident to the same in this country.

In many sections we are arrested and lodged in jails on the most frivolous suspicion of being perpetrators of the most hideous and revolting crimes, and, regardless of established guilt, mobs are formed of ignorant, vicious, whiskey besotted men, at whose approach the keys of these jails and prisons are surrendered and suspicioned party is ruthlessly forced from the custody of the law and tortured, hanged, shot, butchered, dismembered and burned in the most fiendish manner. These mobs no longer conceal themselves in the shadows of the night, but in open day plunder the prisons for the victims of their lawless vengeance and defiantly walk into courts and rob the sheriffs and judges of their prisoners and butcher them without even time to commune in prayer with God, a privilege that no barbaric age has ever denied a soul about to be ushered into the presence of his Maker.

1900 By the turn of the century, in areas controlled by Democrats (the South) thousands of blacks were placed in hardcore prison labor camps. According to historians, the prison camps were worse than slavery—and represented a new resource of free forced labor in the south. The prisoners were required to work from 10 to 14 hours a day, six to seven days a week in temperatures above 100 degrees and below zero. <u>One-fourth of the prison population, were black children ages 6 to 18.</u> Twelve-year-old Cy Williams, was sentenced to 20 years of hard labor for allegedly stealing a horse that he was too small to ride. Eight-year-old Will Evens was sentenced to 2 years of hard labor for taking some change from a counter, and six-year old Mary Gay was sentenced to 30 days of hard labor for taking a hat. While southern authorities sent whites to *jail* for the same offenses (with shorter sentences), they sent blacks to the ***prison labor camps*** with longer sentences. The camps provided free labor for building railroads, for draining snake and alligator infested swamps and rivers, and for

1 mining coal. Conditions in these camps were harsh—blacks were transported from one

2 project to another in rolling cages, similar to those used for circus animals. While thousands

3 died from malaria, frostbite, heat strokes, and shackle poisoning, others were buried alive

4 in mines, blown to pieces during mine explosions, and many others were drowned or shot

5 and beaten to death. <u>Every southern black was a potential prisoner</u>, which meant that the

6 southern owners of railroads and mines had an unlimited resource of free labor. Historians

7 say the prison labor system was the Democrats' **new form slavery** – but more inhumane

8 than the institution of slavery. (See Exhibit 3 video, "Under Democrat Control.")

9

10 **1900** One hundred blacks were lynched in the Democratic controlled South.

11 One Year of Southern Lynching for the Year 1900

12

Name	Date	State
Henry Giveney Ripley	January 9th	Tennessee
Roger Giveney Ripley	January 9th	Tennessee
Walter Cotton	March 24th	Virginia
Williams Edward	March 27th	Mississippi
Moses York	April 16th	Mississippi
Marshall Jones	May 4th	Georgia
Alexander Whitney	May 13th	Georgia
William Willis	May 14th	Georgia
Name Unknown	May 14th	Florida
Name Unknown	May 14th	Florida
Name Unknown	June 10th	Florida
Nate Mullins	June 17th	Arkansas
Robert Davis	June 21st	Florida
John Jennings	July 12th	Georgia
Robert Charles	July 26th	Louisiana

1	Name Unknown	September 11th	North Carolina
2	Thomas J. Amos	September 11th	Louisiana
3	Frank Brown	September 7th	Mississippi
4	David Moore	September 14th	Mississippi
5	William Brown	September 14th	Mississippi
6	Wiley Johnson	October 9th	Louisiana
7	Gloster Barnes	October 23rd	Mississippi
8	Name Unknown	December 19th	Mississippi
9	Mr. Lewis	December 20th	Mississippi
10	John Hughley	April 22nd	Florida
11	S.A. Jenkins	June 17th	Arkansas
12	W.W. Watts	June 5th	Virginia
13	George Ratliffe	March 4th	North Carolina
14	Thomas Clayton	March 10th	Mississippi
15	Allen Brooks	April 3rd	Georgia
16	John Peters	April 20th	West Virginia
17	Name Unknown	May 7th	Alabama
18	Dago Pete	June 3rd	Mississippi
19	Frank Gilmore	June 23rd	Louisiana
20	Elijah Clark	July 23rd	Alabama
21	Jack Hillsman	July 24	Georgia
22	Jack Betts	August 13th	Mississippi
23	Name Unknown	August 19th	Virginia
24	Name Unknown	August 26th	Tennessee
25	Frank Hardenman	October 19th	Georgia
26	Daniel Long	December 8th	Virginia
27	Name Unknown	December 21st	Arkansas
28	John Bailey	March 18th	Georgia

1	Charles Humphries	March 18th	Alabama
2	Henry McAfee	April 19th	Mississippi
3	William Lee	May 11th	West Virginia
4	Henry Harris	May 15th	Louisiana
5	Simon Adams	June 9th	Georgia
6	Senny Jefferson	June 11th	Georgia
7	Jack Thomas	June 27th	Florida
8	John Roe	July 6th	Alabama
9	Logan Reoms	September 10th	Tennessee
10	Winfield Thomas	October 2nd	Alabama
11	Fratur Warfield	October 18th	Kentucky
12	Name Unknown	July 25th	Louisiana
13	August Thomas	July 25th	Louisiana
14	Baptiste Filean	July 25th	Louisiana
15	Louis Taylor	July 25th	Louisiana
16	Anna Marbry	July 25th	Louisiana
17	Name Unknown	July 25th	Louisiana
18	Silas Jackson	July 25th	Louisiana
19	James Suer	October 24th	Georgia
20	James Calaway	October 24th	Georgia
21	Luis Rice Ripley	March 23rd	Tennessee
22	Henry Ratcliff	May 1st	Mississippi
23	George Gordon	May 1st	Mississippi
24	Grant Weley	September 8th	Georgia
25	Mr. Askew	June 10th	Mississippi
26	Mr. Reese	June 10th	Mississippi
27	John Sanders	June 10th	Florida
28	Jordan Hines	June 27th	Georgia

1	James Barco	June 20th	Florida
2	Name Unknown	May 7th	Mississippi
3	Name Unknown	April 5th	Virginia
4	George Faller	December 28th	Georgia
5	Rufus Salter	January 11th	South Carolina
6	Anderson Gause	January 16th	Tennessee
7	Jefferson Henry	July 9th	Louisiana
8	James Crosby	March 4th	Alabama
9	Seth Cobb	June 12th	Louisiana
10	George Ritter	March 22nd	North Carolina
11	Name Unknown	May 26th	Arkansas
12	Mr. Williams	October 8th	Tennessee
13	George Beckham	September 21st	Louisiana
14	Charles Elliott	September 21st	Louisiana
15	Nathaniel Bowman	September 21st	Louisiana
16	Isaiah Rollins	September 21st	Louisiana
17	John Brodie	June 12th	Arkansas
18	Name Unknown	November 15th	Texas
19	Name Unknown	November 15th	Texas
20	Name Unknown	November 15th	Texas
21	William Burts	February 17th	South Carolina
22	Samuel Hinson	May 16th	Mississippi
23	Mr. Abernathy	October 30th	Alabama

Congressional records will show that Democrats voted against every anti-lynching bill that came before Congress from 1871 to the 1950s.

1900 From 1900 to 1917 there were several terrorist attacks on blacks in regions under Democrat control including Alabama, Georgia, Louisiana, and other parts of the South.

Several thousand blacks were lynched, beaten, and shot to death during this period.

1904 Thomas Dixon opened his new stage play (*The Klansman*) in Atlanta, Georgia. The play glorified the Klan and defamed blacks by portraying blacks as savaged men on the prowl for white women. During the week of September 17, an Atlanta newspaper falsely reported rapes of a few white women. Their false reports resulted in several thousand white men gathering in the streets of Atlanta, mercifully beating blacks at random. When blacks fought back, they were killed. The Militia was called in to control the riot.

1909 As an answer to the lynchings and other racist practices by Democrats, three whites came together and formed a new organization. The organization was called the NAACP. African American History Professor, John Hope Franklin said, *"In 1909, liberal whites such as Mary White Ovington, Oswald Garrison Villard, and William English Walling issued a call for a conference to consider the plight of African Americans."* In that same year, these key individuals met and formed what is now known as the NAACP or the National Association for the Advancement of Colored People. In confirming Professor Franklin's findings, the Negro Almanac reports, that the formation of the *"NAACP was largely the brain-child of Ovington, Villard and Walling, three white individuals."*[29] By 1936, these individuals and other white liberals continued to play a major role in the NAACP, focusing primarily on eliminating the lynching of black citizens in those states under Democrat control.

1912 W.E.B Dubois endorsed **Democratic** candidate Woodrow Wilson for President. He asked Wilson to support *black education, blacks' rights to vote and own land, and to stop the onslaught of lynchings*. Shortly after Wilson took office he ignored Dubois' request and gave his blessings to three southern cabinet members to segregate their departments. A New York paper released an article entitled: *"Jim Crow had come to Washington."* One

---

29 *The Negro Almanac Fifth Edition*, 260.

government supervisor boasted that *"There are no government positions for Negroes in the South, a Negro's place is in the cornfield."*

1915 The stage play, *The Klansman,* was made into a motion picture, entitled: *The Birth of a Nation.* The movie strengthened the Klan, and its membership grew. In many places where the **Democrats** ruled, gangs of whites openly attacked blacks on the street, after watching the movie.

1917 Black soldiers in Houston, Texas, who had been harassed for several months by the Houston police, took matters into their own hands after one of their soldiers was arrested and beaten without cause. One hundred black soldiers went to town to retaliate. Shots were fired. Sixteen whites and four fellow soldiers were killed. Nineteen soldiers were court-martialed and sentenced to death. The soldiers were denied the right to appeal their case to Woodrow Wilson, the Democratic President whom W.E.B. Dubois had previously endorsed.

1918 In May of 1918, there was a series of lynchings in Georgia. When Mary Turner, who was nine months pregnant complained that she was going to see to it that the white men who lynched her husband would be prosecuted, the mob dragged her from her home, tortured and hung her. While she was still alive, hanging from the rope, they cut open her womb so her unborn child would spill out and crushed the baby's skull under their heels.

1919 During the Senate debates on the Ku Klux Klan Act of 1871, Republican Senator, William Stoughton asked*: "How long will it be before the Tammany Hall Democracy, who are now furnishing arms to the Ku Klux Klan of the South to murder southern Republicans, will introduce this new element of Democratic success into the northern politics?"* His question was answered on July 27, 1919, when whites attacked and killed Eugene Williams, a black swimmer in Chicago. When the dust settled, 15 whites and 23 blacks were killed*. "Jim Crow," said the* **Chicago Tribune,** *"has come north."*

1919 In Elaine, Arkansas, there were reports that as many as 200 black farmers were massacred, while several others were arrested and executed, simply because they met at a Black church to discuss how they could stop their white landlords from cheating them out of their cotton crops. No one was arrested, tried or convicted for this massacre. (See Exhibit 3 video "Under Democrat Control.")

1921 On May 31, 1921, Tulsa's leading newspaper (*Tulsa Tribune*) released a front-page article alleging that a black man had raped a white woman. Whites went on a rampage, killing 300 blacks, wounding 800 others, arresting as many as 6,000. During the riot, whites burned down 35 city blocks in the middle class black community (which was also known as the Greenwood District or Black Wall Street). Even though blacks lost millions in addition to their lives, no white was arrested and convicted for this event. (See Exhibit 3 video "Under Democrat Control.")

1922 On December 31, 1922, (New Years Eve), a young white woman from Rosewood, Florida, claimed she was raped by a black man. The next day (New Year) several whites from nearby communities swarmed the town killing over 100 blacks and burning down most of the black-owned businesses and homes. The massacre included women and children. Others escaped by spending the night in the swamps. No whites were arrested, tried or convicted for this event (See Exhibit 3 video "Under Democrat Control.") **Democratic** Governor Cary Hardee took no action. Reparations were finally paid in 1993.

1933 Democratic candidate Franklin D. Roosevelt received the black vote and became the 32nd president of the United States. Professor John Hope Franklin says, shortly after taking office, blacks *"discovered that agencies of the federal government were as capable of discriminatory practices or could be used for such purposes, as any others. Black sharecroppers and tenants had difficulty in obtaining relief benefits from the Agricultural Administration because landlords kept their relief checks. While the Federal Housing*

Authority guaranteed a limited number of loans for Negroes to build or purchase homes, its policy was not to interfere with local housing practices that excluded Negroes from certain neighborhoods. Lynchings and other forms of racial violence had continued during the New Deal and the federal government had pleaded that it had no jurisdiction over such matters." President Roosevelt also banned black newspapers from the military, claiming they were "communist." These were the same black newspapers that had urged their readers to give Roosevelt their vote.

1945 Harry S. Truman, a Democrat, was elected president of the United States. President Truman started the process of integrating the military, but no Civil Rights legislation was passed during his administration to stop the continued lynchings and terrorist attacks by the southern Democrats and their Klan supporters. Historians report that southern blacks lived in constant fear, knowing that death at the hands of their terrorists was just a matter of time.

1954 On May 17, 1954, Democrats received a major defeat and a major blow to their racist policy of segregation when the United States Supreme Court rendered its decision on ***Brown v Board of Education***. The decision virtually dismantled the earlier ruling in the case of ***Plessy v Ferguson***. Southern Democrats were furious, and ***continued*** their practices of ***terror*** and ***segregation*** in education in defiance to the ruling.

Black historians told the producers of the PBS's series *The Rise & Fall of Jim Crow* that, in southern regions controlled by Democrats, blacks accepted the fact that one day they would all die from terrorist attacks, ***"they just didn't know how or when."*** Blacks lived in constant terror, day and night. Their future seemed hopeless. Then in 1954, a ray of hope came with the decision of ***Brown v the Board of Education,*** and three years later, more encouragement came with the introduction of the Civil Rights Act of 1957. To many African Americans, this was the dawning of a new day.

1955 A fourteen-year-old black teenager from Chicago named Emmett Till was abducted, severely beaten, and thrown into the river with a weight fastened around his neck with barbed wire, while visiting relatives in Mississippi. Loyalty to the Democrats' *good ole* boy network and fear of retaliatory terrorist attacks from the Democrats' terrorist auxiliaries is what kept some witnesses from testifying. Thus the two men who were on trial were acquitted. In 2004, President G.W. Bush has asked his Justice Department to re-open the Emmett Till case.

1957

1957 Civil Rights

Purpose: It was introduced by Republican President Dwight D. Eisenhower and supported by a ***bipartisan*** Congress. Democrats voiced the greatest opposition. The law was designed to establish a Civil Rights Commission and permit the government to bring lawsuits for civil rights violations, including the denial of the right to vote.

Democrats' Opposition: One of the spokespersons for the Democrats was **William Winstead, the Democrat from Mississippi. Winstead** said*: "This bill contains most of the evil provisions of last year's so-called civil rights bill, plus an additional section which would empower the Attorney General of the United States, to seek injunctions in the Federal district court for the enforcement of alleged violations of civil rights laws."*

Richard Russell, the Democratic Senator from Georgia, argued*: "This law will be administered by a politically minded Attorney General. There can be little doubt that he will be constantly pressed by the Vice President of the United States to apply the great powers of the law in the Southern States, at such places and in such time and manner as the **NAACP, of which the Vice President is the most distinguished member**, may demand."*

"The threat of this vicious legislation will be used to intimate honest officials of the State

1   *and local governments who are earnestly endeavoring to discharge their duties under their*

2   *oaths of the office and the laws of their respective States.*

3

4   *"It is entirely likely that the application of this law will result in forcing the registration*

5   *of a large number of Negro citizens who, in fact, cannot meet the qualifications prescribed*

6   *for all electors under the laws of the State in which they live. It is a thoroughly bad bill,*

7   *and places dangerous powers in the hands of those who are to administer it without much*

8   *comforting proof of their responsibility and fairness."*

9

10   In the Senate opponents were successful in eliminating Part III of the bill which was aimed

11   at striking down the separation of the races in hospitals, schools, hotels, swimming pools,

12   and places of public entertainment. Senator Russell went on to say, *"As I have said, the*

13   *bill is bad, but consider how much worse it would have been if we had not been able to*

14   *eliminate Part III.*

15

16   *"If the original Part III had been applied so as to bring about the social intermingling of the*

17   *races from the kindergarten to the grave, southern civilization would have destroyed beyond*

18   *hope of redemption. This was the supreme tragedy we sought above all else to avert."*

19

20   **William Colmer, the Democratic Congressman from Mississippi,** said, *"Some of us have*

21   *conscientiously and therefore stubbornly opposed this misnamed civil-rights proposal. It is*

22   *nothing more or less than the abolition of the civil rights of all the people under the guise of*

23   *granting civil rights to a highly organized and politically powerful minority group. So, Mr.*

24   *Speaker, as we gather today in this historic Chamber to witness the final act in the tragedy*

25   *of the beginning of the downfall of the Republic, it might be well to briefly sum up the value*

26   *of the winners and losers in this political gamble.*

27

28   *"The actors in this political tragedy are of the summit stature in both political camps, It is*

1 obvious that the Republican high command has deliberately set out to recapture the minority

2 Negro vote stolen from them by the **Democratic** high command some two decades ago."

3

4 Clifford Case, Republican from New Jersey: "Mr. President, the facts, which have been

5 developed in debate in the House and in the Senate, indicated clearly the deprivation of

6 voting rights that exist in this country and the need for further legislation for the enforcement

7 of those rights.... It is particularly appropriate, Mr. President, that these further remedies

8 be by the way of preventive relief. As I indicated earlier, it does not do a person who has

9 been deprived of his right to vote any good to have the person who deprives him of the right,

10 put in jail, and no amount of money damages can compensate a person deprived of the

11 right to vote for that deprivation. In spite of the existence of these theoretical remedies, the

12 right to vote has been taken away from millions of our citizens. It is clear that an additional

13 remedy is required." Debates took place June 5-18, 1957 in the House and from August

14 29-30 in the Senate.

15

16 **1960**

17 **1960 Civil Rights Act**

18 The Purpose: On February 5. 1960, President Dwight D. Eisenhower sent to Congress a

19 message requesting "legislation to strengthen the law dealing with obstruction of justice so

20 as to provide expressly that the use of force or threats of force to obstruct court orders in

21 school desegregation cases shall be a federal offense." He said, "there have been instances

22 where extremists have attempted by mob violence and other concerted threats of violence to

23 obstruct the accomplishment of objectives in school decrees."

24

25 Like the 1957 Civil Rights Act, this bill had **bi-partisan** support. But there were still

26 Democrats that opposed the bill. In his argument **for** the bill, **Democratic Congressman**

27 **Ray Madden of Indiana** said, "Patriotic Negroes of America only ask that their future

28 generations are not called upon to combat the economic and educational impediments

1 *which their ancestors endured."*

2

3 **Congressman Overton Brooks, a Democrat from Louisiana,** countered and said,

4 *"This Civil Rights bill is as vicious an instrument as I have read since I have been in this*

5 *Congress. If enacted into law, it will undoubtedly hurt our people in the South. The bill*

6 *provides that anybody who writes a letter critical of a decree of the Federal courts dealing*

7 *with the integration of schools, with the intent to obstruct the execution of an order of this*

8 *court, is guilty of a Federal crime and punishable by fine and imprisonment. The provision*

9 *regarding fleeing from one State to another to avoid prosecution or imprisonment for the*

10 *crime of bombing or setting fire to a building, whether it be church or otherwise, make*

11 *another step toward taking away from States their fundamental rights."*

12

13 **Congressman William McCulloch, a Republican from Ohio,** argued, ***"For almost a***

14 ***century, the failure to provide political equality for all qualified citizens has been nagging***

15 ***the conscience of the people,*** *and now we are obliged to consider and pass legislation to*

16 *insure and implement such rights to all qualified citizens, which rights so long ago, were*

17 *extended to all, only to be lost or taken away, in a substantial number of states or lesser*

18 *political subdivision of our country."*

19

20 **1964**

21 <u>**1964 Civil Rights Act**</u>

22 The purpose: One of the prime sponsors and supporters of this bill was Republican

23 Senator Everett Dirksen of Illinois. The law which contained 11 different Titles, prohibited

24 discrimination in all public accommodations, if their *operation "affected commerce*

25 *(including hotels and other places of lodging of more than five rooms, restaurants and other*

26 *eating places, gasoline stations, theaters, motion pictures houses, stadiums and other places*

27 *of exhibitions or entertainment)."* It also covered voting, desegregation of public education,

28 Equal Opportunity and a Civil Rights Commission. **This bill was almost identical to the**

Republicans' 1957 Civil Rights Bill and the 1875 Civil Rights Act that the Democrats had overturned by the United Supreme Court.

Background Leading Up to 1964 Civil Rights Acts

In his book, *Why We Can't Wait*, Dr. Martin Luther King said, *"The feeling was growing among Negroes that the [Kennedy] administration had oversimplified and underestimated the civil rights issue.... The administration had fashioned its primary approach to discrimination in the South.... With each new Negro protest we were advised, sometimes privately and sometimes in public, **to call off our efforts and channel all of our energies into registering voters**. On each occasion we would agree with the importance of voting rights, but would patiently seek to explain that Negroes did not want to neglect all other rights while one was selected for concentrated attention. **The Kennedy administration appeared to believe it had by its positive deeds, earned enough credit to coast on civil rights...."**

King went on to say *"that no one would have ever believed that during the first two years of the Kennedy administration"* (1961-1962) that Negroes *"would become as militant as the segregationist."*

What King was referring to was the social unrest that African Americans vehemently expressed during the first two years of the Kennedy administration.

*In 1961, Freedom Riders were attacked and arrested in the South. The Freedom Riders were organized by CORE to test desegregation orders in the South. Blacks protested and Robert Kennedy ordered six hundred Federal Marshals to Montgomery, Alabama, to maintain order.

*In 1962, several thousand federal troops were ordered to the University of Mississippi to

1 maintain order as riots erupted as whites protested the admission of James Meredith, a 29-

2 year old black veteran.

3

4 *In 1962, black churches in Georgia were burned to discourage voter registration.

5

6 In 1963, the nation was in chaos, the situation was out of control. By the week of May 18

7 the Department of Justice had noted that there had been **forty-three** different civil rights

8 demonstrations of various magnitudes. On April 3 Dr. King demonstrated in Birmingham,

9 Alabama. The number of demonstrators increased significantly by May 3. There were more

10 demonstrations after Medgar Evers (a civil rights leader) was assassinated in Mississippi.

11 By May 7 over 2,500 demonstrators had been arrested, many of them were children. On May

12 11 a black leader's home was bombed. During that same period, **Democratic** Governor,

13 George Wallace refused to comply with a presidential order to register two black students to

14 the University of Alabama and four black children were killed when the 16th Street Baptist

15 of Birmingham, Alabama, was bombed.

16

17 New York University Law School Professor, Bernard Schwartz said, *"The events in*

18 *Birmingham, followed by the need to federalize the Alabama National Guard to frustrate*

19 *George Wallace, the Democratic Governor of Alabama, whose efforts to thwart a court*

20 *order admitting two Negro students to the state university, roused the national conscience,*

21 *as almost never before, to the need for speedy action to correct the situation. Most*

22 *important perhaps, they stimulated a previously lukewarm Administration to becoming firm*

23 *supporters of strong civil rights legislation. The tepid attitude of President John Kennedy in*

24 *the matter had been a source of serious discomfort to many of his supporters. ...The troubles*

25 *in Alabama completely altered the Administration's attitude to make a full commitment to*

26 *civil rights that he had until then, so carefully avoided.*

27

28 On June 19, 1963 President Kennedy sent the following letter to Congress, asking Congress

1 to pass his 1963 Civil Rights Bill. The first section of the letter seem to suggest that the

2 president was more concerned with the social disorder that was taking place than he was

3 about the deplorable conditions of the African Americans.

4

5 President Kennedy's Message to Congress

6 For Passage of 1963 Civil Rights Act

7 June 19, 1963

8

9 *Last week I addressed to the American people an appeal to conscience – a request for their*

10 *cooperation in meeting the growing moral crisis in American race relations. I warned of*

11 *"a rising tide of discontent that threatens the public safety" in many parts of the country. I*

12 *emphasized that "the events in Birmingham and elsewhere have so increased the cries for*

13 *equality that no city or state or legislative body can prudently choose to ignore them." "It*

14 *is a time to act," I said, "in the Congress, in State and local legislative bodies and, above*

15 *all, in all of our daily lives.*

16

17 *In the days that have followed, the predictions of **increased violence** have been tragically*

18 *borne out. The "fires of frustration and discord" have burned hotter than ever.*

19

20 *At the same time, the response of the American people to this appeal to their principles and*

21 *obligations has been reassuring. Private progress – by merchants and the unions and local*

22 *organizations – has been marked, if not uniform in many areas. Many doors long closed*

23 *to Negroes, North and South, have been open. Local biracial committees, under private*

24 *and public sponsorship, have mushroomed. The mayors of our major cities, whom I earlier*

25 *addressed, have pledged renewed action. **But persisting inequalities and tensions make it***

26 ***clear that Federal action must lead the way, providing both the Nation's standard and a***

27 ***nationwide solution.** In short, the time has come for Congress of the United States to join*

28 *with the executive and judicial branches in making it clear to all, that race has no place in*

1 *American life or law....*

2

3 **The result of continued Federal legislative inaction will be continued, if not increased,**

4 **racial strife** *– causing the leadership on both sides to pass from the hands of reasonable*

5 *responsible men to the purveyors of hate and violence,* **endangering domestic tranquility,**

6 *retarding our Nation's economic and social progress, and weakening the respect with which*

7 *the rest of the world regards us. No American, I feel sure, would prefer this course of tension,*

8 *disorder, and division – and the great majority of our citizens simply cannot accept it.*

9

10 **For these reasons**, *I am proposing that Congress stay in session this year until it has*

11 *enacted – preferable as a single omnibus bill – the most responsible, reasonable, and*

12 *urgently needed solutions to this problem, solutions which should be acceptable to all fair-*

13 *minded men. This bill would be known as the Civil Rights Act of 1963....*

14

15 President Kennedy died before the bill was passed, and his successor, President Lyndon

16 Johnson, had a difficult time convincing his own party that such legislation was necessary.

17 **Because of the strong opposition by the Southern Democrats**, the debates involving this

18 bill lasted over eighty days. The debates took up some 7,000 pages in the Congressional

19 Record (consisting of over 10,000,000 words) and created the longest filibuster in Senate

20 history. The following are a few of the Democrats who opposed the Civil Rights Bill and

21 the Republicans who supported it.

22

23 Democrats' Opposition: <u>This was another bill that received bi-partisan support</u>. Those

24 Democrats who opposed the bill included **Donald Matthews from Florida.** In his

25 arguments he said, *"In the name of civil rights, this bill would deprive schoolchildren of*

26 *milk and basic education if there appears to be discrimination because of race, color, or*

27 *national origin. How cruel can the humanitarians and the moralists be in the name of*

28 *civil rights? What do we mean by discrimination? The communists have been fed under*

1 *Republican and Democratic administrations, but this will deny daily bread to American*

2 *children in the name of civil rights."*

3

4 **Thomas Abernethy, a Democrat from Mississippi**, argued, *"If enacted, it is certain*

5 *to precipitate a tremendous upheaval in our society, but not the kind of upheaval that*

6 *proponents apparently expect. I predict it will precipitate an upheaval that will make the*

7 *sit-ins, kneel-ins, lie-ins, mass picketing, chanting, the march on Washington, and all*

8 *other elements of the **so-called Negro revolutions**, all of these – I predict – will look like*

9 *kindergarten play in comparison with the counter-revolution that is bound to arise and*

10 *continue to grow and grow and grow."*

11

12 **Howard Smith, a Democrat from Virginia,** added the following arguments: *"I deeply*

13 *regret that out of the fifteen minutes allotted to me, I cannot assign time for protest to the*

14 *many patriotic members of this House who would like to express their distaste, dismay and*

15 *disgust at this invasion of the rights of American citizens. In a few minutes, you will vote*

16 *this monstrous instrument of oppression upon all of the American People.... **Be forewarned***

17 ***that the paid agents and leaders of the NAACP** can never permit this law to be gradually*

18 *and peacefully accepted because that means an end to their well-paid activities."*

19

20 **Democrat Robert Byrd from West Virginia** said, *"Can the senator from Minnesota*

21 *[Humphrey] assure the senator from West Virginia that under Title VI school children*

22 *may not be bused from one end of the community to another end of the community at the*

23 *taxpayers' expense to relieve so-called racial imbalance in the schools?*

24

25 **Democrat Sam Ervin** said, *"This bill is based upon a strange thesis. The thesis is that*

26 *the best way and the only way to promote the civil rights of some Americans is to rob all*

27 *Americans of civil rights equally precious, and to reduce the supposedly sovereign states to*

28 *meaningless zeros on the nation's map."*

1 **Olin Johnston, the Democrat from South Carolina,** argued, *"Mr. President, this is indeed*

2 *the blackest day in the U.S. Senate since 1875, when the Congress passed a civil rights*

3 *bill similar to this one. It was 89 years ago that the [Republican] Congress passed the*

4 *nefarious Reconstruction era civil rights laws, __identical with what we are now discussing,__*

5 *__which were later declared unconstitutional by the U.S. Supreme Court__. The Senate, if it*

6 *passes this measure before us, will be compounding that unconstitutional error made back*

7 *in 1875* [when the Republicans passed the 1875 Civil Rights Act]. *I predict that this bill*

8 *will never be enforced without turning our Nation into a police state and without the cost*

9 *of bloodshed and violence.*

10

11 *"Ten years ago, in **1954, the Supreme Court took it upon itself to amend the Constitution***

12 *of the United States and declared that segregation – that is, required separate but equal*

13 *school facilities for the races – was illegal. Instead of promoting peace and harmony*

14 *between the races, as a result of this decision we have seen racial violence, intolerance,*

15 *bigotry, and hatred compounded and multiplied. Whenever Government decrees a social*

16 *policy for people when people are not behind such a policy, one can only expect as a result*

17 *such violence and trouble.*

18

19 *"Those who advocate passage of this civil rights bill need not expect this legislation to*

20 *do anything for our country except to divide our people and rekindle the hatreds and*

21 *prejudices of one hundred years ago, to be perpetuated into the future for at least another*

22 *one hundred years. Contained in this legislation is not just a so so-called framework for*

23 *engendering equality among people of different races. This bill contains the equipment,*

24 *tools, temptation, and power to establish a vast federal network for controlling the people*

25 *of every community. The damage this will do to our government is incomprehensible....*

26

27 *"When one talks of eliminating discrimination with this piece of so-called legislation, if it*

28 *were not such a serious matter it would be fit for a good joke...."*

1 *"If we sweep away the clutter of emotion and the clatter of the demonstrators and look*
2 *at the legal aspect of this legislation, we can only come to the realistic conclusion that it*
3 *is unconstitutional and will be recorded in history as the greatest robber of the rights of*
4 *individuals and states and the most tremendous hoax ever perpetrated upon the people of*
5 *the United States."*

6

7 **John Sparkman, the Democrat from Alabama,** told Congress: *"Mr. President, we now*
8 *have before us a motion to proceed with the consideration of H.R. 7152, the so called civil*
9 *rights bill....*

10

11 *"Mr. President, never in my long history of opposition to so-called civil rights legislation*
12 *have I risen to attack so formidable an array of legislation that is probably well-intended*
13 *but which could do so much to take away many of the liberties and rights for which we have*
14 *fought throughout the history of this Nation....*

15

16 *"...For months I have been receiving literally thousands of letters from all over the nation*
17 *supporting my stand against this bill. So I rise not just with a mandate from the people of*
18 *Alabama or the South. My mandate comes from the four corners of the country....*

19

20 *"Title II, the so-called public accommodations provision of H.R. 7152 is the most sweeping,*
21 *the most far-reaching attempt to repeal the constitutional concept of individual liberty that*
22 *has been proposed since the cruel period of* [the Republicans'] *Reconstruction.*

23

24 *"In those days when the Southland lay prostrate, crushed, harshly ruled by military governors*
25 [appointed by the Republicans], *the Congress, in which the South was misrepresented in*
26 *many cases by residents of northern states, rammed through the* [Republicans'] *notorious*
27 **Civil Rights Act of 1875.** *This was one of the infamous 'force bills' designed to tear apart*
28 *the very fabric of southern life.*

1   *"Fortunately for the Nation, those aggrieved had recourse to the Constitution. Even though*
2   *amended under questionable circumstances, the Constitution was our salvation because*
3   *when [the Democrats challenged the issue in court] and the Supreme Court put the Civil*
4   *Rights of 1875 to the ultimate test, it was found wanting.*

5

6   **"Mr. President, I for one, am going to devote my best efforts to returning this resurrected**
7   [Republican] **statute to its grave."**

8

9   **Everett Dirksen, Republican** from Illinois, addressed the Senate with the following: *"...*
10   *To my fellow Senators to consider this issue in the light of national interest. It is a phase*
11   *that came close to the late President Kennedy. It is a phase that comes close to our former*
12   *majority leader, who now occupies his exalted position. I want to do what I think is in the*
13   *interest of the present and future wellbeing of probably the only real, true free republic that*
14   *still remains on God's footstool. I shall cooperate. I shall do my best...."*

15

16   **Emanuel Celler, Democrat from New York,** was one of the Democrats that argued in
17   favor of the bill. Celler said. *"This is an opportunity for which we have been anxiously*
18   *awaiting.* **You know, the Lord's best gifts to us are not things, but opportunities, and we**
19   **now have bestowed upon us a golden opportunity to do a great thing.**

20

21   *"Both parties joined hands. We felt we represented a cause. We shunned a political issue.*
22   *I am grateful to the ranking member of the Republican Party on the Judiciary Committee,*
23   *the gentleman form Ohio [Mr. McCulloch]. He and I labored incessantly fashioning the*
24   *bill. I pay tribute to him and his fellow Republicans who stood by him.... The demonstration*
25   *and violence of the recent months have served to point up what many of us have known for*
26   *years: That this nation can no longer abide the moral outrage of discrimination."*

27

28   **William McCullough, Republican from Ohio,** followed with these comments: *"No*

Statutory law can completely end discrimination under attack by this legislation. Intelligent work and vigilance by members of all races will be required, for many years, before discrimination completely disappears. To create hope of immediate and complete success can only promote conflict and result in brooding and despair.... No force or fear, then, but belief in the inherent equality of man induces me to support this legislation.

"I believe in the right of each individual to have his constitutional rights guaranteed. On the other hand, he must always be prepared to shoulder the obligations and assume the burdens of citizenship.

"No one would suggest that the Negro receives equality of treatment and equality of opportunity in many fields of activity today. Well-formed persons, everywhere, admit that in all sections of the country – North, South, East, and West – the Negro continues to face the barriers of racial intolerance and discrimination. Hundreds of thousands of citizens are denied the basic right to vote. Thousands of school districts remain segregated. Decent hotel and eating accommodations frequently lie hundreds of miles apart for the Negro traveler. Parks, playgrounds, and golf courses continue to be off limits to Negroes whose tax money go to support them. Many programs continue to be operated in a discriminatory manner. These and many more such conditions point the way toward the need for additional legislation. I recommend H.R. 7152, as amended, to all my colleagues from wheresoever they come."

1965 One year after the 1964 Civil Rights Acts' debates, **Democratic** Governor George Wallace ordered two hundred State Troopers and members of the Dallas County Sheriff's office to stop five-hundred-plus civil rights marches, seventeen blacks were hospitalized and sixty-seven others were treated for injuries from night sticks, tear gas, and whips.

1965 1965 Voting Rights Act

The 1965 Voting Rights Act began with a speech from **Democratic President Lyndon B. Johnson** to the Congress of the United States on March 15, 1965. The followings are a few excerpts from that speech:

Mr. Speaker, Members of the Congress, I speak tonight for the dignity of man and the destiny of democracy....In our time we have come to live with moments of great crisis. Our lives have been marked with debate about great issues, issues of war and peace, of prosperity and depression. But rarely in any time does an issue lay bare the secret heart of America itself.... The issue of equal rights for American Negroes is such an issue. And should we defeat every enemy, should we double our wealth and conquer the stars, and still be unequal to this issue, then we will have failed as a people and as a nation.

For with a country as with a person, "What is a man profited, if he shall gain the whole world and lose his own soul?"

...To deny a man his hopes because of his color or race, his religion or place of birth – is not only to do injustice, it is to deny America and to dishonor the dead who gave their lives for American freedom. ...Yet the harsh fact is that in many places in this country men and women are kept from voting because they are Negroes....All Americans must have the right to vote. And we are going to give that right.

...Above the pyramid on the great seal of the United States its says – in Latin – "God has favored our undertaking." God will not favor everything we do. It is rather our duty to divine His will. But I cannot help believing that He truly understands and that he really favors the undertaking that we begin here tonight.

The Purpose: **With bipartisan support, the debates started on April 22, 1965** to eliminate

1 the voting irregularities in the South by providing congressional enforcement of the 15th

2 Amendment in the election process.

3

4 **Democrats' Opposition**: Several participated in the debate, but the primary persons who

5 controlled the debates were Republican Senators Everett Dirksen of Illinois and Jacob Javits

6 from New York and Democratic Senators **Sam Ervin of North Carolina and Herman**

7 **Talmadge from Georgia.**

8

9 **Sam Erivin**: *"This bill contains a provision which condemns without judicial trial the*

10 *States of Alabama, Mississippi, Louisiana, Georgia, South Carolina, and Virginia and*

11 *thirty-four counties in North Carolina; does it not?"*

12

13 **Senator Dirksen**: *"Yes; I do not believe it condemns the states. It takes account of a*

14 *condition that has existed in those states. We are seeking to remedy a condition that exists*

15 *with respect to citizens of the United States. We go to the heart of the problem and seek to*

16 *supply a remedy that we think is constitutional and non-punitive."*

17

18 **Herman Talmadge, Democrat from Georgia**: *"We were told last year that with the*

19 *passage of a broad, all-encompassing civil rights bill, which covered almost everything that*

20 *the mind of man could conceive, that there would not be any further need of a civil rights*

21 *bill. Would not the bill deny to the States of Louisiana, Alabama, Mississippi, Georgia,*

22 *North Carolina, and certain carefully selected counties in other areas the right to apply any*

23 *literacy standards whatsoever for their voters?"*

24

25 Regarding literacy test, **Jacob Javits responded:** *"Think of the situation, for example*

26 *in Mississippi, where whites are asked to interpret the following provision of the State*

27 *Constitution: "The Senate shall consist of members chosen every four years by the*

28 *qualified electors of the several districts." Negroes are asked to interpret sections of*

the Constitution dealing with tax exemptions, the judicial sale of land, eminent domain, concurrent jurisdiction of chancery and circuit courts and habeas corpus. [And] **what about deprivation going back for a century, which inhered in segregated schools resulting in a median education level of the sixth grade for Negroes in Mississippi, as compared with an eleventh grade median for whites?** *Then there is the intimidation by public officials; there are the bombings and shooting, the burnings, the beatings; and quite apart from them,* **the denial of surplus food to Negroes who persist in their attempt to register,** *as in Humphreys County, Mississippi; or the boycotting of Negroes who had the temerity to register by cutting off their bank loans and their grocery store credit."* The debates started on April 22, 1965.

1968

1968 Civil Rights Acts

The Purpose: The *bi-partisan* bill was designed to protect Negroes and civil-rights workers by outlawing racially-motivated acts of violence against persons exercising the Fourteenth Amendment rights. It also had a fair housing component to ban discrimination in housing.

Democrats' Opposition: The Democrats opposing the bill included Lawrence Fountain and Sam Ervin, Democrats from North Carolina. Fountain said, *"If this bill becomes law, it will be a clear invitation to this tiny band of agitators to continue to foment strife and fuel civil disorder. We have seen too much of that lately, and why we seem to want to nourish it is beyond me. But that is exactly what the impact of this bill would be."*

Sam Ervin said, *"It would be easy to defeat their efforts if they were evil-minded men professing bad ends. Unfortunately for the cause of sound constitutional government, however, they are men of good intentions, who are willing to do constitutional evil because they believe good will result from it. In so doing, they emulate the example of Mother Eve, who succumbed to the temptation to eat the forbidden fruit because she saw*

1   *'it was pleasant to the eyes,' and believed it to be 'good for food,' and was satisfied that*

2   *it 'would make one wise.'*

3

4   *"The men who seek to destroy or impair these constitutional principles and*

5   *constitutional rights, claim that it is necessary for the federal government to deprive*

6   *all Americans of basic economic, legal, personal, and property rights to give equality*

7   *to twenty million Negro Americans."*

8

9   **John Stennis**, the Democrat from Mississippi, said, *"I wish to be clear that I oppose this*

10   *measure in most of its major particulars, and that I have been one of many who have*

11   *worked to avoid it. I believe particularly with reference to the passage of the open housing*

12   *legislation, that it will prove to be a grave mistake and **one of the gravest that the Senate***

13   ***has ever made."***

14

15   **1972**

16   <u>**1972 Equal Employment Act**</u>

17   The Purpose: To assure and promote equal opportunity in employment. The voting record

18   on this piece of legislation shows that there were Democrats who also opposed this bill.

19   Democrats: 155 voted for and 79 voted against. Republicans: 130 voted for and 26 voted

20   against. This bill was passed during the Nixon Administration. Shortly after the passage of

21   this bill, Nixon issued Executive Order 11478 which paved the way for affirmative action

22   programs that included quotas, goals and timetables.

23

24   **79 Democrats Voted against 1972 Equal Employment Opportunity Act**

25   Abernethy, Abourezk, Andrews (Ala), Aspinall, Baring, Begich, Dveill, Brinkley, Burleson

26   (Texas), Cabell, Caffery, Chappell, Chisholm, Clay, Colmer, Conyers, Daniel, Danmiel

27   (VA), Davis (GA), Davis (S.C.), Dellums, Denholm, Dent, Diggs, Dorn, Dowdy, Drinan,

28   Edmondson, Fisher, Flowers, Dlynt, Ford (W.D. Mich.), Gettys, Giaimo, Grasso, Green,

(Ore.), Griffin, Griffith, Hagan, Haley, Hebert, Henderson, Hull, Hungate, Jones (Ala.), Jones (Tenn), Kazen, Kee, Landrum, Lennon, McMillan, Mahon, Mathis, Mills (W.D. Ark.), Mink, Nedzi, Nichols, O'Hara, Passman, Patman, Poage, Purcell, Randall, Rarick, Roberts, Runnels, Satterfield, Shipley, Sikes, Slack, Staggers, Steed, Stephens, Stubblefield, Stuckey, Teague (Texas), Waggonner, Watts, Whitten, Young (Texas).

21 Democrats Did Not Vote

Abbitt, Albert, Alexander, Anderson (Tenn), Clark, Edwards (La.), Evans (Colo.), Hansen (Wash), Hathaway, Jarman, Karth, Long (La.), McCormack, Mollohan, Montgomery, Murphy (Ill.), Pryor (Ark), Roybal, Sullivan, Symington, Udall.

1972 Nixon's 1972 Equal Employment Opportunities Act granted EEOC power to bring *"Pattern and Practice"* lawsuits starting in 1974.

1973 One hundred and eighty-one (181) years after the Democratic Party was originally formed (1792) and almost one decade after the passage of the 1964 Civil Rights Act, Barbara Jordan, became *the Democrats' first black member of Congress* from the South.

1994 On December 15, 1994, the Honorable Judge David V. Kenyon ordered the Clinton Administration to force one hundred member-shipping companies of the Pacific Maritime Association to develop an Affirmative Action Plan to stop discriminatory practices against African Americans, Hispanic and female longshore workers. The Clinton Administration never complied with the federal court order and the companies never developed the Affirmative Action Plan during his administration (case number CV925765Kn).

1995 In 1995, the Clinton Administration instructed Attorney General Janet Reno to file a reverse discrimination suit against Illinois State University on behalf of a group of white janitors, but refused to help a group of black, Hispanic, and female longshore workers who had filed three class action complaints against Pacific Maritime Association in the

1 Seattle-Tacoma area. Even though the blacks complained that they were forced to work in an
2 environment that had jobs known as *"Nigger Jobs,"* the Clinton Administration turned a deaf
3 ear their cries and refused to help. Despite a court order, ordering the Clinton Administration
4 to force the Pacific Maritime Association to develop an Affirmative Action Plan to correct
5 discriminatory practices, the Clinton Administration ignored the federal court and devoted
6 its time to the reverse discrimination case against Illinois State University. The female and
7 minority workers won their case without the support of the Clinton Administration. (Wayne
8 Perryman was the fact-finding consultant in all three cases.)

9

10 **1996** In 1996, California (a Democratic state) put an end to affirmative action by passing
11 Proposition 209. The new law prohibits racial preferences in government hiring and public
12 school admissions. The Proposition passed with a 54 percent popular vote. The new law,
13 which was aimed at ending affirmative action for blacks and other minorities, was passed
14 in a state that has had a long tradition of being a Democratic state.

15

16 **1998** Washington State, another long-time Democratic state, attacked affirmative action
17 programs with its passage of I-200. The new law prohibited the state from using race or
18 ethnicity in deciding student admission, employment, or contract awards.

19

20 **2001** Associated Press reported that in states controlled by Democrats, African Americans
21 at one time owned over fifteen million acres of land; today they own less than two million.
22 The AP reporters said many of the blacks lost their land through fraud, murder, and biased
23 court decisions.

24

25 **2002** From 1792 to 2002, the Democratic Party (the oldest political party in America
26 and also known as the *Party of White Supremacy*) had *never* elected a **black man** to the
27 United States Senate, they *never* apologized for the wrong that they committed against
28 African Americans, they *continue* to cover up their racist past and up to 1964, they voted

against every major piece of civil rights legislation that was designed to help the **<u>entire black race</u>**.

Democrats' Opposition to Black Education

Professor James McPherson reports that when the AMA (American Missionary Association) sent white teachers to areas controlled by **Democrats** to educate Negroes, the old time southern hospitality was immediately transformed into southern hostility.

Professor McPherson said: *"Southern hostility to Yankee teachers sometimes went beyond ostracism and verbal abuse. In times of political excitement during Reconstruction many missionaries were threatened, beaten, and murdered. The AMA reported several incidents similar to the one in which a group of masked men took a teacher from his house in North Carolina in 1874, tied him up, and after threatening to kill him if he did not leave the state gave him 100 lashes with a bullwhip. The founder and president for nearly 30 years of Shaw University, Henry Tupper of Massachusetts, was often harassed by the Ku Klux Klan and once hid all night in a cornfield with his wife and two children to avoid an assassination attempt.*

"In 1871, a college treasurer went to a nearby town on business, had dinner with a Black family, and after leaving a prayer meeting at a Negro church was ambushed by five men who fired at him seven times and left him for dead. The shots had missed, however; the treasurer returned to his hotel, where at 3:00 AM 30 masked men dragged him from his bed, took him to the woods, and gave him 61 lashes with a hickory whip.

"The 1874 elections were a particularly tense time; as one teacher put it, to be for weeks in a constant expectation of being murdered or burned out, and without losing faith in God, is something of a strain on the nerves.

1 *"In 1879, the Northern Methodists compiled a list of 34 attacks on their missionaries and*

2 *teachers in the past decade; 19 of the victims were White and 15 Black, three of the Whites*

3 *and four of the Blacks were killed.*

4

5 *"The AMA tried for several years to cooperate with local [southern] school boards. So long*

6 *as Republicans were in power this arrangement worked out reasonably well. But when the*

7 **Democrats** *began to regain control of the South the dual support foundered and eventually*

8 *collapsed. In Memphis the **Democrats** dismissed all AMA teachers, forcing the association*

9 *to withdraw from the jointly sponsored Lincoln School and found LeMoyne Institute in*

10 *its place. In Columbus, Mississippi, **Democrats** drove out the Union Academy's northern*

11 *teachers with threats of violence and then closed the school in 1871."*[30]

12

13 Black Colleges

14 The following is a list of a few of the black schools and colleges started by various missionary

15 societies of the North. Again, these schools were financed, funded, and sponsored by

16 prominent Republicans and their abolitionist supporters, while the Democrats with brutal

17 force opposed every effort that the two groups put forth to educate the American Negro.

School	**Date**	**Place**
Morehouse College	1867	Atlanta, GA
Howard University	1867	Washington, D.C.
Spelman Seminary	1881	Atlanta, GA
Shaw University	1865	Raleigh, NC
Fisk University	1866	Nashville, TN
Atlanta University	1867	Atlanta, GA
Virginia Union University	1899	Richmond, VA
Straight University	1869	New Orleans, LA

27

28 30 McPherson, *The Abolitionist Legacy: From Reconstruction to the NAACP*, 174-175.

1	Talladega College	1867	Talladega, AL
2	Clark University	1870	Atlanta, GA
3	Meharry Medical College	1876	Nashville, TN
4	Morgan College	1867	Baltimore, MD
5	New Orleans University	1873	New Orleans, LA
6	Philander Smith College	1883	Little Rock, AK
7	Rust College	1883	Holy Springs, MS
8	Samuel Houston College	1900	Austin, TX

Summary

Looking back over the events that have impacted the lives of African Americans during the past 210 years, one can't help but to compare these events with the events that affected the lives of millions of Jews. Some historians suggest that the Nazi Party's agenda of *racial purity* may have been inspired by the Democratic Party's agenda of *racial supremacy*. The striking similarities between what happened to Jews under the rule of Germany's Nazi Party versus what happened to blacks under the rule of the Democratic Party are worth noting.

In the past, many African Americans have accused the ***entire white race*** for the injustices that they were forced to endure. Others blamed the U.S. Government. But history reveals that it was neither the white race nor the federal government that was behind these injustices. These injustices were meticulously orchestrated by the Democratic Party and their auxiliaries.

Today, a number of Democrats proudly boast about their alleged civil rights accomplishment of the '60s, mainly the passage of the 1964 Civil Rights Act. However, after reviewing all the evidence including actual Congressional Records, one must conclude that had the Democrats attempted to pass these same types of laws in 1864, their legislative efforts in 1964 would not have been necessary. From 1864 and beyond Democrats proudly legislated Black Codes, Jim Crow Laws, and a multitude of other local laws (under State's Rights) to

1 disenfranchise blacks. These laws were specifically designed to **hurt blacks** - they passed

2 no laws to **help blacks**. The underlined truth is this: After almost two hundred years of racist

3 practices, the Democrats didn't pass laws and develop the programs (in the '60s) because

4 they had a change of heart and *fell in love with black folks*. They did it because they *fell in*

5 *love with the black vote*, knowing that was their only ticket to the White House.

6

7 Some have argued that the Republicans also owe African Americans an apology for

8 abandoning them when they reached a compromise (with the Democrats) to remove

9 federal troops from the South, in exchange for giving Rutherford B. Hayes the presidency.

10 History notes that the compromise did indeed take place, and troops were removed from

11 the South. However experts say that, like the problems facing today's American troops in

12 the reconstruction of Iraq, it was impossible to have enough federal troops to cover the

13 entire region (thirteen states) during Reconstruction of the South. History reveals that from

14 1866 to 1877 Democrats and their Klan supporters launched a multitude of terrorist attacks

15 against African Americans while federal troops' were stationed in the region. Professor

16 David Donald of Harvard writes: *"Congress could require federal troops to supervise*

17 *the registration of voters, but Negroes were waylaid and butchered on the roads to the*

18 *registration office...."* The troops' presence had little effect in preventing the reign of terror

19 that was initiated by Democrats and their Klan supporters.

20

21 When it comes to offering apologies, the one factor that may excuse Republicans is the fact

22 that unlike the Democrats, Republicans have always had abolitionists and "radical" members

23 like Senator Charles Sumner, Congressman Thaddeus Stevens, and Lincoln's law partner,

24 William Herndon, to consistently challenge racist individuals within their party. Professor

25 James McPherson of Princeton said, *"The abolitionists became the respected spokesmen*

26 *of the radical wing of the Republican Party."* From 1792 to 1960, the *"radicals"* in the

27 Democratic Party weren't spokespersons *for* African Americans; they were the assassins

28 that brought terror and death *to* African Americans.

After giving the Defendants support for the past forty years, many African Americans believe that an apology for the role that the Defendants played in ***inoculating our nation with the contagious disease of racism*** during the past 210 years is the least that the party can do. The apology should be issued for:

Fraud

Murder

The Formation of Terrorist Organizations

Economic Deprivation

Racist Legislation

Profane Defamation

Substandard Education

Terrorist Intimidation

Landmark Litigation

Brutal Assassinations

And Fraudulent Adjudication

Damages To African Americans

Many African Americans agree with those psychologists who believe that the horrors of institutional racism established to a large degree by the Defendants' racist policies, practices, programs, and Jim Crow legislation still haunt African Americans today.

Professor Nancy Boyd-Franklin, author of *Black Families in Therapy* and the Clinical Associate Professor in the Department of Psychiatry at the University of Medicine and Dentistry of New Jersey, puts it this way. *"It is difficult to convey fully to someone who has not experienced it, the insidious, pervasive and constant impact that racism and discrimination have on the lives of Black people in America today. Both affect a Black person from birth until death and have an impact on every aspect of family life, from child-rearing practices, courtship, and marriage, to male-female roles, self-esteem, and cultural and racial identification. They also influence the way in which black people related to each*

1 *other and to the outside world.*

2

3 *"Slavery set the tone for Black people to be treated as inferior…. The process of discrimination*

4 *is evident at all levels of society from theories about genetic inferiority (Jensen, 1969) and*

5 *cultural pathology (Monynihan 1965) to segregation that existed blatantly in the South*

6 *until the Civil Rights era of the 1960s **and still occurs in subtler forms today**. There are*

7 *continued equities in the United States…that are manifested by the disproportionate number*

8 *of Black people who are poor, homeless, living in substandard housing, unemployed and*

9 *school dropouts."* Source quote from *Black Families in Therapy* p 10.

10

11 It was the goal of the Democratic Party to ***infect*** the entire nation with their racist agenda of

12 ***White Superiority*** and they succeeded. As Professor Nancy Boyd stated, after 168 years of

13 racist indoctrination by Democrats, African Americans still struggle with

14 • Being the last to be hired and the first to be fired.

15 • Being profiled by law enforcement agencies.

16 • Being kept out of high paying decision-making positions.

17 • Having longer prison sentences than their white counterparts.

18 • Being followed around in department stores as though they are a perpetual race

19 of thieves.

20 • Having difficulty with housing – and being denied access to certain

21 neighborhoods.

22 • Having their racial discrimination complaints heard and processed.

23 • Being classified as illiterate, violent, and inferior.

24 Because of these factors, millions of African Americans are forced to depend on the social

25 systems of the government for their survival just like they were forced to depend on the

26 Democrats' racist system of slavery for their survival. This dependency hinders their ability

27 to move from one economic level to the next.

28

1 Under the Democrats' rule when blacks were denied education, when blacks were driven out
2 of (political) office, when their neighborhoods were burned to the ground, and when they
3 were denied the opportunity to patent their inventions, this not only had a psychological
4 impact on future generations, but it also had a profound economic impact as well. Instead
5 of starting life with the economic inheritance of the preceding generation, each generation
6 was forced to start from scratch with virtually nothing.

7

8 Today there is not only an economic gap between blacks and whites; there is also
9 a relationship gap between blacks and whites. In 2004, officers of the court and major
10 corporations are still sponsoring sensitivity training to bridge this gap. Public schools are
11 doing the same with their cultural diversity programs. The attitudes of both blacks and
12 whites in America, to a large degree, were shaped by the practices and indoctrination of
13 the only political party that consistently promoted *White Supremacy* for 168 years (1792-
14 1960), and that party was the Democratic Party. The problem is so severe that, today,
15 the average African American still has a problem of accepting and trusting whites and
16 most whites feel the same way about their African American counterparts. This became
17 evident during the 2003 Democratic Primary, on September 9, when the candidates were
18 asked: If they won the Democratic Primary, *would they select an African American as a*
19 *running mate?* The Democratic candidates avoided the question, and none attempted to
20 answer it. The strained relationship between blacks and whites has had a direct impact
21 on the earning potential of African Americans. The strained relationship is what have kept
22 *qualified* competent African Americans out of important positions like the vice president of
23 the United States. This racial disparity is exactly what the original Democratic Party wanted
24 to achieve—and they achieved it.

25

26 Because of the Democrats' racist policies and practices, millions of African Americans died
27 from the institution of slavery, from inhumane prison labor camps, from Klan terrorist attacks,
28 and from racist experiments like the Tuskegee Experiment. Because of the Democrats'

1 racist polices and practices, millions of acres of land were fraudulently taken from blacks,

2 patents were denied, inventions were stolen, and entire communities were burned to the

3 ground. Because of the Democrats' racist policies and practices, generations of African

4 Americans were either denied the right to attend school or were forced to attend inferior

5 schools. In regions controlled by Democrats our teachers were murdered, our constitutional

6 right to vote was denied, and our people lived in constant fear of terrorist attacks. Over a

7 period of 168 years these racist acts have not only violated their constitutional rights as

8 citizens of the United States (as pointed out in *Brown v Board of Education*); they also

9 have caused African Americans as a race to lose trillions of dollars while building a trillion-

10 dollar-plus economy for the South.

11

12 The Court must remember that it was Democratic President Jefferson Davis that said it was

13 because of the free black labor that *"hundreds of thousands of square miles of wilderness*

14 *were converted into cultivated lands covered with a prosperous people; towns and cities*

15 *had sprung into existence, and had rapidly increased in wealth and population under the*

16 [Democrat's] *social system of the South...; and the productions in the South of cotton, rice,*

17 *sugar, and tobacco, for the full development and continuance of which the labor of African*

18 *slaves was and is indispensable, had swollen to an amount which formed nearly three-*

19 *fourths of the exports of the whole United States and had become absolutely necessary*

20 *to wants of civilized man...."* (Source of quote: *Causes of The Civil War*, page 154, by

21 Professor Kenneth M. Stampp of University of California, Berkley.) The free black labor not

22 only occurred during slavery; it also continued under Black Codes during Reconstruction

23 and was expanded with inhumane prison labor camps in the late 1800s and early 1900s (see

24 exhibit video "Under Democrat Control").

25

26 Despite these factual truths, the modern day Democratic Party has never issued or offered

27 an apology to African Americans or to America, nor have they offered redress.

28

Precedent for an Apology & Reparation Pay

History reveals that reparation would not be a question today had Democratic President Andrew Johnson chosen to sign Senate Bill 60. Since Johnson's veto (of Senate Bill 60), the door for reparations remained closed for 122 years. In 1988, Congress opened that door with the passage of the Civil Liberties Act of 1988. Under this new bill, Japanese interment victims received an apology plus $20,000 each in reparation pay. In 1993, the victims of the Rosewood (Florida) massacre received reparations from the State of Florida. On May 16, 1997, President Clinton issued an apology to the victims of the Tuskegee Experiment and paid the African American victims a total of $10,000,000 in reparations. **In each case, the party that committed the wrong paid the reparations.** Because the precedent has been set, the Plaintiffs in this case feel the Defendants [Democratic Party] should offer an apology and pay reparations for the wrong that they committed against African Americans from 1792 to 2002.

Under the Civil Liberties Act of 1988 the law calls for

1. The acknowledgement of the fundamental injustices of the victims

2. An apology by the group, organization or person who committed the act

3. Providing a public education fund to inform the public on what actually took place

4. Making restitution to those individuals who were wronged

5. And making more credible and sincere declarations of the concern by those who committed the act....

We submit our Prayer for Relief based on the criteria of the Civil Liberties Act of 1988 and Section 1983 of Title 42 of the U.S. Codes.

Prayer for Injunctive Relief

Note: This Prayer for Relief was part of the second lawsuit of April 2005. The first lawsuit was filed on December 10, 2004 and asked for monetary damages.

WHEREFORE, Plaintiffs, on Plaintiffs' own behalf and on behalf of the Class, prays for injunctive relief as follows:

1. That the court order the Defendants to issue a formal public apology to African Americans for the wrong that was committed during the duration of the Defendants' tenure as an organization or political party and in addition to the public apology place the apology on their official website.

2. The Plaintiffs ask that as an extension to their apology the Defendants provide funding to fund educational projects depicting all of the historical events and acts that were highlighted in this lawsuit as well as other historical events not mentioned—any and all events that reflect the true relationship between blacks and Democrats from 1792 to 1965. The projects should include and not be limited to: the production of printed materials, short films, featured films, and CDs–all to be made available to every American public and private K-12 school and public libraries at cost (including shipping and handling). We further ask that the Lead Plaintiff and the consultants of his choice be paid a consulting fee including traveling and all other related expenses to help produce these educational materials. The consulting fee will be the standard consulting fee for similar types of educational projects. Under the Civil Liberties Act of 1988 funds to educate the *public* of the wrongs that took place were part of the redress.

3. Awarding Plaintiff fees and expenses incurred in this action, including reasonable allowance of fees for attorneys and appropriate consultant fees for the research and development of this case and for the previously related case of CV04-2442.

4. Granting such other and further relief as the Court may deem just and proper.

Plaintiff Demands Without Oral Arguments

Under the penalty of perjury of the United States the statements made in this complaint are true and correct, based on the Plaintiff's investigation and research.

Signed this _____ of _____ 2004 & 2005

by

Wayne Perryman Pro Se Plaintiff

Respectfully submitted,

Wayne Perryman, Pro Se

P.O. Box 245

Mercer Island, WA 98040

(206) 232-5575 FAX (206) 232-2904

Democrats' Response

In response to my brief, attorney David Burman (of Perkins Coie law firm representing the DNC) submitted a *Motion to Dismiss*. The following are portions of their basic arguments to dismiss the case (beginning with paragraph 2 of page 3 through pages 4 and 5).

"Conceding the horrors of slavery and racism, and even accepting for the purpose of this motion that the Democratic Party in the past supported or acquiesced in those horrors, nowhere does the complaint make the required showing of any "concrete and personalized injury" necessary to confer standing....

"Plaintiff references the 'insidious, pervasive and constant impact that racism and discrimination have on the lives of black people in America today,' and concludes that 'after 168 years of racist indoctrination by Democrats, African Americans still struggle with' a host of social problems, including employment discrimination, racial profiling, disproportionately long prison sentences and housing discrimination....

"These general allegations of injuries suffered by an entire race, deriving from conduct beginning two centuries ago are insufficient to establish standing...

"The generalized injuries that Plaintiff states have been suffered by all African Americans as a result of the Defendant's alleged actions simply do not constitute actionable claims...

"Plaintiff's Complaint is devoid of any allegations showing how Defendant's alleged conduct has harmed him as an individual. As such he is unable to meet the most basic requirement of standing and his Complaint must be dismissed...."

Appeal to the Ninth Circuit Court of Appeals

No. 05-35890

UNITED STATES COURT OF APPEALS

FOR THE NINTH CIRCUIT COURT

Wayne Perryman on behalf of himself
& African American Citizens of USA

Petitioner –Appellant

V

Democratic National Committee, et al.,

Respondent - Appellee

The Appellant's Reply Brief
No. CV05-0722-JCC

Wayne Perryman
Pro Se Litigant
P.O. Box 256
Mercer Island, WA 98040
Telephone (206) 232-5575
FAX (206) 232-2904

Arguments Regarding Standing

In the **_motion to dismiss_**, both the Defendant and the District Court agreed (therefore **stipulating**) that the Appellant had indeed been injured, but his injuries were the same injuries that were "*inflicted on all African Americans over two hundred years and affect the* *entire African American community."* It should be understood that the court's statement regarding *"injuries affecting the entire African American community"* is precisely the reason why the Appellant filed the suit. The Appellant believes an apology will serve as redress for the two hundred years of racist practices and policies that were planned, programmed and promulgated by the Democratic Party.

In their arguments to dismiss, the Defendant cited *Lujan v Defenders of Wildlife* for their position on *"standing"* and compared this current case with the *African American Slave Descendant Case* where the Plaintiffs were seeking unspecified monetary damages as a redress for slavery. In their arguments, the Defendants overlooked the fact that the Plaintiff in this case, is not seeking monetary damages as redress for slavery nor is he trying to establish *"standing"* based on injuries that ***may occur*** sometime in the ***future***. This case is based primarily on the subsequent events that followed slavery (from 1865 to 1965) and on injuries that have already occurred—not injuries that ***may occur***, which was the primary focus of *Lujan*.

It was never the intent of the court in *Lujan* to ignore **stipulated** injuries that had already impacted an entire race, but rather to prevent individual plaintiffs from seeking redress on **anticipated subjective** injuries that ***may*** occur sometime in the future (as indicated in the affidavits of Ms. Joyce Kelly and Amy Skilbred, two members of the *Defenders*. Id. at 145-146).

In the *Lujan* case, the court determined that Kelly and Skilbred's allegations of **anticipated** personal injuries that may result from the extinction of certain endangered species was *"pure speculation and fantasy."* The court stated that *"The Plaintiff alleges only an injury at some indefinite future time and the acts necessary to make the injury happen are at least partly within the Plaintiff's own control."* Such is not the case in the matter that is currently before the court. The injuries alleged in this case, are injuries that have been clearly established and stipulated, not merely anticipated.

The court added, *"The 'injury in fact' test requires that the party seeking review be himself **among** the injured."* Id., at 734-735. The Plaintiffs, Kelly and Skilbred were not ***among*** the injured, because in the

Lujan case, no injuries had occurred at the time the matter was brought to trial. However in this case, the District Court ruled that as an African American, the Appellant's injuries are the same injuries that the *"entire African American Community suffered over a two-hundred-year period."* In making the statement, the court acknowledged two important facts: (1) Injuries have been sustained by an entire race and (2) The Appellant was **_among_** those who were injured.

In the case of *Lujan* the intent of the court was clear when it made reference to *"particularized," "concrete,"* and *"injuries in fact"* rather than speculative injuries that **_may occur_**. In the *Lujan* case, there were no *particularized, concrete, or injuries in fact*, because there were no injuries. The entire case was based solely on the possibility that injuries may occur as a result of damage to endangered species. In *Lujan*, the court was simply saying plaintiffs can not bring a matter to court on the possibility of an injury sometime in the future. In contrast, the matter that is currently before the court is based on well-documented and well-publicized injuries that have occurred over a span of two hundred years. If there were no **serious injuries** to individuals like the Appellant and the entire *African American Community*, the need for a multitude of civil rights legislation and Presidential Executive Orders during the 1960s would not have been necessary. The fact that such legislation was enacted proves that the injuries were indeed *concrete* and *particularized* rather than insignificant and generalized. This legislation was specifically designed to stop the pain brought about by the racist practices that were a standard part of the Democrats' agenda for over 170 years (1792-1964).

If both the District Court and the Defendant are correct and the Appellant's injuries are the same injuries as those suffered by the *"entire African American community,"* then the central question before the Court of Appeals should be whether or not the injuries inflicted on the *entire African American Community over a two-hundred-year period* are *"injuries in fact"* or *"concrete"* enough to establish *"standing."* S*tanding* would give the court jurisdiction and the legal justification to order the Defendant to issue an apology for redress.

Documented Evidence of Injuries

Since the establishment of our jurisprudence system, there has never been a case before the court where a plaintiff was merely seeking **an apology** as redress on behalf of a race of people *"that had been injured over a two-hundred-year period."* If the *entire African American community's* injuries are not *injuries in fact*, then the injuries to the Jews at the hands of the Nazi Party could not be *injuries in fact*. History reveals that their experiences are strikingly similar to African Americans.

As stated in his brief to the District Court, the Appellant argued that when discussions are raised regarding an *entire race* being affected by racist practices and policies, we often refer to the Jewish Holocaust. But the Jewish Holocaust (although similar to the African American experience), did not occur in the United States nor did it take place over a period of two hundred years. Their inhumane treatment lasted twelve years, not two hundred years.

Some leading historians now suggest that the Nazi Party's agenda of *racial purity* may have been inspired by the Democratic Party's agenda of *racial supremacy*. The striking similarities between what happened to Jews under the rule of Germany's Nazi Party versus what happened to blacks in states that were under the rule of the Democratic Party, are worth noting in establishing *standing* in this case. The following are a few of those similarities:

Oppression

From 1933 to 1945 the Nazi Party oppressed millions of Jews (twelve years). From 1792 to 1964, the Democratic Party oppressed millions of blacks (172 years).

Racist Legislation

The Nazi Party passed racist legislation to deny Jews their rights as citizens. The Democratic Party also passed racist legislation to deny blacks their rights as citizens. The Democrats' legislative accomplishments include: Fugitive Slave Laws, Black Codes, Jim Crow Laws, the Repeal Act of 1894, and a multitude of other repressive legislation at the federal and state level.

Education

The Nazi Party refused to let Jewish children attend public schools with German children. The Democratic Party refused to let black children attend school with white children (and openly supported the Board of Education in Topeka, Kansas, in the case of *Brown v The Board of Education*).

Forced Labor

The Nazi Party forced Jews to work in labor camps giving them nothing or little in return. During slavery, Democrats used Fugitive Slave Laws, and later during Reconstruction, they used Black Codes to force blacks to work for their former slave masters.

Denied Citizenship

Under Nazi rule, the party took away the Jews' citizenship. Under Democratic rule, Democrats exhausted every effort to deny blacks their constitutional rights as citizens starting with the *Dred Scott* decision, the *Slaughterhouse Case*, *Plessy v. Ferguson* and by collectively voting against the 13th, 14th, and 15th amendments.

Forbidding Intermarriage

Under Nazi rule, Jews were prohibited from marrying Germans. Under the Democratic rule (using Black Codes and other legislation) blacks were prohibited from marrying whites.

Businesses Taken and Destroyed

The Nazi Party confiscated and/or destroyed Jewish businesses. Southern Democrats also confiscated land and destroyed black businesses (1867-1945). According to an Associated Press investigation, blacks in regions under Democrat control lost over two million acres of land. Noted historians also report that in Democratic controlled regions several middle class black communities were burned to the ground. Those communities included: Wilmington, North Carolina, Rosewood, Florida, and the Greenwood district in Tulsa, Oklahoma, just to name a few.

Synagogues and Churches Destroyed

Under Nazi rule, synagogues were destroyed. Under Democratic rule, several black churches were burned and bombed during a 172-year period (1792 to 1964).

Terrorist Activities and Murder

The Nazi Party used their SS division to terrorize and murder Jews at random. The Democratic Party also used their terrorist divisions (including the Klan) to terrorize and murder blacks at random.

Hatred

The Nazi Party used education and literature to promote hatred against Jews. The Democratic Party and the Klan used political campaigns to promote hatred against blacks (and later targeted Jews, Catholics, and homosexuals).

Political Offices

Under Nazi rule Jews were prohibited from running for public office. Under Democratic rule, blacks were beaten, killed, and driven out of office to discourage others from seeking public office. The first black to be elected to Congress in a Democratic controlled state was Barbara Jordan in 1973, 181 years after the party was formed.

Destruction of Lives

The Nazi Party took the lives of millions of Jews during a twelve-year period using legislation and terrorist activities. Democrats used slavery, the Ku Klux Klan, and racist legislation to accomplish the same over a 172-year period (1792 to 1964).

Torture

The Nazi Party through their SS division tortured millions of Jews. The Democratic Party through their courts and their terrorist organizations, tortured, hung, shot, mutilated, and burned to death millions of blacks.

Apology

Eventually the Jews did receive an apology. However, the records will show that the Democratic Party has never issued an apology for the atrocities that they committed against blacks, even though they have received requests from the Appellant to do so. Instead, they are spending thousands of dollars in attorney fees to avoid issuing such an apology.

Conclusion

According to psychologists, sociologists, historians, and other experts in human behavior, the sum of all of these racist activities should constitute a ***concrete injury*** and all of these horrific acts can be traced to the Democratic Party.

The Defendants' racist past is well documented in the chronicles of history, Congressional Records, newspaper articles, and in their own Political Platforms. The records will show, the Defendants were more than willing to issue an apology when an all-white United States Senate requested an apology, but when the African American Appellant requested a similar apology using the same evidence that the Senate used, the Defendant told the black Appellant he had to establish *"standing."* This is indicative of their racist way of thinking.

The Defendants have argued that the Appellant's injuries are the same as the injuries inflicted on African Americans over a two-hundred-year period. But what they failed to report is that they were the ones who inflicted these injuries.

Summary

In the *African American Slave Descendant Case*, there were **_no_** injuries to the descendants, as a direct result of **slavery**. In the *Lujan v Defenders of Wildlife Case*, there were no injuries, just a mere speculation that injuries **_may occur_** sometime in the future. But in the matter currently before the Court of Appeals, both the District Court and the Defendants stipulated the Appellant **had been injured** and his injuries are "*the **_same injuries_** that affected the entire African American Community for a period of two hundreds years.*" This stipulation, places the Appellant *among* the injured as *Lujan* requires. Unlike the injuries in *Lujan,* the Appellant's injuries and injuries to the "*entire African American community*" were **_severe_** enough to enact a multitude of civil rights legislation to put an end to them.

These injuries were "*concrete*"; they were "*an invasion of a legally protected interest*"; and they are "*traceable*" to the Democratic Party. The Appellant sincerely believes that a public apology would be the "*proper redress*" for such injuries. Based on these factors, the Appellant asks the Court of Appeals to overturn the District Court's ruling and grant the Appellant's motion for a Summary Judgment.

Respectfully submitted, under the penalty of perjury of the United States, on this 6th day of December 2005.

By

Wayne Perryman, Pro Se
P.O. Box 256
Mercer Island, WA 98040
(206) 232-5575
Doublebro@aol.com

Appeal to the United States Supreme Court

No.

In The
Supreme Court of the United States

Wayne Perryman on behalf of himself
and the African American Citizens of the United States

Petitioner

v.

Democratic National Committee and National Democratic Party

Respondent

ON PETITION FOR A WRIT OF CERTIORARI
to the
United States Supreme Court

PETITION FOR A WRIT OF CERTIORARI

Wayne Perryman
Pro Se Litigant
P.O. Box 256
Mercer Island, WA 98040
Telephone (206) 232-5575
FAX (206) 232-2904
E-Mail Doublebro@aol.com

QUESTION PRESENTED

1. Did the court err when it ignored *Cort v. Ash 422 U.S. 66 (1975),* which, in civil matters, gives a citizen the right to file a private cause of action in order to secure a *remedy* under 18 U.S.C. 610?

2. Did the court err when it determined that the Petitioner's injuries *"Stem from <u>the injury</u> inflicted on the entire African American community two hundred years ago,"* but failed to recognize that the evidence presented in this case did not refer to **one injury** or one event that occurred two hundred years ago, but rather the <u>collective</u> ongoing series of racist practices that were inflicted on the Petitioner and the *entire African American community* <u>over a two-hundred-year period</u>, more specifically from 1792 to 2002?

3. Did the court err when it failed to grant the Petitioner *"standing,"* when the evidence proved the Petitioner met all of the legal requirements of *Lujan v. Defenders of Wildlife 504 U.S. at 560* including tracing the injuries of the *entire African American community* to the Respondent's past racist practices and policies?

4. If the Petitioner's injury is the same injury that the entire class of which he is a member of has suffered during the past two hundred years, can the court consider the **collective** injuries of the entire class to establish *standing*, in a case that is seeking an apology on behalf of that class?

PARTIES TO THE PROCEEDING

Democratic National Committee and National Democratic Party

2

TABLE OF CONTENTS

TABLE OF AUTHORITIES

Cases

United States Statutes & Laws

CITATIONS OF REPORTS OF OPINIONS

ENTERED IN THE CASE

Wayne Perryman on behalf of himself and the African American Citizens of the United States v. Democratic National Committee: National Democratic Party Fed. R. App. P. 34(a)(2) (9th Cir. December 27, 2006). Appendix A-1.

BASIS FOR SUPREMENT COURT JURISDICTION

The Judgment of the Ninth Circuit Court of Appeals was entered on December 27, 2006 (Fed. R. App. P. 34(a)(2)). The jurisdiction of this Court is invoked under 28 U.S.C. 1254(1). The present petition is timely filed under 28 U.S.C. 2101(c) and under rule 13.3 of this court.

The court has jurisdiction under 28 U.S.C. 1254(1) and 18 U.S.C. 610 to review on a writ of certiorari the judgment of the federal court of appeals.

Constitutional Provisions

The Constitution of the United States' Fourteenth Amendment, Equal Protection Clause

STATEMENT OF THE CASE

On April 5, 2004, the Petitioner sent a letter to the Democratic National Committee (DNC) seeking an apology on behalf the African American community for their past racist practices. After receiving no response, the Petitioner filed the first class action case against the DNC on December 10, 2004, case no. CV 04-2442. The Honorable Marsha J. Pechman dismissed the case on April 5, 2005 without prejudice. On April 15, 2005 the Petitioner filed for an Injunctive Relief, seeking only an apology and no monetary damages, case no. CV 05-0722C. On July 22, 2005, the Honorable John C. Coughenour dismissed the case due to the lack of *"standing."* The Petitioner filed

5

a Motion for Reconsideration & Revision of the order. Motion was denied on August 9, 2005. Petitioner appealed the decision to the 9th Circuit Court of Appeal on August 29th 2005. The 9th Circuit Court of Appeals **_Affirmed_** the lower court's decision on December 27, 2006.

INTRODUCTION

The Respondent's past racist practices, <u>which caused</u> injury to the entire African American community during the past two hundred years, had a broad range of support, including support from the very court that is currently reviewing this case. **It was the United States Supreme Court's decisions in key civil rights cases** that gave the Respondent (the Democratic Party) the legal authority to inflict the **alleged** injuries on those whom the District Court referred to as the *"entire African American community."* Those cases include, but are not limited to: the *Dred Scott Decision*, the *Slaughterhouse Cases*, *Plessy v Ferguson* and the **<u>Civil Rights Cases of 1881</u>** that convinced the court that the 1875 Civil Rights Act was unconstitutional (**_<u>Civil Rights Cases 109 U.S. 3 (1881)</u>_**).

In his book the *Statutory History of the United States: Civil Rights Vol. I Vol. II*, Professor Bernard Schwartz of New York University School of Law provides an example of how discrimination against the Negro was sanctioned by the Supreme Court. Professor Schwartz said:

The Fourteenth Amendment provision designed directly to prevent discrimination against the emancipated race was the equal protection clause. In Plessy v. Ferguson, 163 U.S. 537 (1896), however, the Supreme Court construed that clause in a manner which enabled discrimination against the Negro to be condoned by law.... Plessy v. Ferguson gave the lie to the American ideal, so eloquently stated by Justice John Harlan in dissent there: "Our Constitution is color-blind, and neither knows nor tolerates classes among citizens." ...Upon Plessy was built the whole structure of segregation that has been at the heart of the [Democrats'] *Southern system of racial discrimination. So much was, indeed, conceded by the Supreme Court itself, including the 1873* Slaughterhouse *cases 16 Wall. 36 (1873).* (360)

In writing the opinion for the court in *Brown v. Board of Education*, Chief Justice Warren addresses how the **separate but equal doctrine** affected African American children. In that opinion, he wrote:

To separate them [black children] *from other children of similar age and qualifications solely because of their race generates a feeling of inferiority as to their status in the community that may affect their hearts and minds in a way unlikely ever to be undone. The effect of this separation in their educational opportunities was well stated by the finding in the Kansas case by a court which nevertheless felt compelled to rule against the Negro Plaintiff.*

Before rendering the decision in the Kansas case, the court issued the following statement: "*Segregation of white and colored children in public schools has a detrimental effect upon the colored children. The impact is greater when it has the sanction of the law; for the policy of separating the races is usually interpreted as denoting the inferiority of the negro group. A sense of inferiority affects the motivation of a child to learn. Segregation with the sanction of law, therefore, has a tendency to [retard] the educational and mental development of negro children and to deprive them of some of the benefits they would receive in a racial [ly] integrated school system.*" (364)

In the *Slaughterhouse* cases and other subsequent cases including *Plessy v. Ferguson*, it was the court's narrow interpretation of the 14th Amendment that allowed many racist practices to go unchallenged and unpunished under what the Democrats' claimed as state's rights, including their right to own slaves and treat them as property and not as people. In recent years, the court has made great efforts to reverse those decisions with such cases as *Brown v. Board of Education,* but the damage was already done. Now the court is faced with another interpretation of the law which could have a profound impact on the African American community. Will it (as it did with its narrow interpretation of 14th Amendment) revert back to the days of the *Slaughterhouse Cases* and give a narrow interpretation of what is an **"injury** *in fact"* and discount the <u>collective</u> injuries of the *entire African American community*, injuries that resulted from the Respondent's racist practices?

The evidence presented in this case can not begin to tell the full story of the atrocities that were committed by the Respondent. It would take volumes to give an accurate depiction of what really took place during the past two hundred years. If the court finds that the injuries inflicted on the *entire African American community* during the past two hundred years are not *injuries in fact*, it would be very difficult for any reasonable person to ascertain, what constitutes an *"injury."*

Racism in America was politically driven. Without the political backing of those who made up and formed the powerful Democratic Party, a Party that gave their lives and spent billions to preserve the institution of slavery and the system of Jim Crow, slavery would have ended a hundred years earlier, and Jim Crow would have died in the womb of those who conceived it. Contrary to public opinion, racism **was not** something that the entire white race engaged in. Racism was the political agenda of a political party—made up of individuals who chose to use this deadly disease to cover their own insecurities—in their relentless quest for wealth and power.

NINTH CIRCUIT AFFIRMED

On December 21, 2006, in the matter of *Wayne Perryman on behalf of himself and African American Citizens of the United States v. Democratic National Committee: National Democratic Party* (Case No. 05-35890), the Ninth Circuit Court of Appeals *affirmed* the decision of the United States District Court of Western Washington (in case No. CV 05-00722-JCC). On July 22, 2005, the District Court decided that the Petitioner lacked *standing* because his alleged injuries:

- ***Stem from the injury inflicted on all African Americans over two-hundred years ago and affect the entire African American community.***

ARGUMENTS

After reviewing all the evidence, the lower court, the Respondent, and the Ninth Circuit Court of Appeals all stipulated that the Petitioner had been *"injured,"* but felt his *"injury stems from **the injury** inflicted on African Americans 200 years ago and affect the entire African American community."* The court's statement suggests or implies that 200 years ago <u>one single event</u> in history caused "**the injury**." But what the court but failed to recognize is that the evidence presented in this case did not refer to <u>one injury</u> or <u>a single event</u> in history two hundred years ago but rather a series of court decisions and racist acts from 1792 to 2002 that collectively *injured* the *entire African American community.*

Petitioner's legal grounds to secure an Injunctive Relief

While basing their decision on *Cato v. United States, 70 F.3d 1103, 1109 (9th Cir 1995), African-American Slave Descendant Litig., 304 F. Supp. 2d 1027, 1052 (N.D. Ill. 204) and Lujan v. Defenders of Wildlife, 504 U.S. at 560,* the court erred when it ignored *Cort v. Ash* 422 U.S. 66 (1975) which, in civil matters, gives a citizen the right to file a private cause of action in order to obtain a re*medy* under 18 U.S.C. 610.

The Petitioner in this case is a *citizen* and a member of the African American community. He is seeking to *secure* an *Injunctive Relief* in a private cause of action involving a civil matter under 18 U.S.C. 610 (as in the Bethlehem case of *Cort v. Ash*). In ***Cort v. Ash*** the court decided that:

- *A private cause of action, whether brought by a citizen to secure injunctive relief or by a stockholder to secure injunctive or derivative damage relief [is] proper to remedy violation 610 under 18 U.S.C. 610. Id, at 424. We granted certiorari, 419 U.S. 992 (1974).*

9

Perryman Case Differs from Cases Cited by the Court

The court also erred when it compared the current case with those cited in its decision. A careful review of the cases cited by the court will reveal that the only similarities between those cases and the case that is currently before this court is that both involve African Americans.

Cato v. United States and the *African American Slave Descendant* cases were based ***solely*** on the events surrounding ***slavery*** and the ***subjective unproven injuries*** that the Plaintiffs believed resulted from slavery. There was also a question regarding how to determine who was injured. The case that is currently before this court ***is not*** based on slavery or the subjective injuries resulting from slavery. Although it includes or starts with slavery, it concentrates and focuses on the subsequent events that followed slavery in order to establish a *pattern of practice*. Additionally, in the current case there was never a question as to whether or not the *"entire African American community"* (of which the Petitioner is a member) had been injured by these racist practices. In several landmark decisions and legislative mandates, the courts, Congress, historians, and social scientists have all agreed that the racist practices that followed slavery have had a profound negative impact on the *"entire African American community."* They also agree that such practices can be traced to the Democratic Party's policies and practices (the party that was commonly referred to as the *Party of White Supremacy*). In contrast, in *Cato v. United States* and the *African American Slave Descendant* case, the Plaintiffs (1) failed to provide evidence to prove that the racist practices that followed slavery resulted from the residual effects of slavery or that such practices could be traced to the Defendants; (2) nor could they prove that the Defendants actually owned slaves.

The lower court also cited the *Lujan v. Defender of Wildlife* case in deciding that the Appellant did not have "**standing**." The court stated that the Petitioner's injuries were **"generalized"** and the same as those suffered by **the entire African American community**, thus implying that the collective ***injuries to the entire African American commu-***

nity during the past two hundred years were either insignificant or non-existence. In the *Lujan* case, no injuries had occurred at the time of trial. The entire case (*Lujan*) was based on injuries that **may occur** sometime in the future if the extinction of certain endangered species actually took place. To compare the current case with either *Lujan* where there were no injuries, or to *Cato* and the *Slave Descendant* case which failed to show any direct relationship between slavery and the modern-day practices of racism, is to imply or suggest that: (1) the *African American Community was not grossly injured* by the Democrats' racist practices; or (2) that there was no relationship between the Democrats' past racist policies and practices and the injuries suffered by the *entire African American community.*

Racist acts can be traced to the Respondent

(Democrats).

The Petitioner is not trying to establish *standing* based on injuries that may occur sometime in the future (as in *Lujan*), nor is he attempting to tie the injuries of racism to slavery (as in the cases of *Cato* and the *African American Descendant* case). Additionally, unlike the Plaintiffs in the *Slave Reparation* cases, the Petitioner is not attempting to establish *standing* based on the profits of U.S. Corporations or by genealogy association. The Petitioner in this case has provided irrefutable evidence (including the Respondent's own published political platforms from 1844 to 1892) which proves that the injuries suffered by the *entire African Americans community during the past two hundred years* (of which the Petitioner is a member) can be traced to the Democratic Party. The evidence submitted reveals the following:

Democrats as a political party supported slavery and gave their lives to preserve the institution of slavery as indicated in their **Platform of 1844** which said: *Congress has no power to interfere with or control the domestic institutions of the several States; and that such States are the sole and proper judges of everything pertaining to their own affairs.... That all efforts, by <u>abolitionist</u> and others, made to induce*

11

Congress to interfere with <u>questions of slavery</u>....are calculated to lead to the most alarming and dangerous consequences.

Democrats as a political party promoted, supported, and sponsored Fugitive Slave Laws as indicated in their Platforms of 1852, 1856, and 1860 which stated the following: "a. **[1852]** *Resolved: That the forgoing proposition covers and was intended to embrace the whole subject of slavery agitation in Congress; and therefore the <u>Democratic Party</u> of the Union, standing on this national platform, will abide by and adhere to a faithful execution of the acts known as the compromise measures* [referring to the Missouri Compromise to expand slavery] *and the acts <u>for reclaiming fugitives</u> from service or labor. The <u>Democratic Party</u> will resist all attempts at renewing, in Congress or out of it, the agitation of the slavery question, under whatever shape or color the attempt may be made."* **[1856]** *"Resolved: That we reiterate with <u>renewed energy</u> of purpose the well considered declaration of former Conventions upon the sectional issue of <u>Domestic slavery,</u> and concerning the reserve rights of the States."* **[1860]** *"Resolved: That the enactments of the State Legislatures to defeat the faithful execution of the <u>Fugitive Slave Law</u>, are hostile in character, subversive of the Constitution, and revolutionary in their effect...."*

Democrats as a political party promoted, supported, and fought for the decision in the *Dred Scott* case, a decision that classified blacks as property and not as people. After the decision, the following was placed in their **1860 Platform**: *"Resolved, That the Democratic Party will abide by <u>the decision</u> of the United States Supreme Court...."* Historian David Barton reports that the Democratic Party was so pleased with the outcome of the *Dred Scott* case that they printed several copies of the decision and distributed them to the public during their 1860 presidential campaign.

Democrats as a political party successfully promoted and supported the *Slaughterhouse* cases to nullify the 14th Amendment. These cases originated out of the state of Louisiana. At the time, Louisiana was a violent Democrat stronghold (see letter from New Orleans later in the brief).

Democrats as a political party promoted and supported Judge John Ferguson (Democrat) in the case of *Plessy v. Ferguson* to preserve their system of segregation. In this brief, we will provide evidence to prove that Democrats established segregation through legislation (Jim Crow laws), litigation (*Plessy v. Ferguson*) and by assassinations and intimidations (via Ku Klux Klan).

In an effort to continue their long history of denying black children a quality education, Democrats as a political party, opposed the decision in *Brown v. Board of Education of Topeka, Kansas*. History Professor James McPherson of Princeton University revealed such efforts in his book: *The Abolitionist Legacy from Reconstruction to the NAACP*. Professor McPherson said: "*Southern hostility to Yankee teachers sometimes went beyond ostracism and verbal abuse. In times of political excitement during Reconstruction many missionaries were threatened, beaten, and murdered. The American Missionary Association tried for several years to cooperate with local school boards* [of the South]. *So long as* <u>*Republicans*</u> *were in power this arrangement worked out reasonably well. But when the* <u>*Democrats*</u> *began to regain control of the South, the dual support foundered and eventually collapsed.... The 1874 elections were a particularly tense time; as one teacher put it, to be for weeks in a constant expectation* <u>**of being murdered**</u> *or burned out, and without losing faith in God, is something of a strain on the nerves...."*

Democrats as a political party consistently opposed anti-lynching legislations. Many of the lynchings that these laws were designed to put an end to were attended by Democratic senators, congressmen, governors, judges, sheriffs, and mayors. In the book *Without Sanctuary* (with the foreword written by our current Democratic congressman John Lewis), it details several lynchings that were attended by Democratic officials. The following are two lynchings covered in the book: the lynchings of the Sam Hose and Mary Turner. Both are very typical of the 5,000-plus documented lynchings that took place in the Democrats' Jim Crow South where 95 percent of the black population resided.

    a. **[Sam Hose]** *After stripping Hose of his clothes and chaining him to a tree, the self-appointed executioners stacked* *kerosene-soaked wood high around him. Before saturating Hose with oil and applying the torch, they cut off his ears, fingers, and genitals, and skinned his face. While some in the crowd plunged knives into the victim's flesh, others watched with unfeigning satisfaction, the contortions of Sam Hose's body as flames rose, distorting his features, causing his eyes to bulge out of their sockets and rupturing his veins. The only sounds that came from the victim's lips, even as his blood sizzled in the fire. were, "Oh my God! Oh, Jesus." Before Hose's body had even cooled, his heart and liver were removed and cut into several pieces and his bones were crushed into small particles. The crowd fought over these souvenirs. Shortly after the lynching, one of the participants reportedly left for the state capitol, hoping to deliver a slice of Sam Hose's heart to the Democratic governor of Georgia, who would call Sam Hose's deeds, "the most diabolical in the annals of crime."*

b. [Mary Turner] *After tying her ankles together, they hung her from a tree, head downward. Dousing her clothes with gasoline, and burned them [the clothes] from her body. While she was still alive, someone used a knife ordinarily reserved for splitting hogs to cut open the woman's abdomen. The baby fell from her womb to the ground and cried briefly, whereupon a member of the [terrorist] mob crushed the baby's head beneath his heel. Hundreds of bullets were then fired into Mary Turner's body....*

Democrats as a political party opposed the **1871 Ku Klux Klan Act**. The act was designed to stop Klan activities (see portions of the debates on the act later in the brief).

Democrats as a political party consistently opposed every piece of civil rights legislation introduced from 1863 to 1965 including opposing the 13th, 14th, and 15th Amendments as indicated in their **1872 Platform** which stated: *"We pledge ourselves to oppose any reopening of the questions* [regarding our party's compliance with] *the thirteenth, fourteenth, and fifteenth Amendments.*" See Democrats' debates opposing the passage of 13th, 14th, and 15th Amendments further in the brief.

Democrats as a political party opposed the **1867 Reconstruction Act** and fought to destroy Reconstruction as stated in their **1868 Platform** which asked for: *"The abolition of the Freedman's Bureau: and all political instrumentalites designed to secure Negro Supremacy*." The **Platform of 1868** also praised President Andrew Johnson for his efforts in vetoing the 1866 Civil Rights Act and Senate Bill 60, the Reparation Bill to give blacks 40 acres of land. For his consistent efforts to deny African Americans their constitutional rights as citizens of the United States, the party placed the following commendation in their **1868 Platform**: *"…And we do declare and resolve that the President of the United States, Andrew Johnson, in exercising the power of his high office in resisting the aggressions of Congress upon the Constitutional rights of the States and the people, is entitled to the gratitude of the whole American people; and in behalf of the* **Democratic Party**, *we tender him our thanks for his patriotic efforts in that regards*."

Democrats as a political party opposed the **1875 Civil Rights Act**. In their **1876 Platform** they stated the following: *"We denounce the resumption clause of the Act of 1875 and we here demand its repeal."* The Democratic Party used their Platform of 1876 to denounce the passage of the **1875 Civil Rights Act**, but they chose not to denounce their new Jim Crow laws that were legislated during that same year (1875) in regions where over 95 percent of the black population resided.

Democrats as a political party introduced and then passed the **1894 Appeals Act** shortly after they took over Congress. The Appeals Act was designed to overturn portions of previous civil rights legislation.

Democrats had outspoken powerful leaders that openly shared their racist vision and philosophy. Their racist statements and philosophy earned them the title of the *"Party of White Supremacy."* The following are a few examples of statements taken from Congressional Records and from the chronicles of history.

- On April 29, 1861 President Jefferson Davis told his Democratic supporters that: *"Under the supervision of __the superior race__, their [__blacks'__] labor had been so directed not only to allow a gradual and marked amelioration of their own condition, but to convert hundreds of thousands of square miles of wilderness into cultivated lands covered with a prosperous people; towns and cities had sprung into existence, and had rapidly increased in wealth and population under the social system of the South...; which the labor **of African slaves was and is indispensable...."**

- Speaking for the Democratic Party, Democratic Congressman Fernando Wood of New York presented the following argument in their opposition to the passage of the **13__th__ Amendment**. Woods told Congress: *"The proposed amendment to abolish slavery in the states of the Union is unjust, a breach of good faith and utterly irreconcilable.... It involves __the extermination of all white men of the southern States__, and the forfeiture of all the land and other property belonging to them. Negroes and military colonists will take the place of the race [that will be] blotted out of existence."*

- **Regarding the 14__th__ Amendment Democratic Congressman Andrew Rogers from New Jersey** said, the proposed amendment was *"...An attempt to in-graft upon the Constitution of the United States one of the **most dangerous, most wicked, most intolerant, and most outrageous propositions ever introduced into this house**. God save the people of the South from degradation by **which they would be obliged to go to the polls and vote side by side with the Negro!"***

- Speaking for the Democrats on the **15__th__ Amendment**, Congressman Thomas Hendricks said, *" I do not believe that the Negro race and the white race can mingle in the exercise of political power and bring good results to society.... There is*

*a difference not only in their physical appearance and con-
formation**,** but there is a difference morally and intellectually,
and I do not believe that the two races can mingle successfully in the management of government.* *I do not believe that
they will add to the common intelligence of the country when
we make them voters."*

- During the debates on the **Ku Klux Klan Act of 1871** Senator **William Stoughton, the Republican from Michigan,**
said: *"The evidence taken before the Senate committee in
relations to the outrages, lawlessness, and violence in North
Carolina establishes the following propositions: The Ku Klux
Klan organization exists throughout the State, has a **political
purpose**, and is composed of the members of the **Democratic**
or Conservative Party. This organization has sought to carry
out its purposes by murders, whippings, intimidation, and
violence against it opponents. It not only binds its members
to execute decrees of crime, but protects them against conviction and punishment. All of the offenders in this order, which
has established **reign of terrorism** and bloodshed throughout
the State - not one has yet been convicted....We may concede,
Mr. Speaker, that if this system of violence is to continue in the
South, the **Democratic Party** will secure the ascendancy...."*

- During the debates on the **1875 Civil Rights Act**, Democratic
Congressman Willard Saulsbury from Delaware argued this
bill was designed so *"that colored men shall sit at the same
table beside the white guest, that he shall enter the same parlor and take his seat beside the wife and daughter of the white
ma*n*, whether the white man is willing or not, because you
prohibit discrimination against him...."*

- During the 1868 Presidential Campaign, Democrats publicly
referred to Republicans as ***"Nigger Lovers"*** and proudly displayed their campaign posters which said***: "This Is a White
Man's Country - Let the White Men Rule****."*

- In 1898 during a major election in Wilmington, North Carolina, the Democrats' campaign slogan was one word, *"Nigger."*

- Senator Ben Tillman of South Carolina told America: *"We reorganized the **Democratic Party** with one plank, and the only plank, namely, **that this is a white man's country, and white men must govern it."** On March 23, 1909 Tillman told the United States Senate that he defended violence against black men, claiming that "southern white women will not submit to the black man gratifying his lust on our wives and daughters without lynching him."*

- Senator James K. Vardman (1913), another powerful Democratic Senator from Mississippi, said: *"I am just as opposed to the Negro educator, Booker T. Washington as a voter, with all his Anglo-Saxon re-enforcements, as I am to the coconut-headed, chocolate-colored, typical little coon, Andy Dotson, who blacks my shoes every morning."*[31]

[Note: The Plaintiff's one-hundred-page original brief to the District Court included several more pages of citations from Congressional Records along with (video) history documentaries from PBS and the History Channel.]

Our United States Senate also records the racist practices of Democrats. Those records include the Senate's investigations of voting irregularities in areas controlled by Democrats (the South). The investigations became a part of *Senate Report No. 579* of the 48th Congress in 1871. On November 1, 1871, John Childers of Livingston, Alabama, was interviewed by a member of the Senate Select Committee. The following is a portion of his interview as documented by Herbert Aptheker (in his book, *Documentary History of the Negro People in the United States Vol. 2*:

---

31 , *Black Americans*, 59.

Question: *Did you ever hear any threats made by **Democrats** against Negroes of what would be done* [to him] *if he voted the radical* [meaning Republican] *ticket?*

Answer: I have had threats on myself. I can tell them.

Question: *What kind of threats were made to you?*

Answer: *I have had threats that if we all would vote the **Democratic ticket** we would be well thought of, and the white men of the county – the old citizens of the county – would protect us; and every struggle or trouble we got into we could apply to them for protection, and they would assist us.*

Question: *Where did you hear that said?*

Answer: *I have heard it often. At the last election it was given to me. There was a man standing here in the court-house door; when I started to the ballot-box he told me he had a coffin already made for me, because he thought I was going to vote the radical* [meaning Republican] *ticket....*

In the Democrats' **1892 Platform** they voiced strong opposition to federal intervention into the voting practices of the South. Their platform stated that the party was opposed to *"Federal control of elections and Deputy Marshals at every polling place."*

In 1888, several black ministers from New Orleans came together and wrote a letter to Congress. The following is a portion of that letter:

To the People of the United States:

*We, citizens of New Orleans, as well as of neighboring parishes, from which we have been driven away without warrant or law, assembled in mass meeting at New Orleans, La, on Wednesday, August 22, 1888 at Geddes Hall, declare and assert: That **a reign of terror exists** in many parts of the state; that the laws are suspended and the officers of the government,*

from the governor down, *afford no protection to the lives and property of the people against armed bodies of whites, who shed innocent blood and commit deeds of savagery unsurpassed in the dark ages of mankind.*

*For the past twelve years we have been most effectively disfranchised and robbed of our political rights. While denied the privilege in many places of voting for the party and candidates of our choice, acts of violence have been committed to compel us to vote against the dictates of our conscience for the **Democratic Party**, and the Republican ballots cast by us have been counted for the <u>Democratic candidates</u>. The press, the pulpit, the commercial organizations, **and executive authority of the State** have given both open and silent approval of all these crimes. In addition to these methods, there seems to be a deep scheme to reduce the Negroes of the State to a condition of abject serfdom and peonage.*

*These acts are done in deliberate <u>defiance of the Constitution and the laws of the United States</u>, which are so thoroughly nullified that the Negroes who bore arms in defense of the Union have no protection or shelter from them within the borders of Louisiana. During the past twelve months our people have suffered from the lawless regulators as never before and since the carnival of bloodshed conducted by the **Democratic Party** in 1868.*

A single volume would scarcely afford sufficient space to enumerate the outrage our people have suffered, and are daily suffering at the hand of their oppressors. They are flagrantly deprived of every right guaranteed them by the Constitution ...."[32]

---

32 Witcover, Documentary History of the Negro People Vol.2. 741-743

In the book, *The Party of the People: A History of the Democrats* (2003), author Jules Witcover sums it up this way: *"Forcing black suffrage on the South, however was, anathema to many Northern Democrats. They assured their Southern brethren that they had supported the war to preserve the union only, not to give blacks equal rights with whites."* (228)

Democrats' Opposition to Civil Rights Legislation of

the 1960s

The strongest opposition to the passage of the 1964 Civil Rights Act and the Voting Rights Act of 1965 came from the Democratic Party. The debates on the 1964 Civil Rights Act lasted over eighty days and took up some seven thousand pages of congressional records. It also resulted in the longest filibuster in U.S. Senate history, led by Senator Al Gore Sr. The following are just a few of the many Democrats who opposed both the 1964 Civil Rights Acts and the Voting Rights Acts of 1965 as recorded in the congressional records and reported in the book, *The Statutory History of the United States: Civil Rights Vol. I & II*, by Professor Bernard Schwartz of New York University School of Law.

Thomas Abernethy a Democrat from Mississippi, argued, *"If enacted* [the **1964 Civil Rights Act**], *it is certain to precipitate a tremendous upheaval in our society, but not the kind of upheaval that proponents apparently expect. I predict it will precipitate an upheaval that will make the sit-ins, kneel-ins, lie-ins, mass picketing, chanting, the march on Washington, and all other elements of the **so-called Negro revolutions**, all of these – I predict – will look like kindergarten play...."*

Howard Smith, a Democrat from Virginia, added the following arguments: *"In a few minutes, you will vote this monstrous instrument of oppression upon all of the American people.... **Be forewarned that the paid agents and leaders of the NAACP** can never permit this law to be gradually and peacefully accepted because that means an end to their well-paid activities."*

Olin Johnston, the Democrat from South Carolina, argued, *"Mr. President, this is indeed **the blackest day in the <u>U.S. Senate since 1875,</u> when the Congress passed a civil rights bill similar to this one.** It was eighty-nine years ago that the [Republican] Congress passed the nefarious Reconstruction era civil rights laws, <u>**identical with what we are now discussing, which were later declared unconstitutional by the U.S. Supreme Court**</u>. The Senate, if it passes this measure before us, will be compounding that unconstitutional error made back in 1875...."*

The following are a few of the many comments made by Democrats on the <u>**1965 Voting Rights Act**</u>:

Sam Erivin: *"This bill contains a provision which condemns without judicial trial the States of Alabama, Mississippi, Louisiana, Georgia, South Carolina, and Virginia and thirty-four counties in North Carolina; does it not?"*

Herman Talmadge, Democrat from Georgia: *"...Would not the bill deny to the States of Louisiana, Alabama, Mississippi, Georgia, North Carolina, and certain carefully selected counties in other areas the right to apply any literacy standards whatsoever for their voters?"*

Regarding a literacy test, Republican **Jacob Javits responded:** *"Think of the situation, for example in Mississippi, where whites are asked to interpret the following provision of the State Constitution: 'The Senate shall consist of Members chosen every four years by the qualified electors of the several districts.' Negroes are asked to interpret sections of the Constitution dealing with tax exemptions, the judicial sale of land, eminent domain, concurrent jurisdiction of chancery and circuit courts and habeas corpus. [And] **what about deprivation going back for a century, which inhered in segregated schools resulting in a median education level of the sixth grade for Negroes in Mississippi, as compared with an eleventh grade median for whites?** Then there is the intimidation by public officials; there are the bombings and shooting, the burnings, the beatings; and quite apart from them, **the denial of surplus food to Negroes who persist in their attempt to register,** as in Humphreys County, Mississippi; or* *the boycotting of Negroes, who had the temerity to register, by cutting off their bank loans and their grocery store credit."*

Democrats and their Klan Connection

In rendering its opinion in the *African American Slave Descendant* case, the court cited the works of the renowned historian, Professor James McPherson of Princeton University and his book: *The Battle Cry of Freedom*. In the Petitioner's brief, he also cited Professor McPherson and other renowned history professors, all of whom support the allegations that the racist practices alleged in this case not only injured the entire *African American community*, they can all be traced to the Democratic Party. Those scholars include: Professor James M. McPherson of Princeton University, Professor John Hope Franklin of Brooklyn College, Professor David Hebert Donald of Harvard, and Professor Allen W. Trelease of Harvard. These historians report that after the Civil War, when Republicans passed various laws and developed a number of social programs (such as the Freedmen's Bureau) to assist blacks, the Democrats became very angry and resentful. From their deep-seated anger several terrorist organizations were born—and in their efforts to gain the upper hand, the Democrats became the "*daddy*" of the Ku Klux Klan.

- The scholars of the *Encyclopedia Britannica* reported that: "*The **Democrats'** resentment led to the **formation** of the secret terroristic organizations such as the Ku Klux Klan and the Knight of the White Camelia. The use of fraud, violence and intimidation helped Southern conservatives regain control of their state governments; by the time the last federal troops had been withdrawn in 1877, the Democratic Party was back in power.*"[33]

- Professor Allen Trelease in his book, *Reconstruction: The Great Experience*, said: "*Klansmen in disguise rode through Negro neighborhoods at night warning Negroes either to cast **Democratic** ballots or stay away from the poll. The Klan also*

---

33 1992 *Encyclopedia Britannica*, 979.

sent notices to Republican office holders, warning them of death and telling them to either resign or leave the vicinity. Similar notices went to active Republicans of both races and often to the teachers of Negro schools as well. Klan activities created a reign of **terror** *in many localities and sometimes had the desired effect of demoralizing Negroes and Republicans.... <u>Republicans</u> of both races were threatened, beaten, shot, and murdered with impunity. In some areas Negroes stopped voting or voted the* **Democrat** *ticket as the Klan demanded....*" [34]

- Professors John Hope Franklin and Alfred Moss, authors of *From Slavery To Freedom* tell us that, "*The Camelias and the Klan were the most powerful of the secret orders. Armed with guns, swords, or other weapons, their members patrolled some parts of the South day and night. They used intimidation, force, ostracism in business and society, bribery at the polls, arson, and even murder to accomplish their deed. Depriving the Negro of political equality became, to them, a holy crusade in which a noble end justified any means. Negroes were run out of communities if they disobeyed orders to desist from voting; and the more resolute and therefore insubordinate blacks were whipped, maimed, and hanged.... For many white Southerners violence was still the surest means of keeping the Negroes politically impotent, and in countless communities they were not allowed, under penalties of reprisals, to show their faces in town on Election Day. It had looked as though the Civil War would break out anew as the <u>**Democrats resorted to every possible device to overthrow the radicals.**</u>*"[35] Professor Franklin went on to say, "*The personal indignities inflicted upon Negroes were so varied and so numerous as to defy classification or enumeration....*"[36]

- In his book, *The Abolitionist Legacy*, Professor James McPherson reported, "*In 1873, Louisiana became almost a synonym*

---

34 Trelease, *Reconstruction – The Great Experience,*
35 Franklin and Moss, *From Slavery to Freedom,*
36 Franklin, *Reconstruction After The Civil War*, 157.

*for chaos and violence. When Grant sent federal troops to install Kellogg in office [as governor], **Louisiana Democrats** were infuriated. They formed White Leagues which attacked black and white Republicans and took scores of lives."*[37]

- From his book entitled *Charles Sumner*, Harvard Professor David Hebert Donald reached the following conclusion: *"Congress could give the Negro the vote, but all over the South the Ku Klux Klan and other terrorist organizations systematically intimidated the freedmen, flogged or slaughtered their leaders, and drove whites who worked with them into exile. Congress could require federal troops to supervise the registration of voters, but Negroes were waylaid and butchered on the roads to the registration offices. Congress could suppress outright violence by military force, but it could do nothing to protect Negroes from landlords who told them bluntly: If you vote with that Yankee* [Republican] *party you shall not live on our land."*[38]

When the federal government launched various investigations to prosecute those who committed these horrific acts of terror, elected officials from the Democratic Party including Democratic governors, judges, mayors, sheriffs, state legislators, and U.S. senators exhausted every means to block their investigations. Loyal members of the Democratic Party were too loyal to cooperate with the investigations and with rare exception, most African Americans who witnessed the horrific atrocities were too frightened to cooperate and testify.

The Tool of Terrorism

History records that it was only in those southern regions controlled by Democrats that middle class black towns and communities were burned to the ground, towns such as Wilmington, North Carolina; Rosewood Florida; and the Greenwood District of Tulsa, Oklahoma,

---

37 McPherson, *The Abolitionist Legacy*, 40.
38 Donald, *Charles Sumner*, 420.

to name a few. Fear and terror were the ultimate goals of the Democrats and their terrorist organizations. They would terrorize and brutalize blacks so that **the infectious fear of whites** would be passed on to other blacks. It was also passed on to children through their protective parents, thus making black parents **"innocent agents"** of the Democrats' racist agenda to **keep blacks in their place**. See *Smith v. State, 21 Tex. App. 107 17 S.W. 552*; *State v. Carr, 28 Or. 389, 42 P. 215* regarding **innocent agents**.

The Petitioner's mother, like many African American mothers, became the Democrats' ***innocent agent***, much like the Jewish mothers were in Nazi Germany. Both taught their children the *"do's and don'ts"* to survive in a racist society. In a sworn affidavit to the court, the Appellant told the court:

> *When I would hear my mother and Mrs. Ella talk about the racist activities of the south, I would interrupt them and tell them what I would do to those white people if they did that to my mother. My mother would tell me. "Shut up boy. You don't know what you're talking about. Those white folks will kill you." The Democrat-controlled South had taught my mother the necessity of conveying to her children the need to **fear** whites, and to do so because their lives and future depended on such fear.*

> *As a young boy, I can remember how my mother would often whisper when talking to her children about whites. Other times she would have me check underneath the house to see if whites were listening to our conversations. I was taught that listening to the conversations of blacks while hiding underneath their homes was one of the tactics used by those who wanted to gather information about the person they had planned beat or lynch. This may have been the tactic that whites used to apprehend and murder Emmett Till, the black teenager from Chicago. When the Emmett Till's story broke, my mother called all of her children to her side and read a series of stories that appeared in the* Pittsburgh Courier

newspaper (a national African American publication). I was ten years old when I learned that an all-white jury set his murderers free. The point was finally driven home for young black men to stay in their place.

*Stories like the murder of Emmett Till and news of lynchings spread like wildfire throughout the black community. As a child, with the mental pictures of blacks being beaten and lynched embedded in my young mind, it was difficult to sleep at night. I feared that these same types of people or the Ku Klux Klan would break into our home and harm me or a family member just like they had harmed Emmett Till and other blacks. **Every night** I would cry until I either cried myself to sleep or until my parents relented and allowed me to sleep with them. Most children were afraid of monsters; I was afraid of the people who wore regular clothes by day and sheets by night, something the white children never had to worry about. The Democrats' goal of getting black children (like myself) to fear whites and stay in our places was accomplished before I had reached the age of five.*

It was only after fully learning of the Democrats' long history of racist practices, did I understand why my mother raised us as she did. Even up unto the time of my mother's passing on December 28, 2002, she still secured her refrigerator and food cabinets with chains and locks, fearful that whites would come into her home while she was asleep or away and poison her food. I had my deceased mother and other blacks who lived in fear most of their life in mind when I filed this suit.

In his sworn affidavit the Petitioner went on to share with the court other ways how racism and the ***indoctrination of fear*** personally affected his life, including in the area of employment. The Petitioner told the court:

*In job interviewing situations with white interviewers, mistrust and fear would set in and I could never do my best. Consequently, I was passed over for many jobs that I was more than qualified for. Long term unemployment led to bankruptcy, which created a hardship on me and my family. It's hard to explain what it is like to live in **fear** most of your life, **fear** that was necessary for survival in a racist society, **justified fear** that was based on a pattern of racist practices that were sanctioned by the courts and carried out by very a powerful political organization for over two hundred years.*

Professor Nancy Boyd Franklin, a noted professor of psychology, states the following in her book, *Black Families in Therapy.*

It is difficult to convey fully to someone who has not experienced it, the insidious, pervasive and constant impact that racism and discrimination have on the lives of Black people in America today. Both affect a Black person from birth until death and have an impact on every aspect of family life, from child-rearing practices, courtship, and marriage, to male-female roles, self esteem, and cultural and racial identification. They also influence the way in which black people relate to each other and to the outside world.

*Slavery set the tone for Black people to be treated as inferior.... The process of discrimination is evident at all levels of society from theories about genetic inferiority (Jensen, 1969) and cultural pathology (Monynihan 1965) to segregation that existed blatantly in the South until the Civil Rights era of the 1960s **and still occurs in subtler forms today**. There are con-tinued inequities in the United States...that are manifested by the disproportionate number of Black people who are poor, homeless, living in substandard housing, unemployed and school dropouts." (81)*

CONCLUSION & SUMMARY

❖ The Democratic Party *knew or should have known* that the aforementioned racist activities were taking place not only in jurisdictions where their elected officials were in charge, but throughout the country as they had intended.

❖ The Democratic Party *knew or should have known* that their elected officials supported and endorsed these racist practices because many of these practices and policies were outlined in their political platforms and/or were the themes and promises of their political campaigns.

❖ The Democratic Party *knew or should have known* that their legislative practices and their terrorist tactics were having a negative impact on what the District Court referred to as the *entire African American community* and their children.

❖ The Democratic Party *knew or should have known* that they had the power to put a stop to these practices. Not only did they refuse to stop their racist practices; they also never condemned or disciplined Democratic officials who encouraged such practices. Instead they praised them as they did with President Andrew Johnson in their 1868 Platform.

From their support of slavery to the last days of Jim Crow (late 1970s), the Respondent's racist policies and practices cost millions their lives (from the Middle Passage through the Civil War) and negatively affected and altered the lives and future of *the entire African American community during the past two hundred-plus years*.

The Supreme Court has twice held in the cases of *Meritor Sav. Bank v Vinson*, 477 U.S. 57 (1986) and *Harris v. Forklift Systems* 114 S. Ct. 367 (1993) that Title VII of the 1964 Civil Rights Act prohibits hostile work environments on the basis of race, sex, religion, and disabilities. Title VII and First Amendment rulings have covered both the "primary effects" and "secondary effects" of those environments (see *Long v. Board of Education of Jefferson County,* 2000).

The Petitioner in this case wants the court to consider the "primary and secondary effects" of the hostile environment created by the Democratic Party, an environment, in the words of Chief Justice Warren, that *"affects the hearts and minds"* of African Americans *"in a way unlikely ever to be undone."* The hostile environment created by the Respondents was not only accomplished with legislation and landmark litigations; they also used mutilations, decapitations, dismemberments, lynchings, and the beating and burning to death of thousands of African American citizens—all designed to keep an entire race of people in its place.

As stated in the Introduction, *racism* in America was politically driven. Without the political backing of those who made up and formed the powerful Democratic Party, a party that spent billions to preserve the institution of slavery and the system of Jim Crow, slavery would have ended a hundred years earlier and Jim Crow would have died in the womb of those who conceived it. Contrary to public opinion, racism *was not* something that the entire white race engaged in. Racism was the political agenda of a political party—made up of individuals who chose to use this deadly disease to cover their own insecurities—in their relentless quest for wealth and power. Eventually as planned, this disease spread throughout the country.

In stipulating that the Petitioner's injuries are the **_same_** injuries inflicted on the **_entire African American community_**, only one question should remain. Were the *collective* injuries that were inflicted on the **_entire African American community_** of which the Petitioner is a member, *"concrete"* enough to establish *standing*? The answer should be a resounding, **yes,** particularly when you consider all factors in this case, including the Respondent's own political platforms, records from Congress, the expert opinions of our nation's renowned historians, and the multitude of civil rights legislation and landmark cases that were designed to put an end to their racist policies and practices.

In addition to having *standing*, in civil matters under 18 U.S.C. 610, the courts have decided in *Cort v. Ash* that a citizen has the right to file a private cause of action through an Injunctive Relief in order to *secure a remedy*. Based on the standards set by *Lujan* and the previous rulings in *Cort v. Ash*, the Petitioner has the legal authorization to file this class action on behalf of himself and the African American citizens of the United States.

RELIEF SOUGHT

The Petitioner humbly requests that the United States Supreme Court overturn the 9th Circuit's decision and grant the Petitioner the following:

1. That the court order the Defendants to issue a formal public apology to African Americans for the wrong that was committed during the duration of the Defendants' tenure as an organization or political party and in addition to the public apology, we request that the Defendants place the apology on their official website.

2. The Appellant asks that, as an extension to their apology, the Defendants provide funding to fund educational projects depicting all of the historical events and acts that were highlighted in this lawsuit as well as other historical events not mentioned—any and all events that reflect the true relationship between blacks and Democrats from 1792 to 1965. The projects should include and not be limited to: the production of printed materials, short films, featured films and CDs–all to be made available to every American public and private K-12 school and public libraries at cost (including shipping and handling). We further ask that the Appellant and the consultants of his choice be paid a consulting fee including traveling and all other related expenses to help produce these educational materials. The consulting fee will be the standard consulting fee for similar types of educational projects. Under the Civil Liberties Act of 1988 funds to educate the ***public*** of the wrongs that took place was part of the redress.

3. Awarding Appellant fees and expenses incurred in this action, including reasonable allowance of fees for attorneys and appro-

31

priate consultant fees for the research and development of this case and for the previously related case of CV04-2442.

4. Granting such other and further relief as the Court may deem just and proper.

Under the penalty of perjury of the United States the foregoing is true and correct.

Signed this _____ day of February 2007

By

_____

Wayne Perryman

SUPPLEMENTAL BRIEF
FOR UNITED STATES
SUPREME COURT

Case No. 06-1107

==

In The

Supreme Court of the United States

-------------------------------- φ--------------------------------

WAYNE PERRYMAN ON BEHALF OF HIMSELF
AND THE AFRICAN AMERICAN CITIZENS
OF THE UNITED STATES,

Petitioner,

v.

DEMOCRATIC NATIONAL COMMITTEE
AND NATIONAL DEMOCRATIC PARTY,

Respondents.

-------------------------------- φ--------------------------------

**On Petition For A Writ Of Certiorari
To The United States Court Of Appeals
For The Ninth Circuit**

-------------------------------- φ--------------------------------

PETITION FOR A WRIT OF CERTIORARI

-------------------------------- φ--------------------------------

WAYNE PERRYMAN
Pro Se Litigant
P.O. Box 256
Mercer Island, WA 98040
Telephone (206) 232-5575
Fax (206) 232-2904
E-Mail Doublebro@aol.com

Additional Table of Authorities

Federal Election Commission v. Akins (96-1590) 101 F. 3d 731

Friends of the Earth, Inc. et al v. Laidlaw Environmental Services (TOC) Inc. (98-822) 528 U.S. 167 (2000)

Sierra Club v. Morton 405 U.S. 727, 735

Texas & Pacific R. Co. v. Rigsby, 241 U.S. 33, 39 (1916).

Other Authorities

The Audacity of Hope by Senator Barack Obama

The Oxford Companion to the Supreme Court of the United States Second Edition

Alexander Solzhenitsyn's 1978 Speech at Harvard University

Revised Constitutional Provisions

This case is submitted under the provisions of the Constitution of the United States' Fourteenth Amendment's Equal Protection Clause and Due Process Clause.

After submitting the *Writ for Certiorari* and after further research, the *Pro Se* Petitioner discovered two recent cases involving decisions of the current justices that present a different view of what the Supreme Court considers as *"an injury in fact."* Because of this **new** information the Petitioner is submitting this Supplemental Brief under Rule 15.8.

In previous court appearances, the Respondent failed to acknowledge that decisions regarding *standing* have varied as much as the diversity on the bench, and in **recent** cases involving Justices Breyer, Ginsburg, Stevens, and Kennedy, the interpretation of what constitutes *"an injury in fact"* has varied as well. For instance, in the case of the *Federal Election Commission v. Akins (96-1590) 101 F. 3d*

731, the Defendants argued that the Plaintiffs did not have *standing* because none had suffered "*an injury.*" However in the majority opinion, issued by Justice Breyer, the court decided that Plaintiffs did have an *injury in fact* and therefore **standing**, citing that the "*denial of any information which is statutorily required to be provided to citizens by the government*" constitutes an "*injury in fact.*" The court also determined that even though the grievance in the *Federal Election case* was a "***generalized grievance,***" the "***harm***" was *concrete* enough to overcome the Defendant's arguments.

In the case the of *Friends of the Earth, Inc. et al v. Laidlaw Environmential Services (TOC), Inc. (98-822) 528 U.S. 167 (2000),* Justices Ginsburg, Stevens, and Kennedy all agreed that contrary to the arguments presented by *Laidlaw*, the *Friends of the Earth* were also injured. The court was convinced that the Plaintiff's "*reasonable concerns about the effects of the Defendant's pollutant discharges, directly affected the affiant's recreational, aesthetic, and economical interest.*" See, e.g., *Sierra Club v. Morton 405 U.S. 727, 735.* The court felt the affidavits submitted by the Plaintiffs presented dispositively more than the mere '*general averment*" and "*conclusory allegations*" found inadequate in *Lujan v. National Wildlife Federation, 497 U.S. 871, 888* or as the "*some day intentions*" to visit endangered species in various locations, was insufficient in the *Defenders of Wildlife case 504 U.S., at 564.*

In one case, the Supreme Court granted *standing* simply because the Plaintiff was denied information that he or she was entitled to (*Federal Election Commission* case) and in the other case, the court granted *standing* because the court believed the Constitution allows citizens who choose not to fish or swim in a stream because of *reasonable concerns about illegal pollution* also constitutes *an injury in fact* (*Friends of the Earth* case).

To compare the cases cited above with the current case where:

- An entire race of people (of which the Petitioner is a member) was tortured, terrorized, and forced to live in fear for over two hundred years because of beatings, lynchings, assassinations, and intimidations.

- A race of people was forced to live in an environment where constitutional rights were denied, due process was ignored, and a quality education was merely a dream.

- And a race of people was forced to endure injustice while several pieces of racist legislation were passed against them as they watched impatiently while that same political party **vehemently** opposed several pieces of legislation that were introduced on behalf of them.

If it is determined that all of the above do not constitute *"an injury in fact,"* such a decision would be viewed as an insult to the entire race and a travesty of justice, particularly when you weigh the fact that the same court gave an ***injury status*** and ***standing*** to a group that chose not to swim or fish in polluted waters and to another small group that was simply denied some information.

As the court can tell, this current case is not about not being able to fish or swim because of *polluted waters* nor is it about being *denied information* because of a membership with a particular political organization. It is about:

- The *denial of constitutional rights and information* because you were a ***member*** of the *African American community*.

- Not having *a choice* but being forced to live in a *polluted Jim Crow environment* for over two hundred years, an environment a hundred times worse than the conditions at the Abu Ghraib and Guantanomo Bay prisons.

- ***Jim Crow pollutions of racism that infected*** the entire nation and ***affected*** and ***harmed*** the *entire African American community* in a variety of ways, i.e., mentally, physically, emotionally, and economically.

In his book, *The Audacity of Hope*, Senator Barack Obama draws a connection between the Respondents' Jim Crow era, and issues involving **today's** inner city teenage parents and what he refers to as the *"fifteen-year-old young men with a harrowing rap sheet, the shame of men who could not protect their women and support their families, and children who grew up being told they wouldn't amount to anything."* He describes these individuals *"...as those who didn't make it out of history's confinement, of neighborhoods within the black community that house the poorest of the poor, serving as repositories for all the* **<u>scars of slavery and violence of Jim Crow</u>**.... (252)

Two hundred years ago the Respondents found ways to use this very court and the law to enslave us, beat us, terrorize us, and murder us, and now they are using this same court and the law to keep from apologizing to us. African Americans often wondered: ***How could a political organization be so cold, so cruel, so calloused and so inhumane? How could they stand by and watch others suffer and rejoice because of their suffering? How could they brutalize an entire race of people and destroy millions of lives and then hire attorneys so they wouldn't have to apologize? How could the courts and the law allow the Respondents to get away with these horrific acts of terror under the so-called <u>letter of the law</u>? Is the court so insensitive that it can't see right and wrong? Is the law so inflexible that it cannot hold those accountable for their immoral acts and wrongful deeds?***

It was under the *<u>letter of the law</u>* that the constitutional rights of blacks were denied and now it is under the *<u>letter of the law</u>* regarding the issue of *standing* that a formal apology is being denied. Alexander Solzhenitsyn said it best during his speech to Harvard in 1978. In that speech he spoke about the cold insensitive impact of the *<u>letter of the law</u>* and the moral mediocrity that it produces. He told the Harvard students that:

- *Western society has given itself the organization best suited to its purposes, based, I would say, on the <u>letter of the law</u>.... People in the West have acquired a considerable skill in using, interpreting, and manipulating law, even though laws tend to be too complicated for the average person to understand....*

> *Any conflict is solved according to the <u>letter of the law</u> and this is considered to be the supreme solution. If one is right from a legal point of view, nothing more is required; nobody may mention that one could still be entirely right, and urge self-restraint, a willingness to renounce such legal rights, sacrifice and self-restraint, it would sound simply absurd.... A society which is based on the <u>letter of the law</u> and never reaches any higher is taking very scarce advantage of the higher level of human possibilities. The <u>letter of the law</u> is too cold and formal to have a beneficial influence on society. Whenever the tissue of life is woven of legalistic relations, there is an atmosphere of moral mediocrity, paralyzing man's noblest impulses....*

In regards to the letter of the law, the court should be reminded that the rules on **"standing"** and the **"injury in fact"** doctrines originated from the *common law systems of writs* and were intended to apply only to claims brought against the government (and its agencies) for violations of the Constitution (according to *The Oxford Companion to the Supreme Court of the United States*, pp. 956-958). Since that time, for reasons unknown, other the courts have expanded the application of these doctrines to include other types of claims. *Lujan v. Defender of Wildlife 504 U.S. 555 (1992)*, and the *African American Slave Descendant* case, two cases that the Respondents often cite to support their arguments on *standing*, were suits brought against the government and its agencies and therefore necessitated *standing* according to the original intent of the law. It should be noted that unlike *Lujan* and the *African Slave Descendant* case, this case does not involve claims against the government or any of its agencies.

The Petitioner also recognizes that because the current sitting justices were appointed by various Republican and Democratic administrations, the court may not be comfortable deciding a case that involves a political party in which they may or may not be allied with. Like many Defendants in controversial political cases, the Respondents are hoping that rather than a decision on the merits, the court will, as many have in the past, avoid the controversy by using the doctrine of *"standing"* as a surrogate for its decision or invoke the *"prudential"* dimensions of *"standing"* to accomplish the same. However the court must realize that as controversial as this case may be, our nation's citizens (both black and white) have waited patiently since the ending of the Civil War for this matter to be resolved. This case is not about partisan politics nor is it intended to inflict harm on the Democratic Party. It is about addressing a wrong that is long overdue.

For years African Americans struggled with the *"three-fifths"* clause of the Constitution, which basically said blacks were only *"three-fifths"* of a person. Next they had to deal with the court's *Dred Scott* decision that classified blacks as property but not as people. And now they are dealing with arguments claiming that their collective sufferings and injuries during the past two hundred-plus years do not add up to an *injury in fact*.

In the current case, both the Appellate Court and the District Court decided that the Petitioner did not have *standing* even though both courts stipulated that Petitioner had been *injured* and his:

- *Injury stems from the injury <u>inflicted</u> on <u>all</u> African Americans over two hundred years ago and <u>affect</u> the <u>entire</u> African American community.*

The court has consistently overlooked the fact that this case was filed as a class action on behalf of the *"entire African American community,"* a class that according to the court had been *"injured"* and *"affected"* by such *injuries*. As <u>a member</u> of that *"injured"* class, the Petitioner filed this action seeking to obtain an apology on behalf of the *entire African American community* in accordance to the decision in *Cort v. Ash* 422 U.S. 66 (1975), which gives a member of the class the legal authorization to file for an Injunctive Relief under 18 U.S.C. 610 (see *Texas & Pacific R. Co. v. Rigsby, 241 U.S. 33, 39 (1916)*.

Conclusion

For years, our nation and the entire white race have been wrongfully labeled and branded as racist because of the deeds of one political organization. It was this powerful organization that passed legislation, sponsored litigation, and formed terrorist organizations to harm African Americans. It is time to stop the ***blame game*** and place the responsibility on the one group that sponsored the most racist political agenda that our nation has ever known—and that group is the Democratic Party, a political organization that has never apologized nor have they ever attempted to apologize for the two hundred years of atrocities that they committed against an entire race of people.

If the court can find that denial of information in the *Federal Elections Commission* case constitutes an ***injury in fact*** and that the polluted waters of a stream that ***could possibly affect*** the recreational, the aesthetic, and the economic interest of fishermen and swimmers also constitutes an ***injury in fact*** (in the case of *Friends of the Earth)*, the court must find that the Respondents' collective racist activities during the past two hundred years (which according the lower court ***have affected*** and ***injured*** the Petitioner and the *entire African American community), * is an *"injury in fact"* as well.

Respectfully submitted under the penalty of perjury of the United States on this _____ day of March 2007

By

Wayne Perryman, Petitioner

LETTER TO THE UNITED STATES SUPREME COURT

FOR

AFRICAN AMERICANS

from the office
of
Rev. Wayne Perryman

P.O. Box 256 Mercer Island, WA 98040 (206) 232-5575

Doublebro@aol.com

April 23, 2007

Honorable John G. Roberts
Chief Justice
United States Supreme Court
Washington, D.C. 20543-0001

Re: An Apology to African Americans **from** the United States Supreme Court

Dear Justice Roberts:

My name is Rev. Wayne Perryman. I am an inner-city minister, a community servant and the author of several books, including the one that is attached to this letter, which is my gift to you. The book is featured on over 500 conservative websites, it has been the subject of several talk shows including Fox's Hannity & Colmes, and it has touched the lives of thousands of African Americans across the country. If you cannot accept the book as a gift, please accept it and the CD as a supportive document for this letter.

Your honor, over the years African Americans have received apologies from Senator Robert Byrd, Governor George Wallace, and even a recent apology from Don Imus and the Democratic Party of North Carolina, but no apology from the very court that *may have* played an important role in establishing some of the negative attitudes and practices that caused my people harm. Justice Roberts, I am writing to see if you would be kind enough to issue a public apology on behalf of the United States Supreme Court. I am not asking you to compromise the integrity of the court nor am I asking you to vilify those justices who rendered landmark decisions that adversely affected the

African American community. I am just asking the Court to publicly acknowledge that there were decisions in the past that they are not proud of, decisions that caused my people harm.

In doing research for the attached book, which included examining the relationship between the African American community and both political parties, I discovered two important facts:

- **Fact 1**. The Republican Party has a very impressive track record in fighting for the rights of African Americans, both in and out of court. In fact, the Party was started in 1854 to specifically address the problem of slavery. Republicans were also the Party that introduced and passed the 13th, 14th, and 15th Amendments as well as a multitude of other civil rights legislation from the days of Reconstruction through the civil rights era of the 1960s.

- **Fact 2**. The discriminatory practices that African Americans experienced during the past 200 years were often the results of several landmark decisions rendered by the very court where you now serve as Chief Justice. As you know, in many instances, the Republicans' toughest battles in their fight for the rights of blacks weren't fought on the battlefields of Gettysburg and Richmond; they were fought in the chambers of the United States Supreme Court.

History tells us that the Republicans didn't lose these legal battles because their attorneys were incompetent. They were lost because of the biases on the bench. In key Civil Rights cases, it was the sitting Justices that gave the proponents of slavery and Jim Crow the green light to carry out their racist agenda. Those cases include but are not limited to the Dred Scott Decision, the Slaughterhouse Cases, Plessy v. Ferguson, and the Civil Rights Cases of 1883 which diluted the 14th Amendment and nullified the 1875 Civil Rights Act. All of these cases have had a profound negative impact on the African American community and, as in the words of Chief Justice Warren in the Brown Decision, "affected the hearts and minds [of African Americans] in a way unlikely ever to be undone."

With rare exception, most of our former justices, from Chief Justice Taney to Associate Justice Thurgood Marshall were influenced by their own personal beliefs and prejudices as well as by the organizations to which they belonged.

The Honorable Hugo L. Black was a former member of the "Ku Klux Klan" and the "Invisible Empire." Many legal experts believe his 1944 decision for the Court, in the case of *Korematsu v. United States* reflected his bigotry. The case upheld the World War II sanctions against Japanese Americans, whom he referred to as "Japs."

The Honorable James Moore Wayne was a slave owner and felt Congress had no power to prohibit the introduction of slavery into the territories, nor declare as free those slaves brought into the territories.

The Honorable William Burham Woods is known for giving a narrow view of the 14th Amendment and for striking down both 1875 Civil Rights Act (and in the case of the *United States v. Harris*) the Ku Klux Klan Act of 1871, two pieces of legislation designed to provide protection and equality for the emancipated Negro.

The Honorable Roger B. Taney, the pro-slavery judge who served as Chief Justice of the United States Supreme Court from 1836 to 1864, is known for his passionate support of slavery and the pro-slavery organizations that he was affiliated with. Justice Taney also believed blacks were inferior and because of their inferiority, discrimination against them was legally justified.

Chief Justice Melville Weston Fuller believed the 14th Amendment worked no revolutionary change and felt that he could preside comfortably over a Court that turned a blind eye to racial injustice.

The Honorable Robert Cooper Grier identified with Court in slave cases and felt it was constitutional to sanction "double jeopardy" for those who assisted runaway slaves.

The Honorable Stephen Johnson Field claimed that the 14th Amendment did not give African Americans the right to serve on juries and refused to use the amendment to protect African Americans.

<u>The Honorable Peter Vivian Daniel</u> was an extreme defender of "states rights" and the institution of slavery. He was consumed with a hatred for anything "northern."

<u>The Honorable Henry Billings Brown</u> authored the Court's opinion in the case of *Plessy v. Ferguson* which established the "separate but equal doctrine" and paved the way for Jim Crow.

Throughout the history of the Supreme Court there were a number of other judges and cases that reflected the court's bias. In the case of the *United States v. Cruikshank* (1876), the Supreme Court dismissed the indictment against a mob of whites that burned down a courthouse and murdered over one hundred blacks who were holding a public meeting in that building. Even though this massacre was <u>three times</u> worse than the recent Virginia Tech massacre, <u>there were no national observances, no candlelight ceremonies and no flags flown at half mast</u>. After the Supreme Court voted 9 to 0 to dismiss the indictment, violence against blacks multiplied throughout the South.

In the case of the *United States v. Reese* (1876), the Supreme Court put an end to federal enforcement in state and local elections, holding that "the Fifteenth Amendment does not confer the right of suffrage upon anyone." After this decision, southern Democrats established literacy tests and poll taxes to disenfranchise the black voter.

In *Williams v. Mississippi* (1898) the Supreme Court upheld the South's literacy test and poll taxes, which completely nullified the black vote in areas where over 95% of the black population resided (the South).

In the latest edition of the *Oxford Companion to the Supreme Court of the United States*, it confirms the past racial biases of the Court with the following statement:

- Problems with race and race relations—particularly issues concerning the status of African Americans—have played a prominent role in American political life since the colonial era. Given the place of the Supreme Court in the political structure, it was almost inevitable that the Court would be called upon to take an active role in resolving these problems.

Thus it is not surprising that the Court has often been a significant participant in controversies over race relations.

- The response of the Court has been shaped by a variety of factors. The most obvious is the attitude of the individual justices themselves toward the problem of race relations. These attitudes typically reflect the attitudes of the white society as a whole toward blacks....

- The concept of state's rights and its corollary along with limited national government, were critical to the Court's approach to civil rights issues. Focusing on these principles, the Court often imposed strict limitations on both the Reconstruction amendments themselves and the civil rights statutes adopted by Congress.... The Court in civil rights cases held that neither the 13th nor the 14th Amendment granted Congress the authority to pass statutes such as the Civil Rights Act of 1875. Congressional power could control only the action of the states, not of individuals. " (811-813)

In his book the *Statutory History of the United States: Civil Rights Vol. I Vol. II*, Professor Bernard Schwartz of New York University School of Law provides another example of how discrimination against the Negro was sanctioned by the Supreme Court. Professor Schwartz states:

- *The Fourteenth Amendment provision designed directly to prevent discrimination against the emancipated race was the equal protection clause. In* Plessy v. Ferguson, 163 U.S. 537 *(1896), however, the Supreme Court construed that clause in a manner which enabled discrimination against the Negro to be condoned by law.... Plessy v. Ferguson gave the lie to the American ideal, so eloquently stated by Justice John Harlan in dissent there: "Our Constitution is color-blind, and neither knows nor tolerates classes among citizens." ...Upon Plessy was built the whole structure of segregation that has been at the heart of the Southern system of racial discrimination. So much was, indeed, conceded by the Supreme Court itself, including the 1873 Slaughterhouse Cases 16 Wall. 36 (1873). (360)*

In writing the opinion for the court in *Brown v. Board of Education,* Chief Justice Warren addresses how the *"separate but equal doctrine"* affected school-age African American children. In that opinion, he wrote:

- *To separate them* [black children] *from other children of similar age and qualifications solely because of their race generates a feeling of inferiority as to their status in the community that <u>may affect their hearts and minds in a way unlikely ever to be undone</u>. The effect of this separation in their educational opportunities was well stated by the finding in the Kansas case by a court which nevertheless felt compelled to rule against the Negro Plaintiff.*

Before rendering the decision in the *Kansas case*, the court issued the following statement:

- *Segregation of white and colored children in public schools has a detrimental effect upon the colored children. The impact is greater when it has <u>the sanction of the law;</u> for the policy of separating the races is usually interpreted as denoting the inferiority of the negro group. A sense of inferiority affects the motivation of a child to learn. <u>Segregation with the sanction of law,</u> therefore, has a tendency to [retard] the educational and mental development of Negro children and to deprive them of some of the benefits they would receive in a racial[ly] integrated school system. (364)*

In the *Slaughterhouse* cases and other subsequent cases including *Plessy v. Ferguson*, it was the Court's narrow interpretation of the 14th Amendment that allowed many racist practices to go unchallenged and unpunished under what they claimed to be as *"State's Rights,"* including the right to own slaves and treat them as property and not as people.

In an 1848 open letter, the Honorable John McLean wrote: "slavery exists only where it is <u>established by law</u>." Justice McLean, like many other legal minds, sincerely believed that without the sanction of the

Court, slavery would have ended 100 years earlier and Jim Crow would have died in the wombs of those who conceived it. Contrary to public opinion, racism *was not* something that the entire white race engaged in. Racism, in part, was enhanced by a Court that was made up of biased individuals who chose to use their own personal prejudices and party affiliations to impose their standards of race relations on our beloved country. In hindsight, we all now realize that many of the landmark decisions weren't based on merit, but rather on the individual Justices' personal prejudice and their party affiliation. Because of their personal prejudices and their commitment to party loyalty, millions of lives were literally destroyed (from the beginning of slavery to the last days of Jim Crow, 1970s).

Your honor, based on the history of the Court in matters pertaining to civil rights. I humbly request that, as Chief Justice of the United States Supreme Court, you extend an act of kindness to the African American community by issuing a public apology on behalf of the Court.

I pray that the Lord will give you the *Wisdom of Solomon* to do what is right so we can begin the long-awaited healing process between blacks and whites in this great country of ours, and I pray that your decision will help protect and maintain the integrity of the Court as well as the respect of the American people.
Sincerely,

Rev. Wayne Perryman
cc. National Black Republican Association
  NAACP
  National Black Newspaper Association
  National Black Journalist Association
  National Bar Association
  Concerned Black Clergy
  National Medical Association
  National Urban League
  Blacks In Government
  Association of Black Sociologists

Consultants Confidential Inc.

Employment Relations & Civil Rights Consultants
P.O. Box 256 Mercer Island, WA 98040 (206) 232-5575
Doublebro@aol.com

Wayne Perryman
President

June 19, 2007

The Honorable John G. Roberts, Chief Justice
The Honorable Samuel A. Alito Jr.
The Honorable Stephen G. Breyer
The Honorable Ruth Bader Ginsburg
The Honorable Clarence Thomas
The Honorable David H. Souter
The Honorable Anthony M. Kennedy
The Honorable Antonin Scalia
The Honorable John Paul Stevens

To The Honorable Justices of the United Supreme Court:

I am following up on my April 23, 2007 letter to Chief Justice Roberts and my follow-up letter to the other eight Justices on May 18, 2007. In those correspondences, I asked both the court and Chief Justice Roberts if they would be kind enough to consider issuing a public apology to the African American community for past landmark decisions that caused my people harm. Those landmark cases include: the *Dred Scott* case, the *Slaughterhouse* cases, the *Civil Rights* case of 1883, *Plessy v. Ferguson*, the *United States v. Reese*, and the *United States v. Cruikshank (1876)*, to name a few. As of this date, the court has been silent and has provided no specific reply to my request for an apology.

As a national Civil Rights Consultant and an inner-city minister, I work with a number of African American pastors and inner-city gang members across the country, both of whom have no confidence in our criminal justice system and the courts that are an integral part of that system. Your honors, please know that your silence on this issue only exacerbates our fears and gives credence to the belief that the system is racist and insensitive to the African American experience. As African Americans we ask: Is there any compassion on the bench? Or has the court become like many of those whom they have convicted—cold individuals that offer no remorse for the harm that they caused others?

In the landmark cases cited above, the only offense that the African Americans committed was that they were born black. Even though they committed no wrong other than being black, they became victims of the decisions handed down by the very Court where each of you now serves. In this, my third correspondence, I beg of you to please give your most earnest consideration to my request. It could do so much for the African American community and much more for America.

Respectfully Submitted,

Rev. Wayne Perryman

Sent Certified Mail June 19, 2007

Appendix A
The African American
Political Agenda for 2008

Proposed by Rev. Wayne Perryman June 4, 2007

We, the African American Community of America, submit the following political agenda and proposed legislation to correct the past, strengthen our present, and improve our future.

Life Expectancy Act

Fact: For decades the life expectancy of African Americans has been much shorter than their white counterparts. Because of this factor, thousands of African Americans die before receiving one dime of the money that they placed in the Social Security Fund.

The Act: Based on the shorter life expectancy of African Americans, the *Life Expectancy Act* will modify the current age requirements of 65 for social security benefits for African Americans to reflect their shorter life span.

African American Family Preservation Act

Fact: The fact that 65 percent of our African American children grow up in fatherless homes is not totally the fault of the African American male. In order to qualify for government assistance (Section 8 and others), many government programs mandate that a male cannot be part of that household.

The Act: Because the African American husband will be unemployed several times during his lifetime and/or because many of the 780,000 black men will return home from prison with no jobs, we propose the *African American Family Preservation Act,* a law that will provide government assistance (for a limited amount of time) for those two-parent households that fall onto hard times and for fathers paying child support who become unemployed through no fault of their own.

African American Early Childhood Act

Fact: The academic gap (test scores) between black children and white children is still a major problem in our public school system. There are many studies which have shown that the Headstart programs of the '60s can make a major difference and reduce the gap.

The Act: The *African American Early Childhood Act* will provide Headstart programs for inner city children and educational vouchers for all African American children who choose to attend a private school.

African American College Preparation Act

Fact: Many public schools fail to prepare our young men and women to pass the entrance exams for college.

The Act: The *African American College Preparation Act* will not only assist African American students with college preparation classes; it will also provide SAT and ACT preparation for college entrance exams.

African American Media Community Development Act

Fact: For years, major film producers and advertising agencies have used the deplorable conditions of the inner city as a backdrop for films, television programs, and advertising campaigns and for hip hop videos, without leaving one dine to improve the conditions of the community that they have exploited.

The Act: The *African American Media Community Development Act* will require that every media organization (including motion picture companies, television networks, hip hop video companies, and advertising agencies) that uses the deplorable conditions of the inner city as a backdrop in a profit-making project must pay a fee no less than 20 percent of the gross profits of that project to improve the conditions of that community. In addition, all actors and actresses who perform in such projects will be required to pay 25 percent of their gross salaries to improve the conditions in those communities.

African American Freedom of Speech Act

Fact: The African American pastor has always been the chief spokesperson on social, political, and other issues affecting the African American Community. From the Reverend Richard Allen and the Reverend Absalom Jones to the Reverend Dr. Martin Luther King Jr., the black clergy has been the chief spokesperson in the black community, speaking out on various behavioral issues that the Bible classifies as sin. History reveals that these preachers were not only our spiritual leaders; they also were our first elected officials.

The Act: The *African American Freedom of Speech Act* will allow African American ministers to continue to speak out on social and political issues and on various behaviors that are classified as sin (according to Bible) without reprisal from the IRS or any other government agency that currently regulates so-called "hate crimes." This act will exclude from the "hate speech" legislation any behavior that the Bible classified as sin, and this may include all sexual sins including: incest, sex outside of marriage (fornication), adultery, homosexuality, bestiality, and pedophilia.

African American Affordable Health Care Act

Fact: Since the median net worth of all black households (in the year 2000) was $7,500 compared to their white counterpart of $79,400, and since blacks are still the last to be hired and the first to be fired, many African Americans do not have affordable quality health care.

The Act: The *African American Affordable Health Care Act* will adjust medical costs on a sliding scale based on the African American's income. If there is no income, the medical cost will be free.

African American Drug Control Act

Fact: Our manufacturers of alcoholic beverages have targeted the black community with alcoholic beverages (such as the "40") that are not sold in white communities. In addition to these alcoholic beverages, our communities have been plagued with a multitude of illegal drugs (made affordable for the average person).

The Act: The *African American Drug Control Act* will remove from our community alcohol products targeted specifically at the black community. The act will also step up efforts to identify the sources of drugs coming into our communities and close those doors.

African American Racial Profiling Act

Fact: From African American movie stars to the common citizen, racial profiling has been a problem in the black community.

The Act: The *African American Racial Profiling Act* will not only outlaw racial profiling; it will also compensate the individual, when it is proven that the individual has been a victim of racial profiling.

African American Small Business Development Act

Fact: History reveals, when given the opportunity to succeed, African Americans can establish profitable businesses for their community. During the era of Jim Crow, blacks were forced to start businesses to support their communities. From Black Wall Street in Tulsa, Oklahoma, to Wilmington, North Carolina, blacks experienced economic success through the development of small businesses.

The Act: The *African American Small Business Development Act* will force banking and financial institutions to establish new standards to make funds available to African Americans for the purposes of starting small businesses and for purchasing affordable housing.

African American Fact-finding Investigation Act

Fact: Since the passage of the 1964 Civil Rights Act and the Equal Employment Opportunity Act of 1972, the Equal Employment Opportunity Commission has dismissed millions of discrimination complaints filed by African Americans, without launching any investigations.

The Act: The *African American Fact-finding Investigation Act* will require that all EEOC agencies conduct a complete fact-finding investigation on all discrimination complaints filed by African Americans before final determinations are made.

African American Political Report Card Act

Fact: Every four years (two years for congressional races) political candidates flood our communities seeking the black vote.

The Act: The *African American Political Report Card Act* will require all politicians campaigning in African American communities and/or producing ad campaigns targeting the black community, if elected, to report to the black community three times a year about their efforts on behalf of African Americans.

African American Life Preservation Act

Fact: Since *Roe v. Wade,* seventeen million black babies have been aborted. That means the lost of seventeen million future black voters, seventeen million potential black doctors, ministers, scientists, school teachers, and world leaders. Had those seventeen million lived, the black population would be the largest voting population among the ethnic groups in America. The seventeen million deaths amounts to racial genocide.

The Act: The *African American Life Preservation Act* will provide education, funding, medical care, and other resources for both the mother and the baby as an alternative to abortion.

Sources & Resources

Sources

Statutory History of the United States, Editor, Professor Bernard Schwartz of New York University School of Law

Commerce Clearing House: Voting Records on House Bills, Prentice Hall's American Nation

Thirteenth Amendment

Fernando Wood's Comments	Pages 44, 46	Statutory History
James Wilson's Comments	Pages 29, 35	Statutory History

1866 Civil Rights Acts

Willard Saulsbury's Comments	Page 113	Statutory History
Reverdy Johnson's Comments	Page 119	Statutory History
William Fessenden's Comments	Page 119	Statutory History
Martin Thayer's Comments	Pages 130-131	Statutory History
Michael Kerr's Comments	Pages 135-136	Statutory History

First Reconstruction Act of 1867

Ben Tillman's Comments	Page 427	American Nation

1960 Civil Rights Act

Ray Madden's Comments	Page 956	Statutory History
Overton Brooks' Comments	Page 964	Statutory History
William McColloch's Comments	Page 965	Statutory History

1964 Civil Rights Act

Dr. Martin Luther King's Comments	Pages 5-6	Why We Can't Wait
Professor's Bernard Schwartz's Comments	Page 1017	Statutory History
President Kennedy's Message	Page 1055	Statutory History
Emmanuel Celler's Comments	Page 1099	Statutory History
Thomas Abernethy's Comments	Page 1128	Statutory History
Donald Matthews' Comments	Page 1135	Statutory History
Sam Ervin's Comments	Page 1307	Statutory History
Robert Byrd's Comments	Page 1341	Statutory History
Olin Johnston's Comments	Page 1404	Statutory History
Howard Smith's Comments	Page 1421	Statutory History
William McCullough's Comments	Page 1112	Statutory History
Everett Dirksen's Comments	Page 1141	Statutory History
John Sparkman's Comments	Pages 1151-53	Statutory History

1965 Voting Rights Act

President Johnson's Address	Page 1506	Statutory History
Sam Ervin's Comments	Page 1512	Statutory History
Everett Dirksen's Comments	Page 1512	Statutory History
Herman Talmadge's Comments	Page 1542	Statutory History
Jacob Javit's Comments	Page 1575	Statutory History

1968 Civil Rights Act

Lawrence Fountain's Comments	Page 1668	Statutory History
Everett Dirksen's Comments	Page 1684	Statutory History
Sam Ervin's Comments	Page 1686	Statutory History
John Stennis' Comments	Page 1757	Statutory History

1972 Equal Employment Opportunity Act

Republicans' and Democrats' Voting Records from Commerce Clearing House

Other Fact-Finding Investigative Sources

The Abolitionist Legacy from Reconstruction to the NAACP
    Professor James McPherson of Princeton University

The Struggle for Equality
    Professor James McPherson of Princeton University

Charles Sumner
    Professor David Herbert Donald of Harvard University

Disuniting of America
    Former Associate Professor Arthur M. Schlesinger Jr. of
    Harvard University

Without Sanctuary
    Leon F. Litwack

Black Americans
    John Hope Franklin

Why We Can't Wait
    Rev. Dr. Martin Luther King

The Causes of the Civil War
    Professor Kenneth M. Stampp of University of California at
    Berkeley

The Myth of Separation
    David Barton

God's Politician
    Garth Lean

From Slavery to Freedom
    John Hope Franklin and Alfred A. Moss

The Fabulous Democrats
    David L. Cohn

The Republicans: A History of Their Party
    Professor Malcolm Moos of Johns Hopkins University

The Negro Almanac: A Reference Work on African Americans
  Harry Ploski and James Williams

Black Women in America: An Historical Encyclopedia
  Darlene Clark Hine

A Hand Up: Black Philanthropy and Self-Help in America
  Emmett D. Carson

Economic Empowerment through the Church
  Gregory Reed

When the Game Was Black and White
  Bruce Chadwick

Raising Black Children
  Professor Alvin F. Poussaint and James P. Comer

Black Families in Therapy: A Multisystem Approach
  Professor Nancy Boyd-Franklin

Conspiracy to Destroy Black Boys
  Jawanza Kunjufu

The Negro Family in the United States
  Frazier E. Franklin

Black Lies, White Lies
  Tony Brown

The Way of the Bootstrapper
  Floyd Flake

Playing America's Game
  Michael L. Cooper

A History of Black America
  Professor Howard O. Lindsey of DePaul University

Reconstruction after the Civil War
  Professor John Hope Franklin

Reconstruction: The Great Experiment
Professor Allen W. Trelease

The Clash of the Cultures
Joseph A. Raelin

Counseling the Culturally Different
Professor David Sue

A Documentary History of the Negro People in the United States
Vol. I, II, III
Herbert Aptheker (Foreword by W.E.B. DuBois)

Black Business in the New South
Walter B. Weare

Booker T. Washington
Jan Gleiter and Kathleen Thompson

George Washington Carver: An American Biography
Rackham Holt

The American Presidents
Grolier Books

America's God and Country Encyclopedia of Quotations
William J. Federer

The Inaugural Addresses of the Presidents
John Gabriel

The Oxford Companion To United States History [2001 Edition]
Edited by Paul S. Boyer

Oxford The Desk Encyclopedia of World History 2006 Edition

The Marketing of Evil
David Kupelian

The Al Qaeda Reader
Raymond Ibrahim

Party of the People
Jules Witcover

The Buying of Congress
Charles Lewis

Bias
Bernard Goldberg

Thaddeus Stevens
Fawn M. Brodie

100 Years of Lynchings
Ralph Ginzburg

The Holy Bible (King James and Living)

The Holy Quran

Separate but Equal Branches: Congress and the Presidency
Charles O. Jones

The Audacity of Hope
Barack Obama

My Life
Bill Clinton

At Canaan's Edge
Taylor Branch

Islam and The Crusades
Robert Spencer

Of Kennedys and Kings
Harris Wofford

Losing Bin Laden
Richard Miniter

The Oxford Companion To the United States Supreme Court
  Oxford University

The 9/11 Commission Report
  United States 9/11 Commission

Media Sources

PBS Special: The Rise & Fall of Jim Crow

PBS Special: Reconstruction: The Second Civil War

David Barton: Justice at the Gate Reconciliation

History Channel: Voices of Civil Rights

History Channel: Targeted Osama Bin Laden

History Channel: Saddam Hussein and The Nerve Gas Atrocity

History Channel: Engineering Disaster New Orleans

History Channel: True Story of Black Hawk Down

Peter Mier: Obession

Renaissance Women's Production: Emancipation, Revelation, Revolution

PBS Special: Citizen King

U.S. News & World Report, November 13, 2006

Playboy interview with Dr. Martin Luther King

New York Times October 24, 2004

Washington Post November 1, 1993

Time September 23, 1991

Seattle Times December 14, 1993

Seattle Times/Associated Press December 2, 2001

USA Today February 24, 1992

Christianity Today March 1996

Christianity Today June 11, 2001

Ebony November 2000

Ebony January 1993

Newsweek June 1, 1998

Savoy May 2001

The Economist August 18, 2001

New York Times August 22, 2001

World Net Daily Internet

CNN.com

LaTimes.com

Institute for Public Accuracy: Urban Legends References.com

Democrat's political Plaform from 1835 to 1954

Alexander's Solzhenitsyn 1978 Speech to Harvard University

Exclusive interview with Buck O'Neil, founder of the Negro Baseball Museum

Trial transcripts of *Charles Fairchild v. Secretary of Labor, Robert Riech*

News Reports Regarding New Orleans' Disaster by Various News Organizations

- December 1, 2001. The *Houston Chronicle* published a story, *"Keeping its head above water: New Orleans faces doomsday scenario"* which predicted that a severe hurricane striking New Orleans "would strand 250,000 people or more, and probably kill one of 10 left behind as the city drowned under 20 feet of water. Thousands of refugees could land in Houston."

- September 2001. *Popular Mechanics* ran a story called *"New Orleans Is Sinking"* discussing what might happen if a severe hurricane landed on New Orleans.

- October 2001. *Scientific American* published an article by Mark Fischetti called *"Drowning New Orleans."* This article begins, "A major hurricane could swamp New Orleans under 20 feet of water, killing thousands. Human activities along the Mississippi River have dramatically increased the risk, and now only massive reengineering of southeastern Louisiana can save the city… New Orleans is a disaster waiting to happen."

- June 2002. The *New Orleans Times-Picayune* published an award-winning five-part series called *"Washing Away"* by John McQuaid and Mark Schleifstein. *"Washing Away"* covered various scenarios, including a Category 5 hurricane hitting the city from the south. The series also explored the various environmental changes that have increased the area's vulnerability. One article in the series concluded, "Hundreds of thousands would be left homeless, and it would take months to dry out the area and begin to make it livable. But there wouldn't be much for residents to come home to. The local economy would be in ruins."

- October 2004. The *National Geographic* Magazine published a feature titled *"Gone with the Water."* The article's primary focus is on the destruction of the Mississippi delta's wetlands and the effects that this has on the region's ability to withstand a hurricane, in addition to ecological and social impacts. The article begins with a haunting hypothetical worst-case scenario.

- November 2004. The *Natural Hazards Observer* carried an article entitled *"What if Hurricane Ivan Had Not Missed New Orleans?,"* which suggested "The potential for such extensive flooding and the resulting damage is the result of a levee system that is unable to keep up with the increasing flood threats from a rapidly eroding coastline and thus unable to protect the ever-subsiding landscape."

- January 2005. The PBS science show *Nova* aired an episode on the hurricane threat to New Orleans, including interviews with New Orleans officials and scientists involved in the LSU study. The episode is available for online viewing here.

- May 23, 2005. *The American Prospect* carried "Thinking Big about Hurricanes." That article described the likely aftermath of a major storm surge. "Soon the geographical 'bowl' of the Crescent City would fill up with the waters of the lake, leaving those unable to evacuate with little option but to cluster on rooftops — terrain they would have to share with hungry rats, fire ants, nutria, snakes, and perhaps alligators. The water itself would become a festering stew of sewage, gasoline, refinery chemicals, and debris."

- June 2005. The FX docudrama *Oil Storm* depicted a category 4 hurricane hitting New Orleans and forcing residents to evacuate and hide out in the Superdome. The docudrama went on to speculate about a national economic meltdown caused by the decreased oil supply.